C# Text Manipula

François Liger
Craig McQueen
Paul Wilton

® Wrox Press Ltd.

C# Text Manipulation Handbook

First published November 2002

Published by Wrox Press Ltd,
Arden House, 1102 Warwick Road, Acocks Green,
Birmingham, B27 6BH
United Kingdom
Printed in the United States
ISBN 1-86100-823-6

Trademark Acknowledgments

Wrox has endeavored to provide trademark information about all the companies and products mentioned in this book by the appropriate use of capitals. However, Wrox cannot guarantee the accuracy of this information.

Credits

Authors
François Liger
Craig McQueen
Paul Wilton

Commissioning Editor
Andrew Polshaw

Technical Editor
Nick Manning

Technical Reviewers
Mark Horner
Andrew Krowczyk
Saurabh Nandu
Anthony Naylor
Phil Powers DeGeorge
David Schultz
Erick Sgarbi
Imar Spaanjaars

Managing Editor
Emma Batch
Jan Kolasinski

Indexers
Michael Brinkman
Bill Johncocks

Project Manager
Beckie Stones

Production Coordinator
Sarah Hall

Proof Reader
Chris Smith

Cover
Natalie O'Donnell

About the Authors

François Liger

François Liger is a program manager in the .NET Common Language Runtime group at Microsoft, specializing in the international aspects of the .NET Framework. Prior to this role, he had acquired extensive globalization and localization experience, working on MS-DOS, Windows 95, Internet Explorer, MSN, and Hotmail. He has been using Visual Basic since version 1.0, which he helped launch in France.

For Bérengère and Éloi.

Craig McQueen

Craig McQueen is the Vice President, Software Development for M Systems Group. Craig has led the development of several major projects, such as Extranets and B2B Integration at Panasonic Canada, and Web Banking initiatives at TD Bank. He has a Masters degree in Computer Science from the University of Toronto and a Bachelor of Science degree in System Design Engineering from the University of Waterloo. Craig shares his knowledge through writing and speaking. He was a contributing author for six books and has written over twenty articles. Craig is also a frequent presenter at conferences in North America and Europe. He can be reached at cmcqueen@msystemsgroup.com.

Paul Wilton

After an initial start as a Visual Basic applications programmer at the Ministry of Defence in the UK, Paul found himself pulled into the 'Net. Having joined an Internet development company, he spent three years helping create various Internet solutions, including an e-commerce web site for a major British bank. He's currently working freelance and also busy trying to piece together the Microsoft .NET jigsaw.

Paul's main skills are in developing web front ends using DHTML, JavaScript, VBScript, and Visual Basic and back-end solutions with ASP, Visual Basic, and SQL Server.

Lots of love to my fiancée Catherine who ensures my sanity chip remains plugged in.

C#

Text Manipulation

Handbook

Table of Contents

Table of Contents

C#

Text Manipulation

Handbook

Introduction

Introduction

This book addresses exactly how the .NET Framework deals with text; the different ways it can be stored, what happens if a string is changed, why we need a separate `StringBuilder` class, and the implications of the Framework storing all text in Unicode. The book also covers implementation, explaining the various methods available and comparing their performance so that you can make an informed choice when deciding how to manipulate your text. Dealing with text in C# is not as complicated as dealing with text in C++, for instance, but you do have some control over how `String` objects are dealt with via the object-oriented framework, and it is important that you understand exactly how the .NET Framework is dealing with your text.

One of the most important classes available to you for handling strings is `System.Text.RegularExpressions.Regex`. This class provides all .NET developers with the ability to use the powerful pattern matching language that regular expressions provide. By "matching", we mean checking to see if a string follows a certain pattern and so contains the data we expect. This is usually more effective than trying to catch an exception from a method you might want to pass the string to (such as might happen when updating a database with invalid data). In Chapters 5 to 7 we guide you through the regular expression language, explaining what every component means, and instructing you on how to build up complex expressions for matching against complicated patterns in text.

Without regular expressions, performing even a simple check on whether an e-mail address has been entered correctly could consume many lines of code. If we assume that the e-mail address has been stored in the `myInput` string variable, then a Boolean indicating whether a successful match has been made can be achieved with this line:

```
bool IsMatch = Regex.IsMatch(myInput,
    @"^[a-z](\w|\d|[-.])+@([a-z\d-]+\.)+[a-z]{2,4}$",
    RegexOptions.IgnoreCase);
```

This looks very arcane, but when you have read this book, you will see it as very straightforward. For brevity, this expression doesn't restrict myInput quite enough (although we will do this in Chapter 7), but it does specify the pattern as follows: The address must start with a letter, followed by one or more letters, underscores, numbers, hyphens or periods, or combinations thereof, followed by "@", followed by one or more patterns of a letter, followed by a possibly repeated pattern of one or more letters, numbers, or hyphens (followed by a period), and ending with a pattern of between 2 and 4 letters. This would match support@wrox.com, but not support@wrox.

If you are interested in discovering how to use this expression language with C# code, then the authors will guide you through this pattern matching language as they have had much experience with it.

Who is this Book For?

This is the first in the series of Wrox Handbooks targeted at practicing C# developers, who need to learn more to complete a specific task. Check out our web site at http://www.wrox.com for the other C# Handbooks as they appear.

This book will prove useful for anyone who uses text in their applications; this means every developer. The code in this book assumes that the reader has a copy of Microsoft C# .NET Standard Edition or above installed, but the code and concepts used apply to, and will work with, the .NET Framework SDK alone.

Book Outline

This book explains the various methods to handle text. Below is an overview of what the chapters contain.

Chapter 1 – How the System Deals with Text

This chapter explains how text is handled by the .NET Framework. It covers various low-level details such as how strings are stored in memory. After explaining how text is stored, it will become clear why it is important to consider how you are going handle text. This chapter will look at some MSIL, but generally it is an overview of text, and a description of how memory and memory management (and so the duration for which strings consume memory) is handled in .NET.

Chapter 2 – String and StringBuilder

This chapter covers the `String` class in exhaustive detail, explaining how strings are implemented in .NET. It also explains how the `StringBuilder` class works and compares the different methods each of these objects have, to learn which methods are the fastest for certain operations. We also look at the Shared Source CLI implementation provided by Microsoft to try to gain some understanding of why different methods appear slower and faster than others, and so in what circumstances a seemingly slower method may be appropriate.

Chapter 3 – String Conversion

This chapter covers the issues behind converting strings to and from other data types. It discusses how different data types, such as numbers and dates-times are presented differently in different locales, and how to cope with this. We also cover some of the issues behind storing strings in arrays and collections and how to best manipulate strings stored in this way.

Chapter 4 – Internationalization

All text stored by the .NET Framework is in 16-bit Unicode encoding. This chapter describes this to you and explains how to deal with the fact that string characters are now at least 16-bits wide. We cover locales in detail, and the various methods used to present text for different locales, as well as how to manipulate char types, as in Unicode, a complete character could be made up of two 16-bit char types. This chapter provides information on how you can prepare your text for presentation in different languages. We also describe how you can use resource files to keep the text of your application in one place so it can all be translated to a different language quite easily.

Chapter 5 – Introducing Regular Expressions

This chapter introduces you to the regular expression matching language, and how to use it to match patterns of text. First we teach you how to do the same jobs that can be done using `string` methods, but once you are more familiar with the syntax, we cover the unique features that the language provides. We also walk you through the creation of a regular expression tester application that will prove very useful when testing your future expressions.

Chapter 6 – Advanced Regex Concepts

The previous chapter was an introduction to the matching language; here we ramp up the learning curve and as well as providing more examples of regexes, we describe groups, substitutions, and backreferences. Grouping allows the regular expression to match groups of text, which can be captured and given names. Backreferences can be used to pull out previous matches and can be used, for instance, to match an HTML close tag with its corresponding open tag.

Chapter 7 – Regular Expression Patterns

In this chapter we detail various regular expression patterns for matching specific types of common data, such as numbers, dates, etc. We describe how these patterns are formed, and so help you form your own patterns. One of the patterns used is an e-mail address validator, which is a long and complex expression and apart from being useful in itself, its explanation will help explain how simple it is to build up expressions that match a variety of text patterns.

Appendices

There are five appendices; the first two contain tables listing the constructors, properties, and methods of the `String` and `StringBuilder` classes, whereas the third contains much of the regular expression syntax, options, and special characters. The fourth is a bonus appendix containing an article from the *C Sharp Today* web site (http://www.csharptoday.com). The last contains support and code download details for the book.

Nick Manning
Editor – Handbook Series, Wrox Press

C#

Text Manipulation

Handbook

1

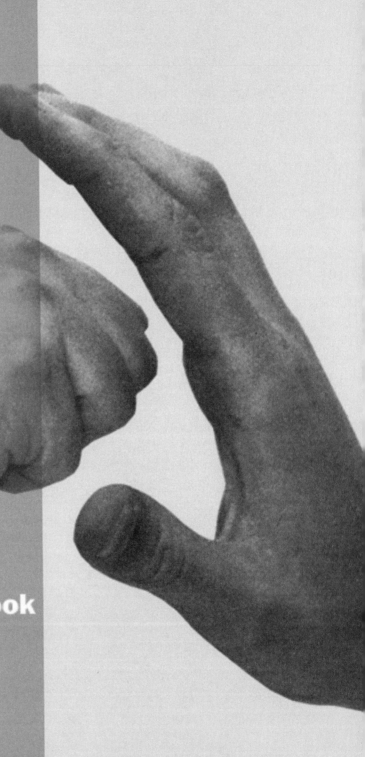

How the System Deals with Text

Text is the most used data type in computer applications. Manipulating and utilizing text effectively is vital for robust and maintainable applications. A robust and maintainable application is one that will perform well, use memory efficiently, and be easy to translate to a different locale, if necessary. Used incorrectly, text processing can result in memory leaks, poor performance, memory exceptions, and difficulty porting an application to another locale.

To provide an understanding of how text is used within MS Windows and the .NET Framework, the following points will be discussed in this chapter:

- ❑ The .NET Framework
- ❑ Text as a data type
- ❑ Characters and strings
- ❑ How an operating system stores text
- ❑ Typical text operations
- ❑ Common text uses
- ❑ Internationalization and Localization

This chapter describes how text is used in a typical computer operating system. Specific descriptions are given of how text is used in the .NET Framework and C#.

This chapter will show some examples to set the context of how text processing was performed before the .NET Framework. By the conclusion of the chapter, you will have an understanding of the underlying issues a computer application faces when processing text. We will also look at how .NET deals with string storage. The rest of the book will show how C# specifically handles text processing.

The .NET Framework

To understand how the system processes text we need to understand particular portions of the system first. The .NET Framework represents a significant shift from the Win32 architecture and as such there are many new concepts.

As you might already know, the .NET Framework consists of an execution environment (a.k.a. runtime) and a class library. The execution environment is responsible for many of the core services required by a .NET application. This includes memory allocation and cleanup. Since strings require a lot of memory management, the implementation of the execution environment will have a significant impact on the performance of applications using string manipulation.

Common Language Runtime

The execution environment is generically called the **Common Language Infrastructure** (CLI). The CLI is a standard that Microsoft has submitted to **ECMA**, which is an organization dedicated to standardizing information and communication systems. The specific standard reference is ECMA-335.

The CLI defines a specification for executable code and the execution environment. The execution environment is also known as a **Virtual Execution System** (VES). Microsoft's implementation of the CLI is the **Common Language Runtime** (CLR). When discussing the Microsoft-specific implementation, CLR is used. When discussing the standard the CLR adheres to, CLI is used. In this book, CLR is used the majority of the time since it is the Microsoft implementation that we are using.

A core part of the CLI is the **Common Type System** (CTS). The CTS defines support for the types and operations found in many programming languages and will be covered in more detail later.

Related to the CTS is the **Common Language Specification** (CLS), which is a set of rules to promote language interoperability. A key goal of the .NET Framework is to enable you to write a program in any language and run it in the same VES. Each language is supposed to be able to operate with any other. The CLS guides tool implementers to ensure the code that they write can move across languages as easily as possible.

The CLR can be thought of as the "manager" of an application written in .NET. The CLR makes sure the application adheres to security rules and provides resources to the application. An application written in .NET is called managed code since the CLR manages how the code runs.

Managed code is stored and transmitted through the **Common Intermediate Language** (CIL) and a file format. CIL is the instruction set that all source code languages are compiled to. So, if you are writing in C#, J#, Visual Basic .NET, or any other .NET language, the compiler will convert the source code to CIL instructions. Microsoft's implementation of CIL is called MSIL.

Managed data is data for which storage is allocated and released automatically by the CLR, and is stored in the managed heap. The automatic releasing is handled through garbage collection.

Managed Heap

The CLR provides automatic memory management, meaning that it takes care of memory allocation and de-allocation. This is a significant benefit for developers, since some of the most common and difficult-to-trace bugs in applications are memory leaks. A memory leak happens when a developer allocates memory and forgets to release it. Memory leaks also happen because it is sometimes not clear who is responsible for releasing that memory. For instance, if a component allocates some memory and returns the memory to the caller – who is supposed to release it and when?

Since strings usually have to be allocated, any memory management benefits translate to benefits for string use.

When an application first starts up, the CLR reserves a block of memory for use by the application. This memory block is the managed heap. All reference types are stored on the heap. As we will confirm later, a String is a reference type, so it is stored in the heap and treated like all other pieces of allocated memory.

Figure 1 illustrates what the heap looks like.

Figure 1

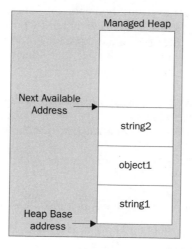

As you can see, the heap has a block of memory with a base memory address. The memory is contiguous and storage is allocated in a linear fashion. Since the heap memory is already allocated, the only thing the garbage collector has to do to return some allocated memory to the system is increment the next available address by the size of the memory being required. This makes for fast allocation of memory.

Allocation is straightforward; releasing memory is much more complicated. In fact, the term garbage collection really refers to releasing memory that is no longer being used. Computer scientists have studied various algorithms for performing garbage collection for years, and the Microsoft developers have chosen one, which in their opinion, is best for their purposes. The .NET documentation outlines the steps the garbage collector takes for releasing memory. They are not repeated here.

.NET Framework Class Library

The .NET Framework Class Library is a collection of types to support programming in the .NET Framework. A type includes classes, structures, and base (primitive) types. For example, both the `System.Text.StringBuilder` class and the `Char` structure are considered types. The class library is quite extensive and includes classes for XML processing, file I/O, drawing, threading, and, of course, string manipulation to just name a few.

Within the `System` namespace there are two important classes:

❑   `Char` – This structure is a Unicode character that has methods for converting characters and categorizing characters, such as whitespace.

❑   `String` – This class is an immutable string of characters that has methods for manipulating the string. See Appendix A for a complete list of the constructors, properties, and methods of the `String` class.

The `System.Text` namespace contains the important `StringBuilder` class that can be used to incrementally construct strings (see Appendix B for a complete list of the constructors, properties, and methods of the `StringBuilder` class). The namespace also contains classes for converting one character encoding to another, such as `Encoding`, `ASCIIEncoding`, and `UnicodeEncoding`.

The `System.Text.RegularExpressions` namespace contains various classes for constructing and executing regular expressions, such as `Capture`, `CaptureCollection`, `Regex`, and `RegexCompilationInfo`.

To summarize, the following are the important points to remember out of this discussion.

❑   Text manipulation functionality is provided by .NET Framework classes

❑   The CLR is responsible for application services including allocating and moving memory to support strings

❑   Memory management is implemented in the CLR as garbage collection

Next, let's look closer at what a data type really is.

Text as a Data Type

A data type in a programming language is data with predefined characteristics. The data type defines the rules regarding which values the data may take on. Most programming languages have some built-in data types. Examples of data types include integer, floating point, and string.

Strongly-typed programming languages, such as the .NET languages, enforce these rules. If you try to assign a value that does not correspond to the data type, an error will be thrown. Typically these rules are enforced by the compiler, meaning that data-type errors are caught early and do not make it to the run-time code.

In addition to the values it can take on, a data type is constrained by the operations that can be performed on it. For instance, using division on a string data type would not make any sense.

In general, text data types have minimal rules. Since there are minimal rules governing the values text can take on, it is often used in situations where a programmer is unsure about the range of values in the data source, such as receiving user input. However, this can cause problems as data may not be stored as efficiently as possible.

In some programming languages, the text data type has become awkward to handle. Visual C++ is one example. The following are some of the possible data-type choices for storing text when using Visual C++.

Description	Examples
Character array	`char myString[32];`
Wide character array	`w_char myString[32];`
Standard C++ library	`std::string myString;`
MFC CString	`CStr myString;`
OLE Automation string	`BSTR myString;`
Class wrapper for BSTR	`CComBSTR myString;`

On top of this, there are functions to manipulate and convert between the different string types. There is no need to have this many ways to represent strings; they are a product of history only. Originally, characters were stored in one byte. As applications became more international, some situations required two bytes to represent all the characters in particular alphabets.

You will note that we have started to use the term "string" to represent text. A character string is the full terminology used and it represents a sequence (or string) of characters. For the rest of the chapter, the term string will be used instead of text.

Since .NET is a new software platform, there was an opportunity to define the `String` data type from scratch and avoid the mess that had evolved in some programming languages.

C# Data Types

All the types in C#, and any other .NET language, are built on the CTS. One goal of the .NET Framework is to give programmers the freedom to develop in a variety of .NET-compliant languages, yet still operate on the same underlying platform. The CTS defines the types that the .NET languages must implement.

Value Types and Reference Types

The two fundamental categories of data types in .NET are value types and reference types.

Value types include integers, enumerations, structures, and characters. Value types are stored directly on the stack, which is a contiguous area of memory set aside by the operating system for fast access to data. The CLR uses a virtual stack for each process that is running. Since the size of a value type is known, there are no problems with storing it on the stack. Value types are accessed directly, rarely through a reference. When a value type is copied, the value is copied to another location.

Examples of reference types include classes, interfaces, arrays, and strings. Reference types are stored in the managed heap, which is an area of memory set aside for dynamic memory allocation where blocks of memory are allocated and freed in an arbitrary order. The sizes of reference types are not known until run time. This is why the heap is used for storing them.

Reference types are accessed through a reference to the managed heap (somewhat like a pointer). This allows the garbage collector to keep track of references and release storage when no more references remain. When reference variables are copied, the reference (which is the memory address) is copied, not the value itself.

Primitive Types

The .NET Framework class library is a collection of types that tightly integrate with the CLR. The class library is object-oriented, meaning that all types have properties and methods. Some types are used so commonly that shortcuts are provided for describing them. These types are called primitive types.

Primitive types are identified through keywords, which are aliases for predefined types in the `System` namespace. A primitive type is indistinguishable from the structure type it aliases: writing the reserved word `char` is the same as writing `System.Char`. Primitive types offer these additional operations over other types:

❑ All primitive types permit values to be created by writing literals. For example, `'A'` is a literal of type `char`.

❏   It is possible to declare constants using primitive types.

❏   When the operands of an expression are all primitive type constants, it is possible for the compiler to evaluate the expression at compile time. Such an expression is known as a constant expression.

The following are examples uses of primitive types declared in a C# program:

```
char myChar = 'A';
string myString = "My String";
int myInt = 42;
```

The string type is unique in that it is the only primitive type that is a reference and not a value type. This causes a flaw in logic; being a primitive type, strings can be declared constant. However, constants cannot be placed on the heap since the heap performs run-time allocation and constants are defined when the program is compiled. A constant string is a special situation and a process called **interning** is performed, which will be discussed later.

Before we look further into the string data type though, let's look at the fundamental unit of strings – the character data type.

Characters and Character Sets

A definition of a character can be found at http://whatis.techtarget.com. This web site defines a character as follows:

In information technology, a character is a printable symbol having phonetic or pictographic meaning and usually forming part of a word of text, depicting a numeral, or expressing grammatical punctuation. In information technology today, a character is generally one of a limited number of symbols, including the letters of a particular language's alphabet, the numerals in the decimal number system, and certain special symbols such as the ampersand (&) and "at sign" (@).

Several standards of computer encoding have been developed for characters. The most commonly used in personal computers is ASCII. IBM mainframe systems use EBCDIC. A new standard, Unicode, is supported by later Windows systems.

That is a good definition. It defines that a character represents a symbol to communicate information to computer users. The only addition is that since characters are historically represented by a byte, they are sometimes used to represent binary information. The definition also indicates there are standards for encoding characters.

ASCII is the character set traditionally used by PCs to store characters. An ASCII character is stored as a 7-bit binary number. That means an ASCII character can take on one of 128 values. The ASCII format is quite old; it was originally developed for teletypes so some of the ASCII values are control characters for the teletype (for example, ASCII value 23, which represents "end of transmission block"). It consumes only 7 bits, because a parity bit was often sent with each character as transports and media were far less reliable in the 1970s.

Since modern computers store information as bytes, each of which is 8 bits, one bit was essentially wasted for each character. One bit may not sound like much, but if all 8 bits are used instead of 7, twice as many characters values can be represented.

As computers evolved, programmers decided to make use of the extra bit and Extended ASCII was born. By using the extra bit, 128 more values could be added to the ASCII character set. These additional characters include accented characters, mathematical symbols, and certain graphics characters.

There are a few varying extended ASCII characters sets. If you are moving characters between platforms, for example from Windows to Macintosh, the extended ASCII characters may have different meanings. For example, the letter ç on MS Windows appears as Á on an Apple Macintosh. Extended characters sets are also referred to as code pages.

If you intend to use the extended ASCII characters between platforms, you should identify the characters set by using a code page. With the Internet, HTML and XML tend to be the text documents that move between platforms. In HTML, you can specify the code page with the following:

```
<META HTTP-EQUIV="Content-Type"
      CONTENT="text/html; charset=ISO-8859-1">
```

In this example, the code page is ISO-8859-1, which is known as Latin1 and covers most West European languages, including English, French, German, Italian, and Spanish.

With XML, a declaration is used to represent the character encoding:

```
<?xml version="1.0" encoding="ISO-8859-1"?>
```

> It should be noted that the first 128 character codes of any of the ISO 8859 character sets are always identical to the ASCII character set.

In the late 1980s, a number of researchers tackled the problem of representing different languages with the same character set. Out of that research, the Unicode Consortium was born in the early 1990s. The Unicode Consortium is responsible for defining the behavior and relationships between Unicode characters, and providing technical information to implementers. Some of its members include Adobe, Apple, Microsoft, IBM, and Sun.

The Unicode Consortium states the following:

> Unicode provides a unique number for every character, no matter what the platform, no matter what the program and no matter what the language.

The Unicode standard defines codes for characters in most major languages written today. Examples of supported scripts include Latin, Greek, Cyrillic, Armenian, Hebrew, Arabic, Devanagari, Oriya, Tamil, and Braille. In addition to scripts, the standard includes punctuation marks, diacritics, mathematical symbols, technical symbols, arrows, and dingbats.

The Unicode Version 2.1 standard provides codes for nearly 39,000 characters from the world's alphabets, ideograph sets, and symbol collections. In addition, there are approximately 18,000 code values reserved for future use. The Unicode standard also contains 6,400 code values that software and hardware developers can assign internally for their own characters and symbols.

The Unicode standard manages to represent so many characters by using an extra byte. Unicode is a 2-byte encoding meaning it can represent 256*256 = 65,536 characters. However, what you get in flexibility you sacrifice with space. A Unicode text file is twice the size of an ASCII file, and the same difference applies to memory usage. As a result, if you are constrained for space, and so may be only using ASCII characters, you should consider how your programming language is representing the characters.

Unfortunately, the original Unicode specification cannot handle all character requirements. The Chinese speaking community alone uses over 55,000 characters. To accommodate this problem, the Unicode Standard has defined surrogates. A surrogate or surrogate pair is a pair of 16-bit Unicode code values that represent a single character. Using surrogates, Unicode can support over one million characters. This will be covered further in Chapter 4.

Characters in C#

C# stores characters as Unicode. A single Unicode characters is represented by the char value type, which maps to the System.Char structure. Since a Unicode character is represented by two bytes, a char type can take on any value from hexadecimal 0x0000 to 0xFFFF.

One of the biggest differences between characters in .NET and those in previous languages is that characters are defined as structures with members. This means that, instead of using functions that operate on a character, we use a character's methods. In addition, constants associated with the data type (such as a minimum value) are tied to the object itself, rather than a separate value listed elsewhere.

One of the more useful methods of the char structure is GetUnicodeCategory(). This static method classifies the type of character passed to it into one of 30 categories, each represented by the System.Globalization.UnicodeCategory enumeration. Example categories include UppercaseLetter, ParagraphSeparator, DashPunctuation, and CurrencySymbol.

The char structure also has a number of methods to classify characters, such as IsDigit() and IsPunctuation(). Here's an example using these methods:

```
string band;
band = "The Albion Band";
Console.WriteLine(char.IsWhiteSpace(band, 3));    // Output: True
Console.WriteLine(char.IsPunctuation('A'));       // Output: False
```

Using the `IsWhiteSpace()` method, a test is performed to see if the fourth character in the string is a whitespace characters (using a zero-based index). The `IsPunctuation()` method tests if the letter "A" is punctuation. Note that we have used single quotes (apostrophes) to delimit the "A" character when defined. This is the language construct used in C# to specify that the object used is of type `char`, and not `string`. See the .NET Framework documentation for all the methods supported by the `char` structure.

You can obtain the character code (also known as code point) for a character by converting the `char` value type to an `int`; you can specify the output in the usual Unicode hexadecimal form by adding a format provider (detailed in Chapter 3) to the number's `ToString()` method:

```
int charCode = (int) 'A';                      // charCode is set to 65.
Console.WriteLine(charCode.ToString("x4")); // Will output 0041
```

Similarly, you can return the character represented by the given character code by converting an `int` into a `char`:

```
int charCode = 100;
char character = (char) charCode;
Console.WriteLine(character);  // Outputs "d"
```

A good way to understand how characters are represented in memory is to write them to a file and then look at them with a binary editor. The bytes in the file are the same as those that get stored in memory. The following example opens a file and writes text to that file in three different encodings. The file extension is `.bin` to force the file to be opened with a binary editor:

```
using System;
using System.IO;
using System.Text;

class Binary
{
    static void Main(string[] args)
    {
        FileStream fs = new FileStream("text.bin", FileMode.OpenOrCreate);

        StreamWriter t = new StreamWriter(fs, Encoding.UTF8);
        t.Write("This is in UTF8");
        t.Flush();
```

```
        StreamWriter t2 = new StreamWriter(fs, Encoding.Unicode);
        t2.Write("This is in Unicode (UTF16)");
        t2.Flush();

        StreamWriter t3 = new StreamWriter(fs, Encoding.ASCII);
        t3.Write("This is in ASCII");
        t3.Flush();

        fs.Close();
    }
}
```

Using the binary editor built in to Visual Studio .NET, you can see that the data looks like the following.

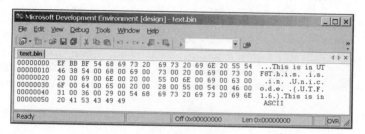

There are a few interesting points to note. In all three encodings, the low bytes are the same. The low byte is the first sixteen bits of the value. For instance, the letter "T" is represented by the value 0x54 in all cases. The Unicode encoding has an extra byte with each character that doubles the amount of space it requires compared to ASCII or UTF-8.

Now that we have covered characters individually, let's look at character strings.

String Data Type

As mentioned, a string is a series of characters. You may already know that with the original version of C, strings could only be represented as an array of characters. The same functions for manipulating arrays of bytes were used to manipulate strings.

The .NET Framework uses a `String` class to implement the `string` data type. The following code shows declaration of a `string` and an array of `string`s:

```
string myString = "My String!";
string[] arrString = {"to", "the", "max"};
```

Strings are a unique data type in that they are the only primitive data type that is of variable length, and this can cause problems. Computers need to know how long data is so that memory can be allocated for it. To understand how this issue has been approached let's look at how text is stored.

Text Storage

Storage of text is dependent on the programming language and software platform being used. To create a computer application, instructions are written in a programming language. The programming language may provide an implementation of these instructions itself or call on the services of an underlying software platform.

When compiled, a program written in C, for instance, converts the instructions directly into machine code. Machine code does not know anything about strings; it only understands allocating memory and copying bytes. As a result, much of the work required to manipulate strings is part of the C programming language.

In the case of .NET, the CLR implements the functionality described within the program. Therefore, the CLR must understand how to do text allocation and copying.

Text can be statically or dynamically allocated. If it is statically allocated, the operating system knows exactly how many characters (and thus how much space) will be required when the program is compiled. If it is dynamically allocated, then the operating system does not reserve any space for the string until run time.

There are two common methods for programming languages to keep track of how long a string is. They can either store the length of the string at its beginning, or the string can contain a special character representing a terminator.

When the length of a string is stored at its beginning, it is often referred to as a **structured string** or a **Pascal string**. As you probably can guess, Pascal is one programming language that takes this approach. The first byte in a structured string is a length byte, which is the number of characters in the string. The actual characters themselves follow the length byte.

Since the length of the string is available immediately, string operations can be much faster. For instance, determining the length of a string is a matter of reading the first byte, whereas with a terminated string the entire string must be scanned to find the terminator. Consider the following pseudo-code:

```
for (int i =0; i < myString.Length; i++)
{
    // Perform some operation
}
```

If the string length were 1,000 then the number of operations for a Pascal string would be 1,000. However, for a terminated string the number of operations would be calculated by the formula myString.Length * myString.Length = 1,000,000! This is an example of how, even though a programmer should be shielded from how a programming language implements operations, it is important to have an understanding of the implications of constructing code a certain way. A better way to implement the operation would be the following:

18

```
int lengthString = myString.Length;
for (int i =0; i < lengthString; i++)
{
    // Perform some operation
}
```

For a terminated string, this would reduce the number of operations back to a linear relationship rather than a quadratic.

Figure 2 shows how a Pascal string is stored in memory:

Figure 2

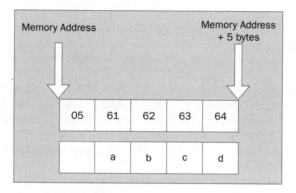

The alternative to prefixing the string with its length is to put a special null-terminator character in the string indicating it is the end of the string. Often a null character of value 0x00 is used, as shown in Figure 3:

Figure 3

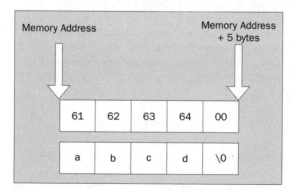

This approach has the flexibility of allowing strings to be of any length, but it also has its problems, as shown in the previous examples; to determine the length of the string you have to go through every character. In addition, as C programmers are already well aware, you can easily cause memory faults by forgetting to terminate the string, or by overwriting the null character.

In both cases, programmers are encouraged to manipulate strings in a particular manner that is efficient for that type of string representation. However, the Pascal form of string manipulation is quite inefficient when used on null-terminated strings, as in C. Thus, code in one language that performs string manipulation cannot be directly translated to another language without introducing inefficiencies.

Since string manipulation is often expensive, software platform designers have often looked into techniques for improving performance. We'll take a look at some of those techniques now.

Caching

To minimize the amount of memory allocation that occurs for strings, some systems implement a caching scheme. Microsoft Automation does this with Automation's representation of Unicode characters, also known as **BSTRs** (Binary Strings).

BSTRs are null-terminated; however, you can query a BSTR for its length rather than scan it, so it can contain embedded null characters. The length is stored as a 32-bit integer at the memory location preceding the data in the string. The theoretical maximum length of a BSTR is 4,294,967,296 characters; however, your operating system may grind to a halt long before this depending upon available resources.

Automation may cache the space allocated for BSTRs. This speeds up the allocation and de-allocation sequence. For example, if the application allocates a BSTR and frees it, the free block of memory is put into the BSTR cache by Automation. If the application then allocates another BSTR, it can get the free block from the cache.

A null pointer is a valid value for a BSTR variable. By convention, it is always treated the same as a pointer to a BSTR that contains zero characters.

The Automation string cache is about 60K, so concatenations that fit in this size are optimized for performance. The cache is designed to operate on strings in an efficient way. Longer strings are allocated to the heap and take considerably longer to be concatenated. The implication is that performance can be significantly increased by concatenating smaller strings first so that the cache is used.

For example, consider the following statement from VB6:

```
sLongString = sLongString + "." + Environment.NewLine
```

The chances that the cache is used will be improved by concentrating the smaller strings first:

```
sLongString = sLongString + ("." + Environment.NewLine)
```

Interning

Sometimes strings are continually reused in an application. Exploiting this characteristic can lead to substantial memory savings and performance gains. The process of interning consists of a data structure and set of algorithms used to achieve these benefits.

Interning offers a performance advantage in the situation where the same strings are used repeatedly. It has some up-front resource cost, but once in place it supports efficient equality checking between strings, since it is comparing pooled objects rather than character sequences.

The CLR automatically maintains a table, called the **intern pool**, which contains a single instance of each unique literal string constant declared in a program, as well as any unique instance of the System.String class you create programmatically.

The intern pool is implemented as a hash table. Using a hash table means a string is represented by a single number or hash. Comparing and searching for strings then becomes very efficient because, instead of comparing strings character for character, only the hash value has to be compared.

The intern pool conserves string storage. If you assign a literal string constant to several variables, each variable is set to reference the same constant in the intern pool, rather than reference several different instances of the System.String class that have identical values.

Strings created using the StringBuilder class can be manually added to the intern pool using the Intern() method. You will see more about interning in Chapter 2.

Other Approaches

For specialized applications, there are algorithms and data structures for storing text efficiently. An example is a **trie**. A trie is a tree structure for storing strings and has been used to store large dictionaries of words for spell checking programming and natural language processing.

Let's look at a simple example of how a trie works. Consider the words "exposition" and "exposure". Stored individually, the total space occupied by these words is 18 characters. However, the first 5 characters are the same. A trie would store the common characters once and then have pointers to the other characters in the words. This reduces the number of characters stored to 13. When a large number of words are stored, the amount of memory saved can be substantial.

Certain programming APIs, such as **Xalan-Java 2,** implement a trie class. If the language does not support it natively, then the programmer would have to build the data structure.

The CLR implementation of the intern pool is as a hash table. However, it could also be implemented as a trie. With the CLI available as a shared source it would be possible for you to make that change as an academic exercise.

.NET Implementation

We have looked at various approaches to storing strings. Now let's use an example to demonstrate how .NET does it.

Consider the following simple program that declares a string variable:

```
public class Class1
{
  static void Main(string[] args)
  {
    string myString = "hello string";
  }
}
```

When viewed with the `ildasm.exe` utility, the IL code that implements this source code looks like the following listing:

```
.method private hidebysig static void  Main(string[] args) cil managed
{
  .entrypoint
  // Code size       7 (0x7)
  .maxstack  1
  .locals init (string V_0)
  IL_0000:  ldstr       "hello string"
  IL_0005:  stloc.0
  IL_0006:  ret
} // end of method Class1::Main
```

This is the extent to which the portable executable knows about loading a string. The IL code just knows that it is supposed to put the characters `hello string` into a `string` object. The actual work of doing this is up to the CLI implementation.

In the file `string.cs` of the Shared Source CLI we can see that the constructor is declared externally:

```
[MethodImplAttribute(MethodImplOptions.InternalCall)]
public extern String(char [] value);
```

To see the actual implementation, we have to switch from C# to C++ code. Within the code of `COMString.cpp`, we can find the code that implements the constructor:

```
STRINGREF COMString::NewString(const WCHAR *pwsz)
{
  THROWSCOMPLUSEXCEPTION();
  if (!pwsz)
  {
    return NULL;
  }
  else
  {
    DWORD nch = (DWORD)wcslen(pwsz);
    if (nch==0) {
      return GetEmptyString();
    }
    _ASSERTE(!g_pGCHeap->IsHeapPointer((BYTE *) pwsz) ||
             !"pwsz can not point to GC Heap");
    STRINGREF pString = AllocateString( nch + 1);

    memcpyNoGCRefs(pString->GetBuffer(), pwsz, nch*sizeof(WCHAR));
    pString->SetStringLength(nch);
    _ASSERTE(pString->GetBuffer()[nch] == 0);
    return pString;
  }
}
```

The AllocateString() call returns a pointer to a StringObject. The C++ StringObject class is the internal representation of a .NET System.String. A portion of the StringObject implementation is listed below:

```
class StringObject : public Object
{
  friend class GCHeap;
  friend class JIT_TrialAlloc;

  private:
    DWORD   m_ArrayLength;
    DWORD   m_StringLength;
    WCHAR   m_Characters[0];
```

We have finally found where the data is stored. It is an array of WCHAR. A WCHAR is a two-byte character. As you can see, an array length and string length are also stored. The array length is the size of allocated memory measured in number of WCHARs. The string length is the number of WCHARs in the string. The array length may be greater than the string length, which means there is unused space in the string.

The m_StringLength field has another responsibility as well. The two high bits of this value indicate if the string has characters higher than 0x7F. If not, it means the characters occupy the standard ASCII character set. If this is the case then the system can use algorithms that will process the string faster. The implication of this is that, if you can keep the characters in a string to the ASCII standard character set, you may get some performance optimizations from the system.

We have seen that ultimately a string is stored as an array of characters. Why not do this to start with in your C# code? The code would look like the following (the string was shortened to make it more readable):

```
public static void Main()
{
    char[] myString = {'h', 'e', 'l', 'l', 'o'};
}
```

The generated IL code looks like the following:

```
.method private hidebysig static void  Main(string[] args) cil managed
{
  .entrypoint
  // Code size       19 (0x13)
  .maxstack  3
  .locals init (char[] V_0)
  IL_0000:  ldc.i4.5
  IL_0001:  newarr     [mscorlib]System.Char
  IL_0006:  dup
  IL_0007:  ldtoken    field valuetype
'<PrivateImplementationDetails>'/'$$struct0x6000001-1'
'<PrivateImplementationDetails>'::'$$method0x6000001-1'
  IL_000c:  call       void
[mscorlib]System.Runtime.CompilerServices.RuntimeHelpers::InitializeAr
ray(class [mscorlib]System.Array,
  valuetype [mscorlib]System.RuntimeFieldHandle)
  IL_0011:  stloc.0
  IL_0012:  ret
} // end of method Class1::Main
```

The <PrivateImplementationDetails> contains a little more code on top of this. That's a lot of instructions to initialize a string. Each individual character is loaded onto the stack and stored in an array location. It seems like an awkward way to initialize a string.

Alternatively, you can specify the character array explicitly as a string as we did earlier. That way is more attractive to look at and there is a lot less IL code in this in case. Notice that a string object was created. That shifts more of the work from IL instructions to the CLR.

The methods used to manipulate arrays can also be used to manipulate char arrays. The following example demonstrates a few operations you can do:

```
using System;

public class Methods
{
    public static void Main(string[] args)
    {
```

```
char[] myString = "hello string!".ToCharArray();
Console.WriteLine(myString);

// Create a substring
for (int i = 6; i < myString.Length; i++)
{
  Console.Write(myString[i]);
}
Console.WriteLine();

// Find the last 'l' in the char array
Console.WriteLine(Array.LastIndexOf(myString, 'l'));

// Reverse the array
Array.Reverse(myString);
Console.WriteLine(myString);

// Sort the array
Array.Sort(myString);
Console.WriteLine(myString);
Console.ReadLine();
  }
}
```

The following output will be displayed on the console:

```
hello string!
String!
3
!gnirts olleh
 !eghillnorst
```

Some operations, such as `Sort()` and `Reverse()`, are not available as part of the `String` and `StringBuilder` classes, which makes a case for representing a string as an array of characters when the need arises.

String Operations

Operations on strings generally fall into the following broad categories:

❑ Concatenating strings

❑ Extracting substrings from strings

❑ Comparing strings

❑ Converting strings

❑ Formatting strings

We will briefly look at these operations in this section, and then see how they combine for common text operations in the next section. The resource cost of the operations will be discussed in terms of performance (time to execute a task) and memory requirements.

Concatenating Strings

Concatenation is probably the most used operation on strings. However, it is probably the most expensive string operation since it demands substantial CPU resources to copy bytes. An application can really suffer from performance problems with string concatenation.

Let's look at a sample piece of code:

```
string str1;
string str2;
string str3;

str1 = "abcde"
str2 = "fgh"
str3 = str1 + str2
```

Figure 4 represents the highlighted operation:

Figure 4

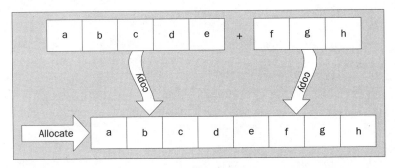

First, new memory has to be allocated to accommodate the new string. Then the characters have to be copied from the source strings to the destination string.

The article *HOWTO: Improve String Concatenation Performance (KB Q170964)* describes an alternative technique to normal concatenation that can improve performance for large strings by twenty times or more. Consider the following simple loop, which contains a concatenation operation in each iteration of the loop:

```
for (int i = 0;i <= N; i++)
{
  Dest = Dest + Source;
}
```

To execute this set of code, the following steps will be needed:

1. Allocate temporary memory large enough to hold the result

2. Copy Dest to the start of the temporary area

3. Copy Source to the end of the temporary area

4. De-allocate the old copy of Dest

5. Allocate memory for Dest large enough to hold the result

6. Copy the temporary data to Dest

The following is the result Microsoft gives:

```
Using standard concatenation
 1000 concatenations took 2348 ticks
 2000 concatenations took 8954 ticks
 3000 concatenations took 20271 ticks
 4000 concatenations took 35103 ticks
 5000 concatenations took 54453 ticks

Using pre-allocated storage and pseudo-concatenation
 1000 pseudo-concatenations took 82 ticks
 2000 pseudo-concatenations took 124 ticks
 3000 pseudo-concatenations took 165 ticks
 4000 pseudo-concatenations took 247 ticks
 5000 pseudo-concatenations took 289 ticks
```

The implication is that good string design would use the "pre-allocated storage and pseudo-concatenation" technique. In Chapter 2, we will see how .NET addresses this problem with the StringBuilder class.

Extracting Substrings from Strings

Instead of making strings bigger with concatenation, we often want to make them smaller. The Trim() method is used to remove leading or trailing whitespace and programmers often use this to clean up user-entered text.

Sometimes specific characters need to be extracted from the string and the Substring() method is how this is done. In reality, using a Trim() method is the same as extracting a substring; you are just relying on the function to determine where the substring should be taken.

In all cases, these functions consist of copying all or a subset of a string to another string. The specific steps are:

1. Determine the number of characters to copy
2. Allocate space for the characters
3. Copy the characters to the new string

Because of the memory allocation and copying operations involved, extracting substrings can also be an expensive operation.

Comparing Strings

String comparison is a common operation. Often a user will have entered some text and the program needs to determine something about what the user has entered. Some string comparisons require an exact match. This is a straightforward operation as it is simply a character-by-character comparison of the two strings. This occurs in C# through the use of the op_Equality() method. Since there is no memory allocation or copying involved, this operation is not as resource expensive.

In many situations, string comparison is used for validation. Often the content is not what is important but rather the format of the data. Writing code to make sure a phone number is of the form XXX-XXX-XXXX, where each X is a value between 0 and 9, would take too much code.

The best way to perform validations like this is to describe the pattern that it should represent and validate the text against that pattern. Pattern matching is implemented with regular expressions, which all .NET languages support through the System.Text.RegularExpressions namespace. Chapters 5 to 7 of this book are dedicated to them, since they provide such a powerful tool.

Converting Strings

Other data types that are not strings are represented in a form that is efficient for the operating system to store. In order to display them in a string, they need to be converted to characters.

.NET uses the ToString() method to return string representations of data types:

```
DateTime myDate = new DateTime(2002, 9,20);
Console.WriteLine(myDate.ToString());
```

This displays 9/20/2002 12:00:00 AM on a US-based system. However, it may be different depending on your locale's date format.

The steps to convert a data type to a string are as follows:

1. Select the conversion algorithm based on the source data type

2. Determine how big the resulting string will be

3. Allocate memory for the string

4. Execute the conversion algorithm to populate the string

The resource requirements for conversion will depend on the algorithm used. Conversion is an expensive operation since, in addition to the resource cost for the algorithm, there are also the requirements of determining the string length and memory allocation. Chapter 3 will provide more details on string conversion with .NET.

Formatting Strings

It is common that various pieces of information are collected together into one string to pass to a user. In addition, programmers often want to control how the conversion from machine representation to character data takes place. This is known as formatting, which is similar to conversion, except that the programmer has more control over the algorithm used for the conversion.

In .NET, to implement a formatting string, you use the `String.Format()` method. With the `Format()` method you can specify either a formatting expression or a named format. The difficulty with formatting in Visual Basic 6, for instance, is that it only allows you to operate on one piece of data at a time. Programmers often want to put a number of pieces of data into one string. The formatting expression present in C is more powerful; it can format a string, perform conversion, and concatenate information at the same time. We will see in Chapter 2 how .NET brings C-like formatting expressions to C#.

Formatting may vary, depending on user preferences or languages settings. For instance, forty dollars is represented as `$40.00` with North American formatting and `40.00 $` with French formatting.

The resource cost for formatting is similar to conversion, since an algorithm needs to be executed and a string needs to be allocated.

In summary, string operations that cause memory allocation and the copying of bytes are resource intensive. String operations that scan strings for information are not as resource expensive. The resource costs can increase dramatically if the operations are performed in a loop. We will see examples of this problem in the next section.

String Uses

Text is used for many different purposes. Let's have a look at a few of them and think about what overhead is associated with each purpose.

Building Strings

One of the more common uses of strings is to build up some information to send somewhere else. Examples include:

❑ Building a log entry to write to a text file

❑ Building an HTML page to send to a browser

❑ Building an XML document to place in a message queue

❑ Building a message for an automated e-mail

❑ Building a SQL statement to pass to a database

With the popularity of the Web, HTML has become a widely used method of creating user interfaces. Since HTML is text-based, programmers use text operations and storage to build and manipulate it. A typical Active Server Page using VBScript would look like the following:

```
<%
    Dim strHTML

    strHTML = "<HTML><BODY>"
    strHTML = strHTML & "My name is: "
    strHTML = strHTML & Request.ServerVariables("SERVER_NAME")
    strHTML = strHTML & "</BODY></HTML>"

    Response.Write strHTML
%>
```

This approach is very easy to understand. You just keep appending information until you have everything you want, and then you send it to the client. However, this approach is not very efficient. When the strHTML variable is declared, the system has no idea how much memory needs to be reserved for it. Only when a value is assigned to the variable does it know how much memory to allocate. With each additional concatenation, the operating system has to allocate more memory and copy the characters. As we have already stated, memory allocation and copying takes time and resources.

The above code snippet potentially initiates four separate memory allocations, which may not seem like a big deal. However, since it is a web page, those allocations happen for each page request. Therefore, if the web page receives five requests per second, this translates to 20 memory allocations per second.

An alternative using similar code in C# would be to put all the string pieces in an array and piece the individual elements together into one string:

```
<%
  string[] arrString = new String[3];
  string strHTML;

  arrString[0] = "<HTML><BODY>";
  arrString[1] = "My name is: ";
  arrString[2] = Request.ServerVariables("SERVER_NAME");
  arrString[3] = "</BODY></HTML>";
  strHTML = arrString[0] + arrString[1] + arrString[2] + arrString[3];

  Response.Write(strHTML);
%>
```

This will result in less memory allocations and fewer copies. If you have an inkling of how large the string will be before you create it, you can specifically allocate that memory. Let's look at an example that does this using the C language:

```
char strBuffer[256];

sprintf( strBuffer, "<HTML><BODY>My name is: %s </BODY></HTML>",
         strServerName );
```

In this case, when the string is declared (actually an array of characters), the amount of memory is fixed. This means that no memory allocations are necessary. However, a problem occurs if strServerName causes the entire string to be greater than 256 characters, as the memory will become corrupt.

To be safe and avoid wasting memory, the memory would have to be dynamically allocated:

```
char *pBuffer;

pBuffer = malloc( sizeof(char)*(sizeof(strServerName)+ 39 ) );

sprintf( strBuffer, "<HTML><BODY>My name is: %s </BODY></HTML>",
         strServerName );
```

This approach requires a memory allocation and is at risk of a memory leak. The programmer must remember to free the memory allocated to the string. This approach is not as intuitive to programmers when building strings either. In the next chapter, you will see how to use the StringBuilder object to build up strings in stages, which is much less cumbersome than concatenating individual elements of an array together.

Parsing Strings

In addition to building strings, developers often have to take strings apart. This is commonly known as parsing. Parsing is breaking structured data into smaller pieces based on rules that describe the layout of the data. One of the most common problems a programmer faces is that of parsing a row of text separated by a delimiter, such as a comma.

In .NET, you use the Split() method. This method operates on a string object and has two overloads. One takes just a char[] array, which specifies each delimiter. The other has the char[] array as its first parameter, and an integer indicating how many elements to return. The method returns a string[] array.

Positional files are another type of text file that often needs parsing. In this case, instead of using a delimiter to separate fields, fields are given a fixed width. EDI transmission is an example of something similar to a positional file. Parsing positional files makes extensive use of the Substring() method, which can be expensive.

For both delimited and positional files, it is often better to use a specialized tool for parsing. The awk tool has been around for a long time in the UNIX environment and has been ported to many other operating systems, including Windows. It supports regular expressions, so it is also useful for search-and-replace operations.

There are other more complicated types of text that may need parsing. Examples include:

❑   Elements in an XML document

❑   Source code of a computer program

❑   Text in a word processing document

These types of parsing problems are beyond the domain of a programming language. Typically, tools are used to do the work of parsing these types of documents. These tools are specialized to perform optimally for the particular parsing problem they were designed to solve.

For example, XML documents can be parsed using an XML parser such as Microsoft's MSXML parser. XML parsers typically have had two approaches to parsing – DOM and SAX. The DOM will parse the text representing the XML document and store it as an object model in memory making it easy for programmers to access the information. SAX is another approach. Instead of having an object model representing the XML document, it informs the calling code when certain text elements have been parsed. These have their own advantages – DOM is necessary for writing XML data as you need a complete XML structure, whereas SAX is fast for locating and replacing data as it doesn't have to search the entire document.

The same approach can be taken for processing text files. If you need all the data in a text file you load the entire file into memory. However, if you are looking for a specific data item or can treat each line of data independently you only need to load one line of data into memory at a time. Also, as soon as the task is complete the processing can be halted instead of reading every line in the file.

32

Internationalization

The terms internationalization and localization are often used interchangeably but they have specific distinct meanings.

Internationalization is the process of planning and implementing products and services so that they can easily be adapted to specific local languages and cultures. The internationalization process is sometimes called "localization enablement". Microsoft has adopted the term **world-ready** to mean internationalization. You may also come across Internationalization referred to as I18N, which is the first letter "I", "1'" to referring to the 18 middle characters, then the last letter "N".

Localization is the process of adapting an application to a particular language, culture, and desired local "look-and-feel". This includes translating the text of the application, and ensuring that formatting (of things such as currencies and dates) is correct for the specific culture.

A culture in .NET is a specific language and region used to specify a language to use, and the various date, time, and number formatting options that region may have. For instance, en-US specifies that the language is English, and that the various data types should be formatted for the US. If en-GB is used, the language is the same, but the currency symbol is £ and dates are written as dd/mm/yyyy, as well as there being other regional differences.

Ideally, a product or service is developed so that localization is relatively easy to achieve. An internationalized product or service is therefore easier to localize. It is a programmer's job to ensure that the software is internationalized. When the software is to be made available in another language, the software is then usually handed to someone else who is a specialist in that area.

A core part of internalization is ensuring text from any language can be placed into the user interface. Certain simple guidelines should be followed when internationalizing text.

When things such as strings, characters, constants, screen positions, file names, and file paths are hard-coded, they can be difficult to track down and localize. It is much better to isolate all localizable items into resource files, and minimize compilation dependencies.

It is best not to declare buffers that are the exact size of a word or a sentence. The problem is that, when text is translated, the translated text may be of a greater size. For example, your application may declare a 2-byte buffer size for the word OK that could refer to the text in an OK button. However, in Spanish the word OK is translated as Aceptar, which would cause your application's buffer to overflow.

String composition should also be avoided. For example, consider translating wrong file and wrong directory into Italian. The results are file errato and cartella erratta, respectively. If you try to perform string composition using the syntax "wrong " + object, it is not going to work.

In addition to these recommendations for strings, character sets also need to be considered. We touched on character sets earlier in the chapter. The characters of a language need to be displayed in order to convey a user interface in that language. There has to be enough data space to accommodate multiple-byte character codes, such as Japanese Kanji. Some languages required more characters to represent concepts and therefore more space has to be accommodated in the user interface.

It is often important to put strings into a resource file. Since this resource file will most likely go to a translator it is also important not to put in resources that may confuse the translator. If you have achieved an internationalized application then localization should consist primarily of translating the user interface. This means the application's executable code should be separated from the text. To accomplish this, resource files are used.

.NET Resource Files

The .NET Framework provides three ways to create resource files: as text files, as XML files, or as binary resource files. Both text files and XML files end up as binary resource files by the time they are inserted in the application. The files are compiled into a resource file with the Resource File Generator (`Resgen.exe`) utility.

A text file can only be used if strings are the only resource to be stored. The text is stored as name-value pairs. Comments are allowed and demarked with a semicolon. The following is a sample text file:

```
[strings]
;prompts
promptAge = Please enter your age.

;error messages
msgNotFound = File not found.
msgNoRecords = No records were found for that query.
```

The advantage of using a text file is that it is straightforward to create and understand. A translator can edit the file in Notepad or any other text editor. The disadvantage is that if a syntax error is introduced into the file it won't be caught until the file is back in the hands of the developer.

The same resource file as XML could look like the following:

```
<?xml version="1.0" encoding="utf-8" ?>
<root>
  <xs:schema id="root" xmlns=""
            xmlns:xs="http://www.w3.org/2001/XMLSchema"
            xmlns:msdata="urn:schemas-microsoft-com:xml-msdata">
    <xs:element name="data">
      <xs:complexType>
        <xs:sequence>
          <xs:element name="value" type="xs:string" minOccurs="0"
```

```
                        msdata:Ordinal="2" />
            </xs:sequence>
            <xs:attribute name="name" type="xs:string" />
          </xs:complexType>
        </xs:element>
      </xs:schema>
      <data name="promptAge">
        <value>Please enter your age.</value>
      </data>
      <data name="msgNotFound">
        <value> File not found.</value>
      </data>
      <data name="msgNoRecords">
        <value> No records were found for that query.</value>
      </data>
    </root>
```

The first section is a header that contains the schema for the actual content. A translator would only work with the content and not touch the header. Since XML is still a text file, it too can be edited in Notepad or any other text editor. However, it would make sense for some specific tools to be used for editing the file. For instance, Visual Studio .NET has an XML editor built in, in which .resx files can be edited.

Any other XML editor can be applied. Many XML editors (such as SoftQuad XMetal) are easy to use. Translators can focus on translating the text rather than worrying about preserving the syntax of the file. An additional advantage is that an XML editor will guarantee that the data written to the file is well-formed XML (and valid if a good editor is used).

Summary

In this chapter, we have reviewed various aspects of using text within a computer application. Using text consists of working with individual characters and contiguous sets of characters – otherwise known as strings.

Many string operations are performance killers because of the memory allocations and character copies that take place. Proper string design is essential to ensure that programmers minimize causing this problem.

In the rest of this book, we will look at the various ways of manipulating text in C#, and advise you on how best to meet your goals.

C#

Text Manipulation

Handbook

2

2

String and StringBuilder

The previous chapter outlined a number of issues for dealing with strings. In particular, since strings are a data type with variable length, there can be issues regarding performance and memory management. This chapter shows how the Microsoft .NET Framework addresses these string-related issues with the String and StringBuilder classes.

To gain an understanding of how text is used with C# we will address the following in this chapter:

❑   How to use the String class

❑   How to use the StringBuilder class

❑   Text operations with C#

❑   Using the String.Format class

❑   Using text within C#

As you will see, there are more ways than one to perform text operations within C#. This chapter gives guidance on which methods are best for various situations, partially through the creation of very simple performance testing applications in the latter half of the chapter.

Tools for this Chapter

To get a better understanding of the inner workings of the String and StringBuilder classes, two sources of information have been used.

The first tool is the Microsoft Shared Source CLI (Common Language Infrastructure) implementation, also known as Rotor, available at: http://msdn.microsoft.com/library/default.asp?url=/library/en-us/dndotnet/html/mssharsourcecli.asp. You do not need to download the shared source, unless you are interested in pursuing the code yourself. Snippets of the code are shown in this chapter.

This is source code for a Microsoft .NET Framework implementation, but is not the same implementation that is the officially released .NET Framework. In fact, Microsoft states: "There are significant differences in implementation between this code and the code for Microsoft's commercial CLR implementation, both to facilitate portability and to make the code base more approachable." However, the source code can give much insight into how the `String` and `StringBuilder` classes may be implemented.

The second tool is the MSIL Disassembler (`ildasm.exe`) used in this chapter to show the Intermediate Language (IL) generated by the compiler. This tool is provided with the .NET Framework SDK. When compiling to code, the compiler translates the C# code into Microsoft Intermediate Language (MSIL), for the CLR to compile to native code. This tool allows you to see the contents of the file before it is compiled to native code.

MSIL includes instructions for loading, storing, initializing, and calling methods on objects, as well as instructions for arithmetic and logical operations, flow control, direct memory access, exception handling, and all other operations the .NET Framework is capable of. Because MSIL is not native assembly code, it is quite easy to read and understand and so MSIL can give programmers insight into how code will perform, as it gives an underlying view of what the actual instructions are that will be executed.

Before code can be executed, it must be compiled to native code, and this happens through the use of a Just-in-Time (**JIT**) compiler – an implementation of one is provided as source with Rotor.

Text Architecture

One of the principal concerns introduced in Chapter 1 was the performance of string operations. This problem reduced to two principal components: memory allocation and byte copying. Therefore, by implementing strategies to minimize memory allocation and byte copying, performance should improve.

To reduce the number of memory reallocations and byte copying, you could allocate much more space than initially required. Then when the string grows, you can just copy the new characters into the space already allocated. This strategy is often used to improve performance. Of course, in this case you can often end up wasting memory. In addition, it is usually not possible to know how much memory you will need until run time. You can rarely be sure of whether the amount of memory allocated is enough, and therefore need a strategy for increasing the space available. In most cases, the developer should be focused on solving the business problem at hand, rather than being concerned about memory allocation. The memory allocation strategy should be integrated into the platform.

Both the Java and .NET platforms have taken similar approaches in text architecture. Both have a class that represents a string, and a class for building strings. The naming is very similar: Java uses String and StringBuffer whereas the .NET Framework uses String and StringBuilder. The namespace locations are similar as well. For .NET, String is located in the System namespace and StringBuilder is located in the System.Text namespace. For Java, both String and StringBuffer are located in the java.lang namespace (which contains the core Java classes).

The .NET Framework String type is immutable. That means that once a value is assigned to it, it cannot be changed. From a coding perspective it may look as if the value is being changed, but the CLR creates another String object behind the scenes and assigns it to the variable. One benefit of it being immutable is that it is thread-safe. Since it cannot be changed, there is no concern of having a read/write or write/write conflict between threads.

When you do need to carry out frequent changes to a string, you should use the StringBuilder class as it will look after the allocation and reallocation of memory for characters as any string operations demand it.

As mentioned in the first chapter, String is the only primitive data type that is a reference type. All the others are value types. Recall that a reference type only stores a pointer to data on the managed heap. In addition, when you are cloning an object of a reference type, you have a new reference but the data is the same. The cloning of a value type results in a new set of data that has the same value.

By making System.String immutable, it can have value semantics, while still being a reference type. For example, consider the following code:

```
using System;
using System.Text;

namespace Wrox.Text.Chapter2
{
  class Immutable
  {
    static void Main(string[] args)
    {
      string s1 = "Rock";
      string s2 = s1;

      Console.WriteLine("s1 = " + s1);
      Console.WriteLine("s2 = " + s2);

      s2 = s2.Replace("ck", "ll");

      Console.WriteLine("s1 = " + s1);
      Console.WriteLine("s2 = " + s2);
    }
  }
}
```

After the second line, both s1 and s2 point to the same set of data on the heap. After the Replace() method has been called, they contain different references. If s2 were not immutable, then both s1 and s2 would contain the value Roll. This is because what would happen is that you would alter the contents of the heap and both s1 and s2 would point to this new data. Instead, what happens is the Replace() method creates a new string (set of data on the heap) and assigns to s2 a reference to it. The original s2 value remains the same and thus s1 does not change either. The contents of a string are never overwritten until after garbage collection explicitly frees the memory.

String Class

System.String was introduced in Chapter 1 as a primitive reference type. The System namespace additionally contains all the core data types for .NET development. It includes fundamental classes and base classes that define commonly used value and reference data types. We will cover these in detail in the following sections.

The following table shows the public members of the String class that are covered in this chapter. The complete list can be found in Appendix A:

Member Name	Member Type	Member Description
Compare(string s1, string s2)	static Method	Performs a case-sensitive comparison of the two given strings according to the current culture.
Compare(string s1, string s2, bool ignoreCase)	static Method	Performs a comparison of the two given strings according to the current culture. If ignoreCase is True, a case-insensitive comparison is performed.
CompareOrdinal(string s1, string s2)	static Method	Performs a comparison of the two given strings without regard to the culture information.
CompareTo(string s)	Instance Method	Performs a case-sensitive, culturally-aware comparison of the given string with the instance string.
Copy(string s)	static Method	Returns a new string with the same value as the given string.
CopyTo(int sourceIndex, char dest(), int destIndex, int count)	Instance Method	Copies a sub-string from the instance string to the given destination string.

Member Name	Member Type	Member Description
EndsWith(string s)	Method	Returns True if the instance string ends with the given string.
Equals(string s)	Method	Returns True if the instance string has the same value as the given object.
Format(IFormatProvider provider, string format, ParamArray args)	Method	Returns a string consisting of the format specification replaced by the argument array according to the given format provider.
Intern(string s)	Method	Returns a reference to the given string. If the string is not interned, this method will intern it. Interning strings is discussed in detail in the following section.
Replace(string oldString, string newString)	Method	Replaces all occurrences of oldString with newString in the instance string.
Split(ParamArray separators)	Method	Splits the instance string into a string array according to the given character separators.
Substring(int startPos, int length)	Method	Returns a sub-string starting at the given position and for given length.
ToString()	Method	Returns a reference to the instance string.
ToString(IFormatProvider format)	Method	Returns a reference to the instance string.

Interning Strings

As mentioned in Chapter 1, the Common Language Runtime maintains an intern pool of strings. If you look at the shared source implementation of the CLI, there seems to be one intern pool per AppDomain.

To see an example of how string interning works, consider the following example:

```
const string s1 = "dog";

// Displays True if the string is interned.
Console.WriteLine(String.IsInterned(s1) != null);
```

You can see this illustrated in Figure 1:

Figure 1

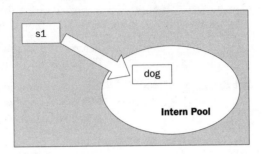

If a string is immutable, as it always is, and it is initialized to a value, then it is effectively the same as a constant. Let's see if the compiler interns it:

```
string s1 = "dog";

// Displays True if the string is interned.
Console.WriteLine(String.IsInterned(s1) != null);
```

When the code is executed, it displays True, indicating that the string has been interned. Let's try another example. In this case we will assign a string as a separate instruction from the initial string declaration:

```
string s1;
s1 = "dog";

// Displays True if the string is interned.
Console.WriteLine(String.IsInterned(s1) != null);
```

A compiler optimization is demonstrated with this example. The compiler can tell that the string will be fixed and therefore interns it. As a result, both previous code examples become the same thing. You might like to know when a string is not interned. Look at the following code:

```
String s1 = "Dog";

// The next line displays True.
Console.WriteLine(String.IsInterned(s1) != null);

s1 = s1 + "s";

// The next line displays False.
Console.WriteLine(String.IsInterned(s1) != null);
```

Here the string is tested twice but returns two different values. Remember that s1 is a reference to a string, not the actual value of the string. The String object is initialized to a value when it is declared. The compiler interns this string because it knows what it is at compile time. The new lines do not add an "s" to the previous string; they create a new string and assign the reference to the new string. Since this string was created at run time, it is not automatically interned.

Figure 2

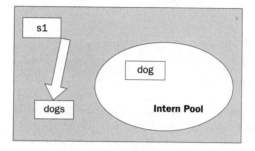

However, you could intern it programmatically:

```
String s1 = "Dog";

// The next line displays true.
Console.WriteLine(String.IsInterned(s1) != null);

s1 = s1 + "s";

String.Intern(s1);

// The next line displays true.
Console.WriteLine(String.IsInterned(s1) != null);
```

In summary, a string will be interned by the system if it knows at compile time what the characters in the string are. As we have seen, the interned string may or may not be a constant.

The other issue left for discussion is what happens to all the strings in the pool. It looks as though there would be memory lost due to non-referenced strings. The garbage collector can check which strings in the pool no longer have any references to them and remove them from the intern pool. For instance, once the s1 variable goes out of scope, there won't be any references to Dog anymore, as long as there is no other string variable in the application with the value Dog.

Construction

In C# there are a number of ways to initialize a string. Consider the following:

```
using System;
using System.Text;

namespace Wrox.Text.Chapter2
{
  class Construction
  {
    static void Main(string[] args)
    {
      const string s1 = "My string 1.";
      string s2 = "My string 2.";
      string s3;
      s3 = "My string 3.";
    }
  }
}
```

Since strings are immutable, there are no functional differences between any of the declarations except that the compiler won't allow the s1 reference to be changed in the code since it is declared as const. In all three cases, once a string value is created in the heap, it cannot be changed. Recall that any perceived changes to a String object create a new String object and the reference contained within the variable then points to this object. In the above example, s1, s2, and s3 are all interned.

When three choices of instruction seem to do the same thing, you may want to know if there are any subtle differences between them. The IL shows us these differences. The code reduces to the following IL. Note that the IL may be slightly different for you since different compiler settings may create different IL code. Don't worry about the exact meaning of each of the IL instructions; what is of interest to us is how the source code is compiled to IL. You can see the IL for the above code yourself by compiling the code above, and typing ildasm Construction.exe:

```
method private hidebysig static void  Main(string[] args) cil managed
{
  .entrypoint
  // Code size        13 (0xd)
  .maxstack  1
  .locals init (string V_0,
           string V_1)
  IL_0000:  ldstr      "My string 2."
  IL_0005:  stloc.0
  IL_0006:  ldstr      "My string 3."
  IL_000b:  stloc.1
  IL_000c:  ret
} // end of method Construction::Main
```

The first thing to notice is that "My string 1." has disappeared. A constant acts like a macro replacement. If it is not referenced, it will not be included in the IL code. If we change the code to use the constant, we will see the value in the IL code:

```
const string s1 = "My string 1.";
string s2 = "My string 2.";
string s3;
s3 = "My string 3.";

Console.WriteLine(s1);
```

The characters are loaded into a String object and the string is output to the console.

```
method private hidebysig static void Main(string[] args) cil managed
{
  .entrypoint
  // Code size       23 (0x17)
  .maxstack  1
  .locals init (string V_0,
            string V_1)
  IL_0000:  ldstr      "My string 2."
  IL_0005:  stloc.0
  IL_0006:  ldstr      "My string 3."
  IL_000b:  stloc.1
  IL_000c:  ldstr      "My string 1."
  IL_0011:  call       void
[mscorlib]System.Console::WriteLine(string)
  IL_0016:  ret
} // end of method Construction::Main
```

The next string, "My string 2.", is operated on with the ldstr (load string) operation. From the Common Language Infrastructure (CLI) document titled, *Partition III – CIL Instruction Set*:

> *"The **ldstr** instruction pushes a new string object representing the literal stored in the metadata as string (that must be a string literal). The **ldstr** instruction allocates memory and performs any format conversion required to convert from the form used in the file to the string format required at runtime. The CLI guarantees that the result of two ldstr instructions referring to two metadata tokens that have the same sequence of characters return precisely the same string object (a process known as "string interning")."*

It is saying that ldstr will take care of all the difficult work. Once the String object is created, it is then stored in the variable. Let's look again at what happens with "My string 3." The keyword string is an alias for the String class. They reduce to exactly the same thing once you get down to the IL instructions. The only difference is that Visual Studio .NET will highlight string since it is a keyword but not String since it is a class name.

With that analysis, const is shown to be the most efficient way to initialize a string, since it minimizes the number of IL instructions.

There are a couple cases when you would use the `String` constructor. One of the constructors allows you to populate the string with fixed characters. For instance, the following creates a string with four "D"s:

```
string s2 = new string('D', 4);
```

You might think that you should be able to create a string like the following:

```
string myString = new string("dog");
```

This does work in VB.NET but not C#. The C# compiler will give you the following result:

```
CodeFile1.cs(11,23): error CS1502: The best overloaded method match
for 'string.String(char*)' has some invalid arguments
CodeFile1.cs(11,34): error CS1503: Argument '1': cannot convert from
'string' to 'char*'
```

The complier converts "dog" to a string primitive type and then attempts to call the `string` constructor with a `String` object. The `String` class does not have any constructors that take a string type, you have to use the `Clone()` method. A rather roundabout way of accomplishing this is as follows:

```
object myObj = "dog".Clone();
string myString = (string) myObj as string;
```

Escaping Strings

As you know, some characters can be challenging to represent as a string. All string variables are assigned by enclosing them in a quotation mark, so the following code causes a syntax error:

```
string myString = "He said, "Dogs and cats."";
```

The compiler believes the string is `"He said, "` and then does not know what to do with the rest of the characters, returning a syntax error. Quotation marks have to be marked with an escape sequence in C# to be properly represented:

```
string myString = "He said, \"Dogs and cats.\"";
```

There may be other characters that you need to represent with an escape sequence. The following table shows the escape sequences that you may use in your application:

Escape Sequence	Unicode Value	Description
\0	x0000	Null
\a	x0007	Alert
\b	x0008	Backspace
\t	x0009	Horizontal tab
\n	x000A	New line
\v	x000B	Vertical tab
\f	x000C	Form feed
\r	x000D	Carriage return
\"	x0022	Double quote
\'	x0027	Quote
\\	x005C	Backslash

C# also supports verbatim string literals using the '@' symbol. By placing an operator in front of the string, the characters are interpreted verbatim (with the exception of the quote-escape sequence). For example, the following code:

```
Console.WriteLine(@"hello \t world");
```

would render the following on the output:

```
hello \t world
```

If the verbatim operator was not present, then a tab character would have been inserted.

StringBuilder Class

As already discussed, the immutability characteristic of the String class allows it to be treated similarly to a value type rather than a reference type. However, this causes it to have the side effect of a new String object being created every time a string operation is required.

The StringBuilder class addresses the problem of numerous objects being created during the repeated modifications to a string. The StringBuilder class allocates space to a string in char units, so that operations may not require additional memory allocations.

The following table shows some of the properties and methods of the StringBuilder class.

47

Member Name	Member Type	Member Description
Capacity	Property	The number of characters currently allocated for the instance. Not necessarily the same value as the length property.
Chars(int index)	Property	Gets or sets the character within the string at the position index.
Length	Property	The number of characters in the string. Can be set smaller than the current string value to truncate it.
MaxCapacity	Property	The maximum number of characters that can be allocated for this instance.
Append(<type>)	Method	Appends the string representation of the given value. There is an overload for each .NET primitive type. For brevity they are not all listed here.
EnsureCapacity(int capacity)	Method	If the current capacity is less than the given capacity, memory is allocated to increase memory to the given capacity.
Insert(int position, string s, int count)	Method	Inserts s at the given position, count number of times.
Replace(char oldChar, char newChar)	Method	Replaces all occurrences of oldChar with newChar in the instance string.
Replace(string oldString, string newString)	Method	Replaces all occurrences of oldString with newString in the instance string.
Replace(char oldChar, char newChar, int startPos, int count)	Method	Replaces all occurrences of oldChar with newChar in the instance string between positions startPos and count − 1.

Member Name	Member Type	Member Description
Replace(string oldString, 　　　　string newString, 　　　　int startPos, 　　　　int count)	Method	Replaces all occurrences of oldString with newString in the instance string between positions startPos and count − 1.
ToString()	Method	Returns a reference to a String object whose value is the same as that contained within the StringBuilder instance.

Length and Capacity

The StringBuilder class contains both Length and Capacity properties. Contrary to what might be expected, the Length property is not read-only. If the Length is set to less than the size of the string, the string is truncated. If it is set greater than the current length, then it is padded with spaces at the end. The following code snippet contained within StringBuilderLength.cs demonstrates this behavior:

```
using System;
using System.Text;

namespace Wrox.Text.Chapter2
{
  class StringBuilderLength
  {
    static void Main(string[] args)
    {
      StringBuilder sb = new StringBuilder("Hot dog!");
      Console.WriteLine(sb.ToString());  // Displays "Hot dog!"

      sb.Length = 3;
      Console.WriteLine(sb.ToString());  // Displays "Hot"

      sb.Length = 10;
      Console.Write(sb.ToString());      // Displays "Hot     "
      Console.WriteLine("(ends)");       // Indicates the string end
    }
  }
}
```

Capacity defines the amount of memory available for text manipulation and the default is 16 characters. If you know that the string is going to be longer than 16 characters, you should explicitly set the capacity, which will save at least one memory reallocation. If you provide a string as a parameter to the constructor, the capacity will be set to the nearest exponent of 2. For example, if the string length is 17, the capacity will be 32. The Rotor source code has a CalculateCapacity method in comstringbuffer.cpp. This method is called when a new StringBuilder is created with an initial string. The following C# Shared Source CLI code implements the capacity calculation:

```
//Double until we find something bigger than what we need.
while (newCapacity < requestedCapacity && newCapacity > 0)
{
    newCapacity*=2;
}
```

In the case of a new string the `requestedCapacity` is the length of the string. The `Capacity` property is independent of `Length`. However, `Capacity` will always be equal to or greater than `Length`.

The following code, contained within `StringBuilderAppend.cs`, demonstrates how the `Capacity` property changes as the string grows. The `Append()` method concatenates the given number of specified characters together with the string:

```csharp
using System;
using System.Text;

namespace Wrox.Text.Chapter2
{
    class StringBuilderAppend
    {
        static void Main(string[] args)
        {
            StringBuilder sb = new StringBuilder();
            Console.WriteLine(sb.Capacity + "\t" + sb.Length);

            sb.Append('a', 17);
            Console.WriteLine(sb.Capacity + "\t" + sb.Length);

            sb.Append('b', 16);
            Console.WriteLine(sb.Capacity + "\t" + sb.Length);

            sb.Append('c', 32);
            Console.WriteLine(sb.Capacity + "\t" + sb.Length);

            sb.Append('d', 64);
            Console.WriteLine(sb.Capacity + "\t" + sb.Length);
        }
    }
}
```

The following output is generated on the console:

```
16      0
32      17
64      33
128     65
256     129
```

In this case, there were four memory reallocations. If the initial `Capacity` had been set to 256 characters, then there would have been no reallocations. Looking at the shared source implementation in the file `stringbuilder.cs`, we can see exactly where the new capacity is calculated:

```
newCapacity = (currentString.Capacity)*2;
if (newCapacity < requiredLength) newCapacity = requiredLength;
if (newCapacity > m_MaxCapacity) newCapacity = m_MaxCapacity;
```

The maximum capacity can be obtained from the property
StringBuilder.MaxCapacity. On released implementations of the Microsoft .NET
Framework, this is equal to Int32.MaxValue, which is 2,147,483,647 ($2^{31}-1$). That is
quite a few characters and you will run into many other problems, such as lack of
system memory space, before you reach that limit.

The default capacity, maximum capacity, and how the capacity grows, are
implementation specific. For example, the behavior of the shared source
implementation may be different from the released implementation (although the
default capacity is still 16). It is important to take advantage of system behavior to
optimize performance but you need to be aware that if the code is running on another
implementation, you may not get the same benefits.

If you find yourself writing code like the following:

```
if (myString.Capacity < myCapacity) myString.Capacity = myCapacity;
```

you can replace it with the following equivalent function:

```
myString.EnsureCapacity(myCapacity)
```

If the current capacity is less then the new one, memory will be reallocated. The
current capacity can be reduced as long as it is not less than Length. If so, a
System.ArgumentOutOfRangeException exception is thrown.

ToString()

We obtain the actual string contained within StringBuilder by calling its
ToString() method. You can retrieve the whole string, or part of it. The following
code demonstrates both methods:

```
StringBuilder sb = new StringBuilder("This is my string.");
String s1 = sb.ToString();
String s2 = sb.ToString(5,5);

Console.WriteLine(s1);    // Displays "This is my string."
Console.WriteLine(s2);    // Displays "is my"
```

The first call to ToString() causes a new String object to be created, and the
characters are copied to it. This keeps the value semantics of the String class.
However, you do get the small performance overhead of allocating the string.

The shared source CLI shows that the second ToString() method calls the Substring() method of the String class. This may not be the case with the final release, as many of the classes may not even be written in C#, but in native code:

```
public String ToString(int startIndex, int length)
{
  return  m_StringValue.Substring(startIndex, length);
}
```

Many of the other StringBuilder methods are duplicated with the String methods. In addition, some of the methods in one class call the methods in the other class. We will look at them together in the following section to compare different approaches.

String Operations

All programming languages have support for string operations. Operations on strings fall into the following broad categories:

❑   Concatenating strings

❑   Extracting substrings from strings

❑   Comparing strings

❑   Formatting strings

We will look at the operations in detail and then see how they combine for common text operations. The resource cost of the operations will be discussed in terms of performance (time to execute a task) and memory requirements.

While performing these operations, you will often have to choose between the String class and the StringBuilder class. Some guidelines will be provided here.

> The relative merits of using Char arrays instead of the String and StringBuilder classes have not been discussed here. Based on some tests, it was found that operations on Chars generally ran slower. The shared source CLI provided a clue as to why this might be the case, and it appears as though a Char array gets transformed into a string before operations are performed on it. Only use Char arrays if the operation would make it simpler, and even then it is advisable to test for any performance penalties.

Concatenating Strings

Let's revisit one of the concatenation examples from Chapter 1 that builds a simple HTML document. The straight translation to C# would look something like the following:

```
using System;
using System.Text;

namespace Wrox.Text.Chapter2
{
  class HTMLConsole
  {
    static void Main(string[] args)
    {
      string htmlString;
      Console.Write("Please enter your name: ");
      string userName = Console.ReadLine();

      htmlString = "<HTML><HEAD></HEAD><BODY>";
      htmlString += "My name is: ";
      htmlString += userName;
      htmlString += "</BODY></HTML>";

      Console.WriteLine(htmlString);
    }
  }
}
```

Code like this is common because it is written in the way most people think. It is a linear way of programming; start with a string and add each of the pieces until the string is finished. However, this is not the optimal way of doing this. From what we know about the String class, the steps taken by the system are the following:

1. The compiler interns the string in the first allocation.

2. In the next line, a concatenation is performed. A new string is allocated, and the interned text and the new text are copied into the string.

3. In the next lines, more concatenations are performed, which again result in new strings being created and characters being copied.

To construct the HTML page, one string is taken from the intern pool and three new ones need to be created. Let's take the same example with our knowledge of how the system stores strings and try to improve performance:

```
using System;
using System.Text;

namespace Wrox.Text.Chapter2
{
  class HTMLConsoleImproved
```

```
{
    static void Main(string[] args)
    {
        const string prefixString =
            "<HTML><HEAD></HEAD><BODY>My name is: ";
        const string suffixString = "</BODY></HTML>";

        Console.Write("Please enter your name: ");
        string userName = Console.ReadLine();

        string htmlString = prefixString + userName + suffixString;

        Console.WriteLine(htmlString);
    }
}
}
```

Since some of the text is known beforehand, it is declared as constant. This ensures that it will be placed in the intern pool. At run time, it will not have to be allocated. This approach takes two strings from the intern pool and allocates one string. Memory will be conserved as well, since the constant text is stored once, instead of being allocated many times for each thread running the code.

Based on some performance testing, assigning a new string one million times, this approach was shown to be almost three times as fast as the previous one.

Another approach is to provide a format string. Format strings will be discussed in detail later, but the important point to know for the time being, is that the {0} specifier will be replaced with the replacement parameter:

```
String htmlString = String.Format(
    "<HTML><BODY>My name is: {0} </BODY></HTML>", userName);
```

This approach looks good. There are no explicit string concatenations and the text is easy to read. Unfortunately, it does not perform very well. The Format() method is resource intensive. As a result, it is not a good approach for simple string concatenation. Later in the chapter, we will look at when it is appropriate.

Finally, let's look at using the StringBuilder class to perform concatenation:

```
StringBuilder MHTML = new StringBuilder();

MHTML.Append("<HTML><HEAD></HEAD><BODY>My name is: ");
MHTML.Append(userName);
MHTML.Append("</BODY></HTML>");

Console.WriteLine(MHTML.ToString());
```

In this case, no string is explicitly created. The `StringBuilder` class looks after all the memory allocation. This approach performs reasonably well but it still seems to take twice as long as the second approach we looked at. However, that is because the creation of a `StringBuilder` object takes longer than that of a string. If we re-execute all these methods again, just on 10,000 cycles, then we notice something more interesting still. The `StringBuilder` takes a hundredth of the time even the interned pool concatenation takes. This is partially because interning isn't making much difference here; it still has to create a new `String` object with every cycle. However, without interning, it would take even longer, depending on how much memory is available, as there would be three times as many `String` objects being created with each cycle and so garbage collection would need to interrupt the execution repeatedly.

The `Capacity` can also be supplied to the constructor of the `StringBuilder`. This can improve performance by giving the class a hint as to approximately how much memory will be required. This way it may not have to perform any further allocations. When this was attempted with the same performance tests, the loop took a hundredth less time again. The task was just moving items into memory, and the speed is only dependent on your memory, motherboard, and processor.

There are other ways to perform concatenation but the major ones have been covered here. The optimal is to ensure that the "pieces" of your string that do not change are declared as constants. So, in summary, for just a single concatenation, don't use `StringBuilder`, as the overhead in creating the object will outweigh the performance advantages of the concatenation. For a single concatenation, use constants and other interned strings wherever possible as that can increase performance threefold.

Extracting Substrings from Strings

The `StringBuilder` class does not have a method to support substrings so you must use the `String` class to retrieve substrings. The method has two overloads: you can either provide just the start index or a start index and length. If the length is not specified it will return the substring from the start index to the end of the string. The following code demonstrates its use:

```
string myString = "It's been a long time.";

// Displays "been a long time."
Console.WriteLine(myString.Substring(5));

// Displays "been"
Console.WriteLine(myString.Substring(5, 4));
```

Comparing Strings

You might think comparing strings would be straightforward; however, a few choices need to be made. The `String` class has four methods for comparing strings, `Compare()`, `CompareTo()`, `CompareOrdinal()`, and `Equals()`.

The `Compare()` method is a `static` version of the `CompareTo()` method. The `Equals()` method is what is called whenever the "=" operator is used, and so is equivalent to it. The `CompareOrdinal()` method compares two strings without considering the local language or culture; cultures are covered in detail in Chapter 4:

```
using System;
using System.Text;

namespace Wrox.Text.Chapter2
{
  class CompareTiming
  {
    static void Main(string[] args)
    {
      const int NUM_ITER = 10000000;
      int result;
      bool bResult;

      // Interned and strings match
      string s1 = "satisfaction";
      string s2 = "satisfaction";

      // Not interned and strings do not match
      //string s1;
      //string s2;
      //s1 = "satisfaction";
      //s2 = "dissatisfaction";

      int startTime;
      int endTime;
      int count;

      // Compare() method
      startTime = Environment.TickCount;
      for (count = 0; count < NUM_ITER; count++)
      {
        result = String.Compare(s1, s2);
      }
      endTime = Environment.TickCount;
      Console.WriteLine("Compare: " + (endTime - startTime));

      // CompareTo() method
      startTime = Environment.TickCount;
      for (count = 0; count < NUM_ITER; count++)
      {
        result = s1.CompareTo(s2);
      }
      endTime = Environment.TickCount;
      Console.WriteLine("CompareTo: " + (endTime - startTime));

      // CompareOrdinal() method
      startTime = Environment.TickCount;
      for (count = 0; count < NUM_ITER; count++)
```

```
    {
        result = String.CompareOrdinal(s1, s2);
    }
    endTime = Environment.TickCount;
    Console.WriteLine("CompareOrdinal: " + (endTime-startTime));

    // Equals() instance method
    startTime = Environment.TickCount;
    for (count = 0; count < NUM_ITER; count++)
    {
        bResult = s1.Equals(s2);
    }
    endTime = Environment.TickCount;
    Console.WriteLine("Equals (instance): " + (endTime-startTime));

    // Equals() static method
    startTime = Environment.TickCount;
    for (count = 0; count < NUM_ITER; count++)
    {
        bResult = String.Equals(s1, s2);
    }
    endTime = Environment.TickCount;
    Console.WriteLine("Equals (static): " + (endTime-startTime));
    }
  }
}
```

The results of this test should look something like those in the following table. The actual values will be different between environments and even executions, but the relative difference between the functions should be the same. Just make slight alterations to the code to make the strings unequal and non-interned, as the table requires:

Method	Strings Match ?	Number of Strings Interned	Execution Time (ms)
Compare()	Yes	2	3665
CompareTo()	Yes	2	3676
CompareOrdinal()	Yes	2	941
Equals() – Instance	Yes	2	1051
Equals() – Shared	Yes	2	11
Compare()	No	2	2894
CompareTo()	No	2	2905
CompareOrdinal()	No	2	420
Equals() – Instance	No	2	421

Table continued on following page

Method	Strings Match ?	Number of Strings Interned	Execution Time (ms)
Equals() – Shared	No	2	541
Compare()	Yes	0	2894
CompareTo()	Yes	0	2904
CompareOrdinal()	Yes	0	421
Equals() – Instance	Yes	0	420
Equals() – Shared	Yes	0	531
Compare()	No	1	2884
CompareTo()	No	1	2904
CompareOrdinal()	No	1	431
Equals() – Instance	No	1	420
Equals() – Shared	No	1	531

As you can see, the results vary widely depending on which method is used and the strings being compared.

There are some interesting observations about the results. The Compare() method, for instance, was consistently faster than the CompareTo() method, although only very marginally. Since the Compare() method is static, there are fewer overheads in calling it than with an instance method as an instance does not have to be created.

The CompareOrdinal() method is substantially faster than the Compare() and CompareTo() methods. Since the CompareOrdinal() method does not have to worry about culture-specific information, it does not have the overhead of conversions and international support that the other two methods have. This can be used on strings that you know will not be localized, such as various operating system and network variables.

Finally, the Equals() method's performance varies widely depending on the strings being compared. Looking at the static source implementation gives a hint as to why:

```
public static bool Equals(String a, String b)
{
  if ((Object)a == (Object)b) return true;
  if ((Object)a == null || (Object)b == null) return false;
  return a.Equals(b);
}
```

Comparing two objects performs best when comparing their hash codes, which is a very quick operation. If two strings are the same, then they will have the same hash code and, as a result, the equality test is very fast. If they are not the same, the call is forwarded and a character-by-character comparison occurs. There must be some further code in the .NET Framework, as when the two strings were interned and identical, the `static` method received an enormous performance boost. This is probably because the references would be identical and so, if it tests for this, the operation would be exceptionally fast.

In general the instance method of `Equals()` is marginally faster, and the equals operator is slowest of all. The one exception is where both strings are interned and identical, in which case the `static` method is much faster. Bear this in mind when choosing what method to use.

Two other useful comparison methods are `EndsWith()` and `StartsWith()`. In the shared source snippet, you can see that these methods use the `Compare()` function; therefore you can expect the performance to be similar. Additionally, if you rewrite the code sample used above to compare these methods, there is a speed difference only if you declare all your variables, like the string lengths, before it starts timing it:

```
public bool EndsWith(String value)
{
   if (null == value) throw new ArgumentNullException("value");

   int valueLen = value.Length;
   int thisLen = this.Length;

   if (valueLen > thisLen) return false;

   return (0==Compare(this, thisLen - valueLen, value, 0, valueLen));
}

public bool StartsWith(String value)
{
   if (null == value) throw new ArgumentNullException("value");

   if (this.Length < value.Length) return false;

   return (0 == Compare(this, 0, value, 0, value.Length));
}
```

We can assume above that there is therefore no advantage behind using `Compare()` as opposed to `EndsWith()` or `StartsWith()`.

Formatting

As discussed in the first chapter, formatting is used to create an end-user view of a value from the internal machine representation of the value. Formatting can be described as the conversion of any data type to a string. The advantage of formatting is that the programmer can specify how the conversion happens.

All base data types implement the IConvertible interface. This interface has a ToString() method, which must be implemented by the classes implementing the interface. As you may or may not know, this method is different from the overload provided through System.Object, but they both return a string representation of the class implementing the interface. Since all base data types implement this interface, you can always retrieve a string representation of the data type. In addition, number, date, and enumeration primitive types also implement the System.IFormattable interface, which contains an additional overload for the ToString() method, and we will be describing it in this section.

This overload is defined as follows:

```
public string ToString(string format, IFormatProvider provider)
```

The first parameter is the format specifier, and the second is the format provider. If the format string is absent, then the System.IConvertible.ToString() method is actually called, which just contains the IFormatProvider argument and uses a default format. We will look at these two arguments in detail in the next section. If neither parameter is provided, then a default format specifier and default format provider will be used by System.Object.ToString(). The richness of formatting in .NET means that you should not ever have to perform character-by-character construction of strings.

Formatting is divided into numeric formatting (which includes currency), date-time formatting, enumeration formatting, and custom formatting. There are many formatting options on all the types. Only some of the commonly used ones are shown in this chapter. Inspect the .NET Framework SDK's documentation to see all the options available for formatting strings.

Formatting Numbers

For the first example, we will rely on the Pi constant defined within the System.Math class. The formats are listed in the order of default, scientific notation, and fixed-point:

```
double val = Math.PI;

Console.WriteLine(val.ToString());       // displays 3.14159265358979
Console.WriteLine(val.ToString("E"));    // displays 3.141593E+000
Console.WriteLine(val.ToString("F3"));   // displays 3.142
```

The default format provides information, but isn't too friendly for a user. Scientific notation is an option, but in this case does not help much either. Specifying the number of decimals to display makes the value more presentable. In addition, the value is rounded instead of truncated.

Many developers may also be interested in hexadecimal formatting. It is doubtful that end users would want to see numbers represented in hexadecimal, but certainly if you are logging errors or trace statements then you may want to record them in hex:

```
int val = 65535;

Console.WriteLine(val.ToString("x"));      // displays ffff
Console.WriteLine(val.ToString("X"));      // displays FFFF
```

It is also possible to format numbers as percentages:

```
Single val = 0.653F;

Console.WriteLine(val.ToString("p"));      // displays 65.30 %
Console.WriteLine(val.ToString("p1"));     // displays 65.3 %
```

The default formatting puts a space between the number and percent sign. This is customizable by changing the format provider:

```
Single val = 0.653F;
object myObj = NumberFormatInfo.CurrentInfo.Clone() as
NumberFormatInfo;
NumberFormatInfo myFormat = myObj as NumberFormatInfo;

myFormat.PercentPositivePattern = 1;

Console.WriteLine(val.ToString("p", myFormat));    // displays 65.30%
Console.WriteLine(val.ToString("p1", myFormat));   // displays 65.3%
```

The first thing to notice is that a new format structure is created by cloning the existing one. Moreover, the NumberFormatInfo class is a member of the System.Globalization namespace, which would have to be imported into your program. The pattern for formatting percentages is changed by setting the PercentPositivePattern property. The new format structure is then passed to the ToString() method. Demonstrations of customizing more of the format will be provided in subsequent examples.

Currency is included as part of number formatting. Results may differ depending on your culture setting. For instance, the currency symbol in the UK is £:

```
double val = 12345.89;

Console.WriteLine(val.ToString());         // displays 12345.89
Console.WriteLine(val.ToString("C"));      // displays $12,345.89 in US
```

There is complete flexibility in the formatting. The following example demonstrates the construction of a nonsense currency:

```
double val = 1234567.89;
int []groupSize = {2, 1, 3};
object myObj = NumberFormatInfo.CurrentInfo.Clone();
NumberFormatInfo myCurrency = myObj as NumberFormatInfo;
```

```
myCurrency.CurrencySymbol = "@";
myCurrency.CurrencyDecimalSeparator = "/";
myCurrency.CurrencyGroupSeparator = "-";
myCurrency.CurrencyGroupSizes = groupSize;

// displays @1-234-5-67/89
Console.WriteLine(val.ToString("C", myCurrency));
```

Formatting Dates

The procedure for formatting dates is the same as for formatting numbers; the format strings are just different.

> *The appearance of the output in this section may differ depending on what your machine culture settings are.*

```
DateTime dateValue = DateTime.Now;

// Displays a date like 9/18/2002 12:14:40 PM
Console.WriteLine(dateValue.ToString());

// Displays date like Wednesday, September 18, 2002 12:14 PM
Console.WriteLine(dateValue.ToString("f"));

// Displays September, 2002
Console.WriteLine(dateValue.ToString("y"));

// Displays 12:14:40 PM
Console.WriteLine(dateValue.ToString("T"));
```

Again, you have complete control of how the date string is formatted as the following example illustrates:

```
DateTime dateValue = DateTime.Now;
string []myDays = {"RelaxDay", "ToughDay", "BlahDay", "LazyDay",
                   "ProductiveDay", "PartyDay", "HomeDay"};

object myObj = DateTimeFormatInfo.CurrentInfo.Clone();
DateTimeFormatInfo myDateTime = myObj as DateTimeFormatInfo;

myDateTime.DayNames = myDays;
myDateTime.FullDateTimePattern = "dddd, dd MMMM yyyy HH:mm:ss";

// Displays LazyDay, 18 September 2002 12:19:47
Console.WriteLine(dateValue.ToString("F", myDateTime));
```

This example shows two things. First, how you can override the days of the week and provide your own; second, how you can explicitly provide a format string to control how the date string is put together.

Formatting Enumerations

Finally, let's take a look at converting enumerations to strings. Consider the following enumeration declaration:

```
enum Music
{
  Rock = 1,
  Blues = 2,
  Jazz = 3,
  Classical = 4
}
```

You can obtain string information about the enumeration as illustrated in the following code:

```
Music myMusic = Music.Blues;

Console.WriteLine(myMusic.ToString());        // displays Blues
Console.WriteLine(myMusic.ToString("d"));     // displays 2
```

You can obtain text from system enumerations the same way:

```
DayOfWeek day = DayOfWeek.Friday;

Console.WriteLine(String.Format("My favorite day is {0:G}", day));
```

This will display the following on the console:

```
My favorite day is Friday
```

The format string "G" displays the enumeration as a string.

Formatting Choices

Since both StringBuilder and String provide format functionality, you may wonder which to use. Looking at the static source for the String.Format() method, we see that it creates a StringBuilder object, and calls the AppendFormat() method:

```
public static String Format(IFormatProvider provider, String format,
                            params Object[] args)
{
  if (format == null || args == null)
      throw new ArgumentNullException((format==null)?"format":"args");
  StringBuilder sb =
      new StringBuilder(format.Length + args.Length * 8);
  sb.AppendFormat(provider, format, args);
  return sb.ToString();
}
```

Since `Format()` is a `static` method, there isn't much overhead in calling it. Your choice then comes down to which method makes most sense, and is most readable in the context of the code you are writing.

We will say a little more about formatting in Chapter 4. String formatting can prove very useful when dealing with internationalized strings, but it wouldn't be useful to go into much detail here.

Uses of Strings

We have covered a number of the operations performed with strings. Let's combine some of the operations together to create some practical applications.

Building Strings

We have looked at the issue of building a string that contains HTML. Let's revisit this using the `String` and `StringBuilder` classes. This example illustrates the retrieval of data from a database and displaying it in an HTML table. This is not a demonstration of the best way to do this task; rather it shows how to build up strings. ASP.NET offers superior ways of displaying data, such as with the `DataGrid` control.

With that said, recall that the problem with the method illustrated in Chapter 1, and earlier in this chapter, was too much memory allocation and string copying. The following code addresses the problem using the `String` and `StringBuilder` classes. This has been written as a console application, but it can easily be adapted for ASP.NET, or Windows Forms by just replacing the `Console.ReadLine()` and `Console.WriteLine()` lines:

```
class HTMLTableConstruction
{
  static void Main(string[] args)
  {
    // Connection string is specific to your database environment.
    const string CONN_STRING =
        "user id=sa;password=;database=pubs;server=localhost";
    string SQLQuery;
    StringBuilder sb = new StringBuilder(256);
    string authorName = "";

    // Retrieve author name - Replace with Request(fieldName) for
    // ASP.NET application
    Console.Write("Please enter author's last name: ");
    authorName = Console.ReadLine();

    // Remove any spaces that might exist before or after the name.
    authorName = authorName.Trim();
```

```
// Create the SQL query.
SQLQuery = String.Format("SELECT * FROM Authors " +
    "WHERE au_lname LIKE '{0}%'", authorName);

// Intern the table tags so as to increase performance
const string OPENTABLE = "<table>";
const string CLOSETABLE = "</table>";
const string OPENTABLEROW = "<tr>";
const string CLOSETABLEROW = "</tr>";
const string OPENTABLECELL = "<td>";
const string CLOSETABLECELL = "</td>";
const string OPENTABLEHEADER = "<th>";
const string CLOSETABLEHEADER = "</th>";

SqlConnection conn = new SqlConnection(CONN_STRING);
conn.Open();
SqlCommand cmd = new SqlCommand(SQLQuery, conn);
SqlDataReader dr = cmd.ExecuteReader();

int numFields = dr.FieldCount;

sb.Append(OPENTABLE + "\n");

// Create the table headings.
for (int count = 0; count < numFields-1; count++)
{
  sb.Append(OPENTABLEHEADER + dr.GetName(count) +
      CLOSETABLEHEADER);
}

// Iterate through the rows and add the data to the HTML table.
while (dr.Read())
{
  sb.Append("\n" + OPENTABLEROW);

  for (int count = 0; count < numFields-1; count++)
  {
    sb.Append(OPENTABLECELL + dr[count].ToString() +
        CLOSETABLECELL);
  }

  sb.Append(CLOSETABLEROW);
}

conn.Close();
sb.Append("\n" + CLOSETABLE + "\n");
Console.WriteLine(sb.ToString());
  }
}
```

The first interesting piece of code is the SQL statement for the query:

```
// Remove any spaces that might exist before or after the name.
authorName = authorName.Trim();

// Create the SQL query.
SQLQuery = String.Format("SELECT * FROM Authors " +
    "WHERE au_lname LIKE '{0}%'", authorName);
```

The `Trim()` method is used to remove any leading or trailing whitespace from the entry; this would be essential in a WebForms application. There is a small performance hit here, because a new string is created for the trimmed string. Next, the `Format()` method is used to create the SQL statement. Concatenation using interned strings could have been used here instead of the `Format()` method. A specific situation where you would use the `Format()` method over concatenation is if you needed to format the text you were inserting into the SQL Statement. We then define a number of constants, to ensure that the system interns them (although it would happen anyway), before passing the SQL statement to a `Command` object, where the command is executed on the connection:

```
SqlCommand cmd = new SqlCommand(SQLQuery, conn);
SqlDataReader    dr = cmd.ExecuteReader();

int numFields = dr.FieldCount;

sb.Append(OPENTABLE + "\n");

// Create the table headings.
for (int count = 0; count < numFields-1; count++)
{
   sb.Append(OPENTABLEHEADER + dr.GetName(count) +
      CLOSETABLEHEADER);
}
```

The HTML is built inside one `StringBuilder` object. Notice that when it is declared it is given a default capacity of 256 characters. Remember that if a capacity is not provided, then the default is 16. The total characters are going to be more than that so we can minimize the amount of memory reallocation by providing a value closer to the size of the result:

```
StringBuilder sb = new StringBuilder(256);
```

The HTML is made part of the `StringBuilder` object using the `Append()` method. The first `Append()` method call contains a fixed string and character. The compiler will recognize this and reduce it to a single string. The strings in the second `Append()` call cannot be evaluated until run time, so we get a performance hit here. Once the header information is in place, we can iterate through the rows:

```
// Iterate through the rows and add the data to the HTML table.
while (dr.Read())
{
   sb.Append("\n" + OPENTABLEROW);
```

```
for (int count = 0; count < numFields-1; count++)
{
  sb.Append(OPENTABLECELL + dr[count].ToString() +
      CLOSETABLECELL);
}

sb.Append(CLOSETABLEROW);
}
```

This loop is where most of the work is, as there is another nested loop inside. In most cases, the `StringBuilder` object copies the characters into the memory it has allocated for the string. When it hits the capacity, it needs to reallocate and copy. Considering that it doubles the capacity each time, this should not be an issue.

The `AppendFormat()` method could be used instead of string concatenation as illustrated below:

```
// Iterate through the rows and add the data to the HTML table.
while (dr.Read())
{
  sb.Append("\n" + OPENTABLEROW);

  for (count = 0; count < numFields-1; count++)
  {
    sb.AppendFormat("<td>{0}</td> ", dr[count].ToString());
  }

  sb.Append(CLOSETABLEROW);
}
```

This is an effective approach if you want to specify the format of the fields to display. It is also somewhat more readable. However, formatted strings are slower to manipulate than concatenation:

```
conn.Close();
sb.Append("\n" + CLOSETABLE + "\n");
Console.WriteLine(sb.ToString());
```

Finally, the HTML is completed, and in an ASP.NET application the string would be sent to the client. In this application, it just outputs to the console.

Tokenizing

Tokenizing is the process of extracting specific content from text. Compilers use tokenizing extensively since they need to separate the language keywords from the delimiters. Tokenizing is also used in natural language processing to remove words from sentences. Consider the following sentence:

"I just want the words, not the punctuation, and not the spaces, from
this sentence."

One approach is to process the sentence character by character. This is tedious and error-prone. Although Java has a `StringTokenizer` class to make this process easy, the .NET Framework does not supply a class like this, so you have to write more code. The following snippet extracts the words from the sentence and outputs them to the console:

```
class Tokenizing
{
  static void Main(string[] args)
  {
    string myString = "I just want the words, not the punctuation," +
                      " and not the spaces, from this sentence.";
    char [] separators = {' ', ',', '.', ':', ';', '?', '!'};

    int startPos = 0;
    int endPos = 0;

    do
    {
      endPos = myString.IndexOfAny(separators, startPos);

      if (endPos == -1) endPos = myString.Length;

      if (endPos != startPos)
          Console.WriteLine(myString.Substring(
                            startPos, (endPos - startPos)));

      startPos = (endPos + 1);
    } while (startPos < myString.Length);
  }
}
```

You will see the following output on the console:

```
I
just
want
the
words
not
the
punctuation
and
not
the
spaces
from
this
sentence
```

First, the variables are declared. The characters identified as the token separators are stored in an array. Variables for the start and end position of each token are declared:

```
string myString = "I just want the words, not the punctuation," +
                  " and not the spaces, from this sentence.";
char [] separators = {' ', ',', '.', ':', ';', '?', '!'};

int startPos = 0;
int endPos = 0;
```

The `IndexOfAny()` method is the key part of this tokenizing routine. Given a list of separators and a starting position, it finds the next character location that contains one of the separators. The method returns `-1` when no separators are found. In this case, the end position is set to the end of the string:

```
do
{
   endPos = myString.IndexOfAny(separators, startPos);

   if (endPos == -1) endPos = myString.Length;
```

The token is extracted from the string using `Substring()` and written to the console. The start position is updated to one character past the end position before the next token is searched for:

```
   if (endPos != startPos)
       Console.WriteLine(myString.Substring(
                         startPos, (endPos - startPos)));

   startPos = (endPos + 1);
} while (startPos < myString.Length);
```

Most of the routine is efficient since it is a linear walkthrough of the characters in the string. The expensive part is the `Substring()` operation, since that creates a new string.

Reversing a String

There are times when you may need to reverse a string. Some languages offer this as built-in functionality, but not the .NET Framework. The following example demonstrates a good approach to solving this problem:

```
class Reverse
{
   static void Main(string[] args)
   {
      string myString = "If there's a bustle in your hedgerow";
      char [] myChars = myString.ToCharArray();
```

```
      Array.Reverse(myChars);
      Console.WriteLine(myString);
      Console.WriteLine(myChars);
   }
}
```

The code displays the following on the console:

```
If there's a bustle in your hedgerow
woregdeh ruoy ni eltsub a s'ereht fI
```

Any class derived from `Array` can use the `Reverse()` method to reorder the elements in the array. To reverse the string we create a character array from the string and call the `Reverse()` method. The resulting array has the characters in reverse order.

However, as you'll discover in Chapter 4, one character can be made up of a pair of chars. Reversing this pair would make such a character invalid.

Insert, Remove, and Replace

A category of operations on strings is to insert, remove, or replace portions of a string. Both the `String` and `StringBuilder` classes support these operations. Most of these operations can also be performed using regular expressions. We look at regular expressions in Chapters 5 to 7.

For the examples here, we will use the following sample file (`albums.txt`) as a source of strings. You will notice that the following code reads the file as Unicode. Be sure that the text file is saved in the same format as it is read. Notepad for instance allows you to Save As Unicode:

```
Led Zeppelin, Led Zeppelin [I], 1969
Frank Zappa, We're Only in It for the Money, 1968
Beatles, Sgt. Pepper's Lonely Hearts Club Band, 1967
Jimi Hendrix, Are You Experienced?, 1967
```

The following code will be the test harness for loading the data and processing it. The results are sent to the console:

```
class ProcessFile
{
   static void Main(string[] args)
   {
      const string NAME = "album.txt";
      Stream readLine;
      TextWriter writeLine;
      StringBuilder sb;
```

```
readLine = File.OpenRead(NAME);
writeLine = Console.Out;

StreamReader readLineSReader =
    new StreamReader(readLine, Encoding.Unicode);

readLineSReader.BaseStream.Seek(0, SeekOrigin.Begin);

while (readLineSReader.Peek() > -1)
{
    sb = new StringBuilder(readLineSReader.ReadLine());
    // insert string operation here
    Console.WriteLine(sb.ToString());
}
}
}
```

If we use the following code to add a column on the end:

```
sb.Append(", Rock");
```

it will display the following on the console:

```
Led Zeppelin, Led Zeppelin [I], 1969, Rock
Frank Zappa, We're Only in It for the Money, 1968, Rock
Beatles, Sgt. Pepper's Lonely Hearts Club Band, 1967, Rock
Jimi Hendrix, Are You Experienced?, 1967, Rock
```

The first column could be removed using the following code:

```
sb.Remove(0, sb.ToString().IndexOf(',') + 1);
```

This results in the following output (notice there is still a space at the start of each line):

```
Led Zeppelin [I], 1969
We're Only in It for the Money, 1968
Sgt. Pepper's Lonely Hearts Club Band, 1967
Are You Experienced?, 1967
```

The delimiter could be replaced with the following code:

```
sb.Replace(",", " |");
```

This gives the following output:

```
Led Zeppelin | Led Zeppelin [I] | 1969
Frank Zappa | We're Only in It for the Money | 1968
Beatles | Sgt. Pepper's Lonely Hearts Club Band | 1967
Jimi Hendrix | Are You Experienced? | 1967
```

71

In this case, there is a performance hit. To make the output look better, a space and a pipe replace the comma. This means the system cannot do a simple character-for-character replacement. Other characters have to be moved and potentially more memory allocated.

Finally, we can prefix each line with line numbers using this code. This assumes lineNumber is declared and initialized to zero somewhere previously:

```
sb.Insert(0, lineNumber.ToString("000 "));
lineNumber++;
```

This results in the following output:

```
000 Led Zeppelin, Led Zeppelin [I], 1969
001 Frank Zappa, We're Only in It for the Money, 1968
002 Beatles, Sgt. Pepper's Lonely Hearts Club Band, 1967
003 Jimi Hendrix, Are You Experienced?, 1967
```

Choosing Between String and StringBuilder

For insert, remove, and replace operations you have a choice between the String and StringBuilder classes. The following table shows some performance results of these operations when the code was executed on a 1.3 GHz Intel Celeron processor, with 256 MB of memory:

Class	Method	String Interned	Execution Time (ms)
String	Insert()/Remove()	Yes	691
String	Insert()/Remove()	No	851
StringBuilder	Insert()/Remove()	N/A	441
String	Replace()	Yes	981
String	Replace()	No	982
StringBuilder	Replace()	N/A	761

By running these tests, you can see that StringBuilder is consistently faster than String for Replace(), Remove(), and Insert() operations. If we're using the String class, operations on an interned string are faster than a non-interned string for Insert() and Replace() operations, but not by enough to make a significant difference.

The main reason `StringBuilder` performs much better than the `String` class is because `String` has to allocate a new string and copy the characters. `StringBuilder` can perform the operations in the same memory space. `StringBuilder` suffers in performance only if it reaches its capacity and needs to allocate more memory. However, it suffers no more than `String` does and it reallocates memory far less often than `String`, if at all. As with the performance tests for concatenation, all you have to be aware of is that creating a `StringBuilder` can take longer. Using a similar test to the one shown below, on the same machine, using the same number of iterations, it was found that on a 114 character string, the creation of a `StringBuilder` took just 790 ms longer. The gap increases depending on the size of the string.

The following code was used to obtain the results for the previous table:

```
using System;
using System.Text;

namespace Wrox.Text.Chapter2
{
  class PerfTest
  {
    const int NUM_ITER = 1000000;

    static void Main(string[] args)
    {
      string s1 = "It's been a long time since I rock and rolled.";
      string s2;
      string s3;
      StringBuilder sb = new StringBuilder(s1);

      // Make sure we have a string that's not interned.
      s2 = s1.Replace('.', '!');

      int startTime;
      int endTime;
      int count;

      // INSERT/REMOVE - String, interned.
      startTime = Environment.TickCount;
      for (count = 0; count < NUM_ITER-1; count++)
      {
        s3 = s1.Insert(12, "really ");
        s1 = s3.Remove(12, 7);
      }
      endTime = Environment.TickCount;
      Console.WriteLine("INSERT/REMOVE - interned String: " +
          (endTime - startTime));

      // INSERT - String, not interned.
      startTime = Environment.TickCount;
      for (count = 0; count < NUM_ITER-1; count++)
      {
```

73

```
      s3 = s2.Insert(12, "really ");
      s1 = s3.Remove(12, 7);
   }
   endTime = Environment.TickCount;
   Console.WriteLine("INSERT/REMOVE - non interned String: " +
       (endTime - startTime));

   // INSERT - StringBuilder
   startTime = Environment.TickCount;
   for (count = 0; count < NUM_ITER-1; count++)
   {
     sb.Insert(12, "really ", 1);
     sb.Remove(12, 7);
   }
   endTime = Environment.TickCount;
   Console.WriteLine("INSERT/REMOVE - String Builder: " +
       (endTime - startTime));

   // REPLACE - String, interned.
   startTime = Environment.TickCount;
   for (count = 0; count < NUM_ITER-1; count++)
   {
     s3 = s1.Replace("rock and rolled", "had the blues");
   }
   endTime = Environment.TickCount;
   Console.WriteLine("REPLACE - interned String: " +
       (endTime - startTime));

   // REPLACE - String, not interned.
   startTime = Environment.TickCount;
   for (count = 0; count < NUM_ITER-1; count++)
   {
     s3 = s2.Replace("rock and rolled", "had the blues");
   }
   endTime = Environment.TickCount;
   Console.WriteLine("REPLACE - non interned String: " +
       (endTime - startTime));

   // REPLACE - StringBuilder
   startTime = Environment.TickCount;
   for (count = 0; count < NUM_ITER-1; count++)
   {
     sb.Replace("rock and rolled", "had the blues");
   }
   endTime = Environment.TickCount;
   Console.WriteLine("REPLACE - String Builder: " +
       (endTime - startTime));
  }
 }
}
```

Summary

Text manipulation using the `String` and `StringBuilder` classes has been extensively covered in this chapter. When faced with performing operations on text, you often have a number of approaches to choose from. This chapter gave you background on how the `String` and `StringBuilder` classes operate, to try to guide you in making the best decisions.

The following tips are recommended to optimize performance of string operations:

❑   Store strings as constants whenever possible to ensure the intern pool is used and so to minimize the number of machine instructions required.

❑   If the `String` class will do the job effectively, use it instead of `StringBuilder`. For example, if the operation is a single string assignment.

❑   If you are looping to build up a large block of character data, use `StringBuilder`.

❑   Only use `Compare()` if you require international strings. Otherwise, use `CompareOrdinal`.

❑   Use `Equals()` rather than `CompareOrdinal()` if you only need to know if the strings are the same.

❑   Always use the `Equals()` method, rather than the "=" operator.

This chapter did not properly address Internationalization, which also has an impact on how you structure your string manipulation solutions. Another approach to solving some of the problems listed in this chapter is through using regular expressions. Internationalization within C# is covered in detail in Chapter 4, whereas Regular Expressions are explained in Chapters 5 to 7. In the next chapter we look at the issues involved when moving strings between data types and storing them in arrays and collections.

C#

Text Manipulation

Handbook

3

String Conversion

When writing code, there are many cases when information needs to be converted from one data type to another. For instance, you may need to convert a date input by a user from a string to an actual date representation on which calculations can be done, or you may need to transform a number to a string so that it can be displayed using a format that shows two decimal places and a currency symbol. The .NET Framework provides you with easy ways to achieve these goals.

The ToString() Method

Every object, because it inherits from the System.Object base class, has a ToString() method that provides a string that represents the object. This includes the system base types, such as Integer or Double as they are also objects. The default implementation for the ToString() method returns the fully qualified name of the type of the instance of the object-derived class. For instance, if you use the following code, it will return a string that contains "System.Object":

```
Object obj = new Object();
MessageBox.Show(obj.ToString());
```

However, this method can and should be overridden, whenever it makes sense to do so, so that this method returns a human-readable, culture-sensitive string that represents the current object. For instance, the `int` class implements the `ToString()` method in this way. The following code provides a useful string representation of the integer value.

```
int i = 123456;
MessageBox.Show(i.ToString());
```

Also, please note that derived classes that require more control over the formatting of the returned string should implement the `IFormattable` interface, which uses the thread's current culture for its `ToString()` method. You'll read much more about cultures in the next chapter, but if you remember, this specifies what region-specific information is to be used. For instance, an instance of the `Double` class, whose value is zero, might return `0.00` or `0,00` after its `ToString()` method call, depending on the current culture.

Now that we know that objects can be converted to strings by using the `ToString()` method, let's see how to convert numeric values to strings.

Representing Numeric Values as Strings

Let's review the numeric formats that are supported by the .NET Framework and how numeric data, including percentage and money amounts, can be formatted and represented as strings. Before we explore the `NumberFormatInfo` class, let's look at some of the more interesting numeric features enabled by the .NET Framework. The simplest way of representing a number as a string can be seen below:

```
12345.ToString();
```

This will output `12345` as a string. While this is useful, the formatting, or rather lack thereof in this case, isn't very impressive. This is because we did not specify a proper format for the string, and by default, the `ToString()` method will use the standard formatting for numbers, with no specification of decimal separator and no grouping.

Now, we can go one step further and specify some formatting information here as well, such as:

```
12345.ToString("n");
```

In this case, we provided formatting information (the "n" value) to indicate that we want 12345 to be formatted as a number when being represented as a string. The formatting will now take into account the currently selected CurrentCulture (see next chapter for more details on cultures) at the thread level in order to provide us with a string that represents this number.

If the current culture were en-US, you would get the following result:

```
12,345.00
```

If the current culture were fr-FR, the result would be:

```
12 345,00
```

You can format numeric results by using the String.Format() method, or for Console applications, you can use the Console.Write() method, which in turn calls the String.Format() method. The format is specified using format strings.

The following code sample uses the currency format (selected by the "C" specifier when using the ToString() method) to display the actual value of the integer. Since the author is located in the United States and the machine is configured as a regular en-US machine, the value is displayed using the symbol for US dollars:

```
using System;
using System.Windows.Forms;

namespace Wrox.Text.Chapter3
{
  class ToStringCulture
  {
    static void Main(string[] args)
    {
      int MyInt = 100;
      string MyString = MyInt.ToString("C");
      MessageBox.Show(MyString);
    }
  }
}
```

The output will be as follows:

If you type this code and run it on your machine, in the UK, with English settings properly configured, then the output will be in Pounds Sterling:

This happens because the application uses the current culture set at the current thread level if no culture information is passed to the ToString() method.

The following code example uses the CultureInfo class to specify the culture that the ToString() method and format string will use. This code creates a new instance of the CultureInfo class called MyCulture and initializes it to the French culture using the string fr-FR. This object is then passed to the ToString() method as an additional parameter along with the "C" string format specifier that we used in the previous example to produce a French monetary value:

```
using System;
using System.Globalization;
using System.Windows.Forms;

namespace Wrox.Text.Chapter3
{
  class ToStringCulture2
  {
    static void Main(string[] args)
    {
      int MyInt = 100;
      CultureInfo MyCulture = new CultureInfo("fr-FR");
      string MyString = MyInt.ToString("C", MyCulture);
      MessageBox.Show(MyString);
    }
  }
}
```

This will result in the following:

This is interesting as the culture is being taken into account. The current CultureInfo object implements the IFormatProvider interface and has a NumberFormatInfo member that is actually responsible for providing the information, such as the grouping symbol, the actual size of the groups, the decimal separator symbol, and more. Actually, the NumberFormatInfo class also implements the IFormatProvider to supply formatting information to applications.

NumberFormatInfo

The NumberFormatInfo class defines how numeric values are formatted and displayed, depending on the culture. This class contains information, such as currency, decimal separators, and other numeric symbols.

To create a NumberFormatInfo for a specific culture, create a CultureInfo object for that culture and retrieve the CultureInfo.NumberFormat property. If you want to create a NumberFormatInfo for the culture of the current thread, use the CurrentCultureInfo property.

To create a NumberFormatInfo for the invariant culture, use the InvariantInfo property for a read-only version, or use the NumberFormatInfo constructor for a writable version. Note that it is impossible to create a NumberFormatInfo for a neutral culture (a culture that only deals with a language and has no region/country information), because there is no indication of formatting associated with a neutral culture.

Numeric values are formatted using standard or custom patterns stored in the properties of a NumberFormatInfo. To modify how a value is displayed, the NumberFormatInfo must be writable, so that custom patterns can be saved in its properties. Since the default NumberFormatInfo object associated with a CultureInfo as a member of this class is not writable, we will need to clone this object, using the Clone() method to create another instance that we can modify.

The format string takes the form Ann, where A is the format specifier, and nn is the precision specifier. The format specifier controls the type of formatting applied to the numerical value, and the precision specifier controls the number of significant digits or decimal places.

If the format string is not specified, or set to Nothing or an empty string, the general format specifier ("G") is implicitly used.

The table below provides a list of all the standard format specifiers and examples of their use:

Format Character	Format Description	Example	Output
C or c	Currency	1000.ToString("C");	$1,000.00
		-1000.ToString("C");	($1,000.00)
D or d	Decimal	1000.ToString("D");	1000
E or e	Scientific (exponential)	100000.ToString("E");	1.000000E+005

Table continued on following page

Format Character	Format Description	Example	Output
F or f	Fixed-point	`1000.ToString("F4");`	`1000.0000`
		`1000.ToString("F0");`	`1000`
G or g	General	`1000.ToString("G");`	`1000`
N or n	Number	`1000.ToString("N");`	`1,000.00`
X or x	Hexadecimal	`1000.ToString("X");`	`3E8`
		`1000.ToString("x");`	`3e8`
		`0x1000.ToString("x");`	`1000`
P or p	Percentage	`1.ToString("P");`	`100.00 %`
r or R	Roundtrip. This is used to ensure that the string representation can be converted back to a number. It is not available for the `Integer` type but works for `Double`.	`double d = 1000.0;` `d.ToString("R");`	`1000`

Note that the format character is not case sensitive, except in the case of "x" and "X", where the case of the format character determines the casing used for hexadecimal numbers. The formatting information displayed in the table above only applies to the en-US culture. If another culture were used, output could be different.

The `NumberFormatInfo` class implements the `ICloneable` interface, so that `NumberFormatInfo` objects can be duplicated using the `Clone()` method. This is very useful when you intend to customize an instance of the `NumberFormatInfo` class associated with a `CultureInfo` in order to provide custom formatting. The example below shows exactly this. This short program retrieves the current culture and customizes it so that the new currency symbol is "*" and the new group separator is "|". Then it outputs a value of `123456` using this format.

The `CurrencyPositivePattern` requires some explanation. The .NET Framework uses a set of patterns, referenced by numbers (it is actually an enumeration), which indicate where the currency symbol is located (in front of the string or at the end of it) and whether a space is to be inserted before the currency symbol or not:

```
using System;
using System.Globalization;
using System.Threading;
```

```
namespace Wrox.Text.Chapter3
{
  class ChangeCultureFormat
  {
    static void Main(string[] args)
    {
      // retrieve current culture information by cloning it so that
      // we can manipulate its NumberFormat member

      CultureInfo ci =
          (CultureInfo)Thread.CurrentThread.CurrentCulture.Clone();
      NumberFormatInfo nfi = ci.NumberFormat;

      // Set our format to "123|456*"
      nfi.CurrencyPositivePattern = 1;
      nfi.CurrencyGroupSeparator = "|";
      nfi.CurrencySymbol = "*";
      nfi.CurrencyDecimalDigits = 0;
      ci.NumberFormat = nfi;

      // Set the thread culture to our modified CultureInfo object
      Thread.CurrentThread.CurrentCulture = ci;

      // Display the actual value using the proper formatting
      Console.WriteLine(123456.ToString("C"));
    }
  }
}
```

The output when executing this should be:

```
123|456*
```

Representing Date and Time as a String

The `DateTime` value type represents dates and times with values ranging from 12:00:00 midnight, January 1, year 1 A.D. (or C.E. – Common Era, which is the new cross-culture name for "A.D.") to 11:59:59 P.M., December 31, 9999 C.E.

The `DateTime` type implements the `IFormattable` interface, allowing it to be formatted as a string with one of the overloads of `DateTime.ToString()`. The standard format provider class used for formatting `DateTime` objects in the .NET Framework is `DateTimeFormatInfo`.

The DateTimeFormatInfo Class

This class defines how `DateTime` values are formatted and displayed, depending on the culture. It contains information, such as date patterns, time patterns, and AM/PM designators. To create a `DateTimeFormatInfo` for a specific culture, create a `CultureInfo` for that culture and retrieve the `CultureInfo.DateTimeFormat` property. To create a `DateTimeFormatInfo` for the invariant culture, use the `InvariantInfo` property for a read-only version, or use the `DateTimeFormatInfo` constructor for a writable version. Like the `NumberFormatInfo` class, it is impossible to create a `DateTimeFormatInfo` for a neutral culture.

Format strings are interpreted as standard format specifiers if they contain only one of the single format specifiers detailed in the bullet points below. If the specified format character is a single character and is not found in the following list, an exception is thrown. If the format string is longer than a single character in length (even if the extra characters are whitespaces), the format string is interpreted as a custom format string. The patterns produced by these format specifiers are influenced by the settings in the Regional Options of the Windows Control Panel as these affect the current culture, unless the user preferences are overridden.

The `DateSeparator` and `TimeSeparator` characters associated with the `DateTimeFormat` property of the current culture define the date and time separators displayed by format strings.

However, in cases where the `InvariantCulture` is used (when referenced by the "r", "s", and "u" specifiers), the characters associated with the `DateSeparator` and `TimeSeparator` characters do not change depending on the current culture, but remain attached to the invariant culture.

The .NET Framework provides a long list of formats that are supported for date and time (the full list is available on MSDN). Here are the most common ones, which are also mapped to member functions of the `DateTimeFormatInfo` class (with some sample data for the en-US culture):

❑ "d": the short date pattern (5/20/2002, for example). Also available directly through the `DateTimeFormatInfo.ShortDatePattern` property.

❑ "D": the long date pattern (Monday, May 20, 2002, for example). Also available directly through the `DateTimeFormatInfo.LongDatePattern` property.

❑ "t": the short time pattern (3:51 PM, for example). Also available directly through the `DateTimeFormatInfo.ShortTimePattern` property.

❑ "T": the long time pattern (3:51:04 PM, for example). Also available directly through the `DateTimeFormatInfo.LongTimePattern` property.

Of course, besides standard formats, custom ones are also supported. The following code example illustrates how to use a custom format string with `DateTime` objects:

84

```
using System;
using System.Globalization;
using System.Threading;

namespace Wrox.Text.Chapter3
{
  class CustomDateTimeFormat
  {
    static void Main(string[] args)
    {
      DateTime dt = DateTime.Now;
      DateTimeFormatInfo dfi = new DateTimeFormatInfo();
      CultureInfo ci = new CultureInfo("nl-BE");

      // Use the DateTimeFormat from the culture associated with
      // the current thread.
      Console.WriteLine(dt.ToString("d"));
      Console.WriteLine(dt.ToString("m"));

      // Use the DateTimeFormat from the specific culture passed.
      Console.WriteLine(dt.ToString("F", ci));

      // Make up a new custom DateTime pattern, and use it
      dfi.MonthDayPattern = "MM-MMMM, ddd-dddd";
      Console.WriteLine(dt.ToString("m", dfi));

      // Reset the current thread to a different culture.
      Thread.CurrentThread.CurrentCulture = new CultureInfo("fr-BE");
      Console.WriteLine(dt.ToString("d"));
    }
  }
}
```

The results will be similar to the following, depending on your current date, time, and culture:

```
10/7/2002
October 07
maandag 7 oktober 2002 11:19:42
10-October, Mon-Monday
7/10/2002
```

Representing Other Objects as Strings

So far, we have dealt with numbers and date and time but what if we were creating a class and wanted to make sure that our class can be represented as a string properly? Well, this is only slightly more complicated: our class will inherit from the Object class and so we just need to provide overload(s) for the ToString method in the class.

Here we will create a Coordinate class that contains two values, X and Y:

```
class Coordinate : Object
{
  private int mx;
  private int my;

  public Coordinate(int X, int Y)
  {
    mx = X;
    my = Y;
  }

  public override String ToString()
  {
    return "(" + mx.ToString() + ", " + my.ToString() + ")";
  }
}
```

This is the really simple and naive approach. A more elaborate approach would be to enable formatting parameters. It would be interesting to support the different formatting options available for the numeric format so that we could, for instance, display the coordinate as hexadecimal numbers.

In order to do so, we simply need to implement an overload for the ToString() method that implements the IFormattable interface, and change the current ToString() overload so that it uses the one that implements the formatting support. This is done here with the code below:

```
using System;
using System.Globalization;
using System.Threading;

namespace Wrox.Text.Chapter3
{
  class Coordinate : Object, IFormattable
  {
```

```
    private int mx;
    private int my;

    public Coordinate(int X, int Y)
    {
      mx = X;
      my = Y;
    }

    public override String ToString()
    {
      return ToString("g", CultureInfo.CurrentCulture);
    }

    public String ToString(String format, IFormatProvider fp)
    {
      // Implements IFormattable.ToString
      return String.Format("({0}, {1})",
                            mx.ToString(format, fp),
                            my.ToString(format, fp));
    }
}

class CoordinateExample
{
  static void Main(string[] args)
  {
    Coordinate c = new Coordinate(1000, 2000);
    Console.WriteLine(c.ToString());
    Console.WriteLine(c.ToString("X", null));
    Console.WriteLine(c.ToString("N", new CultureInfo("en-GB")));
  }
}
}
```

The default ToString() method uses the current culture and the "g" format, which is the general number format.

The output of this sample application is:

```
(1000, 2000)
(3E8, 7D0)
(1,000.00, 2,000.00)
```

Representing Strings with Strings

There are many cases where we need to transform strings into other strings. While this may sound strange, let's just see why we may want to do this.

Let's assume that we have the following code:

```
using System;

namespace Wrox.Text.Chapter3
{
  class StringConcatenation
  {
    static void Main(string[] args)
    {
      string[] list = {"car", "pen"};
      string message;

      foreach (string item in list)
      {
        message = "This is my new " + item;
        Console.WriteLine(message);
      }
    }
  }
}
```

The output of this code is:

```
This is my new car
This is my new pen
```

This looks perfectly fine. However, in many cases, this code is wrong when dealing with international strings. It is wrong because it makes an assumption, which is that all languages work like English. Many languages work in different ways.

Japanese, for instance, uses a different word order, where the verb is at the end of the sentence for sentences like the ones above. In addition, in other languages such as French and Italian, nouns have gender (masculine or feminine) and adjectives change depending on the gender and the number of the nouns they refer to.

It is now easy to see why the code above would not always work appropriately. The simple concatenation used above is not good enough and we need a better mechanism. This is exactly what the `String.Format()` method provides, as shown in the next chapter.

From String to Other Types

We have seen how to format data from a numeric value or a date time object to a string. However, there are cases where we need to do the opposite transform, which is transforming a string into a `DateTime` or a number. This is exactly what the `Parse()` and `ParseExact()` methods are for.

Converting Strings to Numbers

All numeric types (such as `Integer` and `Double`) provide a `Parse()` method that enables you to convert strings to numbers very easily, while taking into account the formatting that may have been applied to the string representations. The `Parse()` method accepts a format provider, which allows you to specify and parse culture-specific strings. This means that you can also apply the same customization that can be applied for formatting.

If no format provider is specified, then the provider associated with the current thread is used. If you want to specify a format, you need to make sure that the `NumberStyles` enumeration flags (provided by the `System.Globalization` namespace) that you pass to the `Parse()` method will actually match the format you want to use, otherwise a `FormatException` will be thrown. For instance, in the en-US culture, a string that contains a comma cannot be converted to an integer value using the `Parse()` method if the `NumberStyles.AllowThousands` enumeration is not passed.

The following code example is invalid and it will raise an exception. It shows an improper way to parse a string containing non-numeric characters:

```
using System;
using System.Globalization;

namespace Wrox.Text.Chapter3
{
  class BadParsing
  {
    static void Main(string[] args)
    {
      CultureInfo myCultureInfo = new CultureInfo("en-US");
      string myString = "1,000";

      try
      {
        int myInt = int.Parse(myString, myCultureInfo);
        Console.WriteLine(myInt);
        // raise exception
      }

      catch(System.FormatException ex)
      {
        Console.WriteLine(
            "Commas cannot be included in string to convert");
        Console.WriteLine("Exception was: {0}", ex.ToString());
      }
    }
  }
}
```

We only need to modify this code slightly to make it work properly by specifying the `NumberStyles.AllowThousand` flag when parsing the string:

```
using System;
using System.Globalization;
using System.Threading;

namespace Wrox.Text.Chapter3
{
  class GoodParsing
  {
    static void Main(string[] args)
    {
      CultureInfo myCultureInfo = new CultureInfo("en-US");
      string myString = "1,000";
      int myInt = int.Parse(myString, NumberStyles.AllowThousands,
                            myCultureInfo);
      Console.WriteLine(myInt);
    }
  }
}
```

We can also use a custom format to do some parsing. In order to show this, let's extend the sample we used when demonstrating how to format numbers using a custom format and just add parsing capabilities to this sample.

This short program retrieves the current culture and customizes it so the currency symbol is "#" and the group separator is ":". It will then output an integer (2364) based on a string with these characters inserted. This can be extremely valuable when dealing with, for instance, an HTML form that could receive input from users in another locale:

```
using System;
using System.Globalization;
using System.Threading;

namespace Wrox.Text.Chapter3
{
  class CustomizeCulture
  {
    static void Main(string[] args)
    {
      // Retrieve current culture information by cloning it
      // so that we can manipulate its NumberFormat member
      CultureInfo ci =
          (CultureInfo)Thread.CurrentThread.CurrentCulture.Clone();
      NumberFormatInfo nfi = ci.NumberFormat;

      // Set our format to "2:364#"
      nfi.CurrencyPositivePattern = 1;
      nfi.CurrencyGroupSeparator = ":";
      nfi.CurrencySymbol = "#";
      nfi.CurrencyDecimalDigits = 0;
      ci.NumberFormat = nfi;
```

```
            // Set the thread's culture to our modified CultureInfo object
            Thread.CurrentThread.CurrentCulture = ci;

            // Display the actual value using the proper formatting
            Console.WriteLine(2364.ToString("C"));

            // Now parse a string using our custom format
            int myInt = int.Parse("2:364#",
                            NumberStyles.AllowCurrencySymbol |
                            NumberStyles.Currency |
                            NumberStyles.AllowThousands);
            Console.WriteLine("{0:N}", myInt);
        }
    }
}
```

The `Parse()` method is called with a combination of the `Currency`,
`AllowCurrencySymbol`, and `AllowThousands` `NumberStyles` flags in order to
match the format that is currently specified using the current thread's culture.

This sample output is now:

```
2:364#
2,364.00
```

Converting String to Date and Time

In this section we cover the subtleties in converting a string to date and time, because
dates are formatted differently in different locales.

Parsing Date and Time

The `DateTime` object has both a `Parse()` and a `ParseExact()` method that can be
used to convert a string representation of a date or time into a `DateTime` object. The
difference between the `Parse()` method and the `ParseExact()` method is that the
`Parse()` method converts any valid string representation, whereas the `ParseExact()`
method only converts strings that match the format that you specify. If you are using
standard `DateTime` patterns (as defined earlier by the `DateTime` format table) then
both methods can be used.

Parse()

The code below shows how to use the `Parse()` method to parse a string that contains
a date:

```
using System;
using System.Globalization;
using System.Threading;
```

```
namespace Wrox.Text.Chapter3
{
  class Parse
  {
    static void Main(string[] args)
    {
      string myString = "10/28/2002";
      DateTime myDateTime = DateTime.Parse(myString);
      Console.WriteLine("{0:F}", myDateTime);
    }
  }
}
```

Provided the current culture is set to English (United States), the output will be:

```
Monday, October 28, 2002 12:00:00 AM
```

It should also be noted that a `CultureInfo` could be passed so that the date/time information is parsed according to the specified culture. If we modify the code slightly to pass an English (United Kingdom) culture, as indicated below, we get different results:

```
using System;
using System.Globalization;

namespace Wrox.Text.Chapter3
{
  class ParseUK
  {
    static void Main(string[] args)
    {
      CultureInfo myCultureInfo = new CultureInfo("en-GB");
      string myString = "28/10/2002";
      DateTime myDateTime = DateTime.Parse(myString, myCultureInfo);
      Console.WriteLine("{0:F}", myDateTime);
    }
  }
}
```

The output for this will be:

```
Monday 28 October 2002 00:00:00 AM
```

It is important to note that because date format depends on the culture being used, it is not always possible to figure out what date is meant if the culture information is not provided. For instance, 02/01/2002 may be either January 2, 2002 or February 1, 2002, depending on the culture that is used. Since this can easily lead to incorrect dates being stored, it is a good practice to always set the culture info explicitly in any date handling code, and to ensure that the date is stored in a culture-independent format – which is exactly what the invariant culture provides in the .NET Framework (see next chapter for more details on this).

Another interesting feature of the `Parse()` method is that, by default, any information about the date or time that is not contained in the passed string is filled with the current date and time value for this information.

ParseExact()

The `ParseExact()` method only converts the specified string pattern to a `DateTime` object and if the string that is passed does not match the pattern, then a `FormatException` is thrown. In the following code example, the `ParseExact()` method is passed a `String` object that matches the en-US short date pattern:

```
using System;
using System.Globalization;

namespace Wrox.Text.Chapter3
{
    class ParseExact
    {
        static void Main(string[] args)
        {
            CultureInfo myCultureInfo = new CultureInfo("en-US");
            string myString = "10/28/2002";
            DateTime myDateTime = DateTime.ParseExact(myString, "d",
                                                      myCultureInfo);
            Console.WriteLine("{0:d}", myDateTime);
        }
    }
}
```

The output of this code varies depending on the current culture settings. On a US locale, for instance, the output will be: `10/28/2002`. On a UK locale, the output will be: `28/10/2002`.

Moving Strings Between Collections and Arrays

This is a small section on members of the `System.Collections` namespace, and objects of type `System.Array`. Because collections and arrays store their members differently, some mention is worthwhile here.

An object can always be cast to an object it inherits from, and it can be cast to its own data type. This is useful if you want to perform a string operation on an item contained in an array or collection.

Arrays

A `System.Array` object can be defined as fixed or variable size, and the object itself
does not contain the contents of any other objects. If you define an array of value
types, then it will contain the values, but as `System.String` is a reference type, then
an array of strings will only contain references to the location of the strings. In addition,
an array can only contain items of the same type. This is because the .NET Framework
prefers to know the exact size of the array. Value types are of fixed size, so an array
that contains ten integers, for instance, will consume 40 bytes of memory. This means
that the heap can allocate exactly the space needed for the array. An array of ten
strings would consume the same amount of memory as an array of ten integers, as
references are also 32-bit. As all references are the same, then you can define an array
of type `System.Object` and it will consume the same amount of memory for strings
and all other objects.

We can see this in practice in the following code. Remember that in arrays, unlike
collections, `GetValue(index)` is used to return the contents at the specified index, and
`SetValue(item, index)` is used to set or change the contents at the specified index:

```
using System;

namespace Wrox.Text.Chapter3
{
  class ArrayExample
  {
    static void Main(string[] args)
    {
      string[] firstArray = {"what", "did", "you", "do"};

      for (int count = 0; count < firstArray.Length; count++)
      {
        Console.WriteLine("{0} - Type: {1}",
                  firstArray.GetValue(count),
                  firstArray.GetValue(count).GetType());
      }

      Console.WriteLine("Type of firstArray is {0}",
                firstArray.GetType());
    }
  }
}
```

There are some interesting things to point out about this code. Firstly, when the array
is first defined, it happens in a few stages. Four areas of the heap are allocated to
contain the strings "what", "did", "you", and "do". Then, the `Array` object is
constructed, and is limited to 4 elements. The references to the four strings are then
inserted in each of the elements of the array. If you change any of the elements in this
array, it will create a new `String` object and insert a reference to it.

Now, look at the first `Console.WriteLine()`. There is no need to cast this to type string as the compiler can see that it is a string at compile time. In the next part of the line, we use a formatting string to output the results of `GetType()`. Because `GetType()` returns a `System.Type`, it would have to be cast to a string, and the formatting instruction does this explicitly. This `for` loop returns `System.String` four times. The second `Console.WriteLine()` uses a formatting string again to return the type of the array. Here, rather than returning `System.Array`, or `System.Object`, it returns `System.String[]`, thus indicating that it is an array object that contains elements of type `System.String`. Arrays are simple to deal with, as the `GetValue()` method always returns the expected type.

Now, if we were to resize this array, what would happen is that a new `Array` object would be created of the specified size, and the contents of the first would be copied into the first elements of the second. This is quite inefficient, and so the .NET Framework has provided collections so that we can store different objects of different types, and like the `StringBuilder` object discussed in the last chapter, attempt to reduce the amount of memory copying that occurs.

ArrayLists

An `ArrayList` is the `StringBuilder` of the array world. Like the `StringBuilder`, on initialization it permits 16 elements when the default constructor is used, and it also allows a value to be passed to its constructor so you can specify that it be resized to contain a different number of elements. An `ArrayList` object will store any object of type `System.Object` – which is everything. This is a boon as it means that any object can be contained, but it is also a burden as it means that objects returned would often need to be cast to their original type for the compiler not to complain about operations you wish to perform. This is generally a good idea anyway, as you may not know for certain what the type is that is contained at a specific position within the `ArrayList`. An `ArrayList`, like an array, stores its elements at specific indices, but it can contain different types, and fewer memory allocations occur if more items need to be added. Unlike an array, an `ArrayList` uses the `Add()` method to append a new item, the `Item()` method to retrieve an item at a specific index, and numerous other methods, like `Insert()`, `Remove()`, `RemoveAt()`, `Sort()`, and `IndexOf()` to perform more powerful operations. `Insert()` and `RemoveAt()` will move the contents of the `ArrayList` up or down one, depending on the method, and so they can be quite expensive. Let's look at an `ArrayList` in action:

```
using System;
using System.Collections;

namespace Wrox.Text.Chapter3
{
    class ArrayListExample
    {
        static void Main(string[] args)
        {
```

```
            ArrayList myList = new ArrayList();

            myList.Add("Humpty Dumpty sat on the wall");
            myList.Add("Humpty Dumpty had a great fall");
            myList.Add("All the king's horses and all the king's men");
            myList.Add("Couldn't put humpty together again");
            myList.Add(6);
            myList.Add(6.3);
            myList.Add(true);

            for(int count = 0; count < myList.Count; count++)
            {
              Console.WriteLine("{0}\tType: {1}",
                                myList[count],
                                myList[count].GetType());
            }
          }
        }
      }
    }
```

This will output the following:

```
Humpty Dumpty sat on the wall    Type: System.String
Humpty Dumpty had a great fall   Type: System.String
All the king's horses and all the king's men    Type: System.String
Couldn't put humpty together again    Type: System.String
6         Type: System.Int32
6.3       Type: System.Double
True      Type: System.Boolean
```

As you can see, the items returned are the expected types, and the String.Format() method (used by Console.WriteLine) happily converts the other types into strings.

IDictionary Objects

These include HashTable and all other key-value pair collections. Thankfully, these work in exactly the same way as the other collections. The key can be any object. String.Format() will work on any of the string items contained in any collection.

Summary

In this chapter you have learned the best methods for converting between strings and other data types, taking into account that different data types may be entered differently, or output differently in different locales. We have covered the details of converting from numbers and dates, which may need formatting in a completely different way depending on the locale. We have also covered the reverse of this, sending a formatted string to a specific data type.

The last section showed how collections contain strings – as references to objects. It showed some of the issues involved when referencing the members of `Arrays`, `ArrayLists`, and `IDictionary` collections. In short, there was very little to learn about these objects. The collections only contain references to separate `String` objects.

The next chapter covers the culture-specific issues touched on this chapter in more detail, and describes how to make use of Unicode in the .NET Framework.

C#

Text Manipulation

Handbook

4

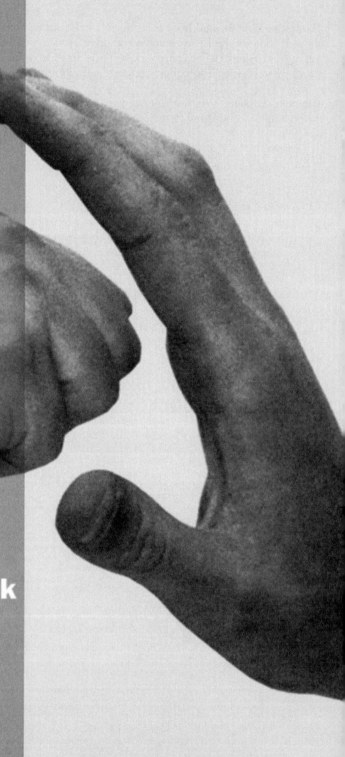

4

Internationalization

Dealing well with text is one of the major challenges of building a truly international application and involves many aspects, from ensuring that the localizability requirements are met, to performing upper and lowercasing, sorting strings, displaying strings and characters, dealing with Unicode intricacies such as surrogate pairs and combining characters, and more. Fortunately, the .NET Framework provides a set of classes that actually help you handle text correctly for the diverse cultures supported by the .NET Framework. In brief, this chapter covers:

❑ Unicode – what it is and how it is encoded in .NET

❑ What cultures are

❑ The different kinds of cultures and how they are dealt with

❑ Sorting and the various issues involved with sorting for different cultures

❑ Dealing with Unicode characters, including surrogate pairs and combining characters

By the end of this chapter, you will understand exactly how strings are dealt with in .NET, and how to make use of the new Unicode default set to ensure your applications are internationalized. You will also become aware of the issues of dealing with Unicode, such as the different ways different languages sort their alphabets. Before we explore all these features and the classes that .NET provides to assist you, let's investigate the standard the .NET Framework uses for dealing with characters and strings – Unicode.

Unicode

While applications and users deal with text, computers as you probably know only operate with numbers – so computers treat letters, digits, and other characters by assigning a value for each one. This is done through encodings, which are simply a way to match characters to arbitrary values. Traditionally, characters have been stored as binary numbers ranging from decimal 0 to 127, complying with the ASCII standard.

Later, additional encodings, such as the MS-DOS or Windows code pages (code pages are just another name for encodings), were created that stored characters as 8-bits, opening up the range from 128 to 255 so that additional characters could be accommodated from languages with different or wider alphabets, such as Russian, Greek, Spanish, and French. However, not all additional characters could be provided at the same time, so support for different languages was divided between different encodings. In Microsoft Windows, one encoding (code page 1252) provided support for all Western European languages, by providing the characters in the ASCII range and diacritics used for Western European languages (such as é, ç, ü, ñ…). However, not all characters used in Eastern and Central European languages could be accommodated so other encodings were necessary for Central and Eastern European languages, such as Russian and Greek.

In addition, other encodings (such as Shift-JIS used in Japan) were devised for East Asian languages, which use many more characters. These encodings mix characters encoded on one byte and those encoded on two bytes, making most string operations, such as the ones to find the next character, far more difficult. While all these encodings provided a way to deal with one, and sometimes several languages at a time, provided they were written using the same set of characters, none of them provided a way to deal with all languages at the same time. This was because none of these encodings provided enough characters for that purpose, and this limitation has had drastic consequences. The European Union, for instance, had to use several encodings to support its languages. Also adding to the complexity was the fact that a value would represent a different character in a different encoding, as well as a character maybe having different values in different encodings, creating many problems when exchanging data between different machines.

Because of these issues, a better solution was required. This solution is Unicode. Developed by the Unicode consortium (http://www.unicode.org), the Unicode standard provides the capacity to encode all the characters used for all the written languages in the world. Each character is assigned a name and a value that is unique. This unique value is called a **code point** and is usually expressed as a hexadecimal number following the prefix "U" and the "+" symbol. For example, the code point U+0042 represents the character "B" in the Unicode standard, and is given the character name of "LATIN CAPITAL LETTER B".

The original goal of Unicode was to use a single 16-bit encoding, providing code points for more than 65,000 characters. However, these 65,000 characters are not enough to encode all the characters used by all of the languages of the world. Therefore, the Unicode standard supports an additional mechanism that allows for over a million characters, which should provide enough space for all the written languages of the world, present or past. This makes the Unicode standard somewhat more complicated and it will be detailed in the section *Dealing with Characters*, later.

Finally, characters are grouped logically in the·Unicode standard, by ranges that correspond to the different writing scripts used by the different languages in the world. The coding starts at U+0000 with the standard ASCII characters, and then from U+0080 onwards, represents ranges defined for Greek, Cyrillic, Hebrew, Arabic, and most other scripts – ultimately it should support every script.

Encoding Formats

The Unicode Standard defines three encoding formats (Unicode Transformation Formats or UTF encodings) that can be used to encode the same data in byte (8 bits), word (16 bits), or double word (32 bits) orientation. All three formats encode the same data and the data can be converted easily and without any loss between these three encoding formats.

UTF-8 is a popular encoding for HTML and XML as its encoding scheme is backwards compatible with ASCII for the characters in the ASCII range. With UTF-8, Unicode characters are converted into bytes. Its main advantage is that Unicode characters that correspond to the familiar ASCII character set are also encoded on a single byte, which has the same value as its ASCII counterpart. For instance, the Unicode string "ABC" is encoded as a series of bytes 0x41, 0x42, 0x43, just as it would be if the string were an ASCII string. Unicode characters that are outside the normal 256-character range of UTF-8 (that is, characters whose code points are higher than U+00FF) are encoded using two or three bytes. The .NET Framework provides support for the UTF-8 encoding through an encoding class.

UTF-16 (16-bits) is the most common Unicode encoding and this is the one people refer to implicitly when speaking about Unicode as it was Unicode's original encoding. It represents most characters as single 16-bit code units, and some as a pair of 16-bit units. This topic will be explored further in the *Dealing with Characters* section. Strings within the .NET Framework use UTF-16, but for the most part, this is transparent to the developer.

UTF-32 (32-bits) is useful when the developer needs to use fixed-width characters, as it provides a way to encode all Unicode characters simply by using 32 bits. However, it is an expensive format because each character is encoded using four bytes, and it is therefore not as common as the other two encodings. The .NET Framework does not provide built-in support for UTF-32.

Finally, another encoding format, UTF-7, is mentioned here for completeness. This encoding format provides a representation of the Unicode character repertoire, with each character encoded as a series of 7-bit entities. This format uses shift characters to encode characters that are not represented as characters in the ASCII range. These shift sequences are pairs of ASCII characters that are rarely seen, and indicate that the next 2 or 3 characters are to be interpreted as a character outside the ASCII range. This format should really only be used in the context of 7-bit transports, such as mail and news transports. The .NET Framework provides an encoding class that lets you convert Unicode characters used internally by the .NET Framework to UTF-7 sequences.

.NET Framework Encoding Classes

Having seen the basics of Unicode, we will now look at the encoding classes provided by the .NET Framework. The System.Text namespace provides a series of encoding classes that allow you to convert strings between Unicode (UTF-16) and other encodings. Why do this? Because converting from an existing code page to Unicode is one way you can exchange data between a legacy application that relies on the operating system's codepage and an application developed on the .NET Framework or vice-versa.

The Encoding Class

The Encoding class is the base class from which the other encoding classes are derived. It provides methods to convert arrays and strings of Unicode characters, to and from arrays of bytes that are encoded using a Windows code page. In simple terms, it is the mechanism that enables you to convert Unicode characters to bytes that can be recognized as characters by applications developed for legacy versions of Windows that did not support Unicode, such as Windows 98.

The following code example shows how to use the encoding class to convert strings between Unicode and code pages 1252 (Windows Latin 1), which is the code page used for English and 932 (Shift-JIS, Japanese), the code page used for Japanese. You will notice that converting Japanese characters using the ConvertToEncoding() method yields different results if the code page specified is 1252 or 932. When code page 1252 is specified, these characters are not recognized as there is no support for Japanese in code page 1252 as it only deals with the Latin script used to write Western European languages. Therefore Japanese characters are converted to question marks in this case, whereas when the 932 code page is specified, then the proper Japanese characters are being generated:

```
using System;
using System.Text;
using System.Windows.Forms;

namespace Wrox.Text.Chapter4
{
  class ConvertEncoding
  {
    [STAThread]
```

```csharp
static void Main(string[] args)
{
  ConvertToEncoding("Hello, world", 1252);
  ConvertToEncoding("Hello, world", 932);

  String japaneseString = "\u307B\u308B\u305A\u3042\u306D";
  ConvertToEncoding(japaneseString, 1252);
  ConvertToEncoding(japaneseString, 932);

  Byte[] bytes = { 65, 66, 67, 233, 230 };
  ConvertFromEncoding(bytes, 1252);
}

static public void ConvertToEncoding(String text, int codePage)
{
  // Get the encoding for the specified code page and
  // get the byte representation of the specified string
  Encoding targetEncoding = Encoding.GetEncoding(codePage);
  Byte[] targetBytes = targetEncoding.GetBytes(text);

  // display the bytes and their values
  String message = String.Format(
      "String \"{0}\" has been converted to: ", text);

  for (int count = 0; count < targetBytes.Length; count++)
  {
    message += String.Format("{0} ", targetBytes[count]);
  }

  MessageBox.Show(message);
}

static public void ConvertFromEncoding(Byte[] bytes, int codePage)
{
  // Get the encoding for the specified code page and
  // convert the byte array to Unicode
  Encoding sourceEncoding = Encoding.GetEncoding(codePage);
  String targetString = sourceEncoding.GetString(bytes);

  // display the bytes and the string
  String byteString = String.Empty;
  for (int count = 0; count < bytes.Length; count++)
  {
    byteString += bytes[count].ToString() + " ";
  }

  String message = String.Format(
      "Bytes \"{0}\" have been converted to string: {1}",
      byteString, targetString);
  MessageBox.Show(message);
}
  }
}
```

The output of this code sample, assuming you have international fonts installed (which can consume 230 MB of space on a Windows XP system) should be as follows:

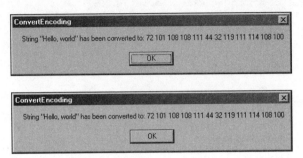

As you can see from the two screenshots, the string "Hello, world" is converted to bytes in an identical manner using both 1252 (Western Europe) and 932 (Japan) code pages. This was expected as the bytes they are converted to are the ASCII values for these characters and the ASCII characters are present in all code pages.

The screenshot above shows that in code page 1252, the Japanese string has been converted to a set of characters of value 63, (a question mark). This is because these characters are not present in this code page and are therefore not understood when the conversion from Unicode to code page 1252 occurs. In this case, data is lost as the conversion replaced the characters that could not be converted with the question mark character.

In the screenshot below, the Unicode Japanese characters have been correctly converted to their equivalent representations in code page 932, as these characters are present in this code page, which was designed to support Japanese:

Finally, the conversion can also be performed the other way round, and characters from code page 1252 can be converted successfully into Unicode characters:

The code uses the `Encoding.GetEncoding()` method, passing a code page as its argument to obtain the actual encoding that is used to format the byte array. Then it uses the `Encoding.GetBytes()` method to convert arrays of Unicode characters into array of bytes. A reversing method, called `GetChars()`, can be used to convert arrays of bytes to arrays of Unicode characters.

A number of `Encoding`-derived classes are also provided in the `System.Text` namespace, including:

❑ The `ASCIIEncoding` class, which encodes Unicode characters as single 7-bit ASCII characters and only supports characters whose values are in the [U+0000-U+007F] range, that is the actual ASCII range. If you are trying to convert a Unicode character that is not in this range, you will get an exception and the character will not be encoded. For instance an 'é' will generate an exception as its value is outside the ASCII range.

❑ The `UnicodeEncoding` class, which encodes each Unicode character as two consecutive bytes. Different operating systems use different byte orders when storing data internally; some use the big endian order where the most significant byte is stored first and some use the little endian order where the most significant byte is stored last. For instance, the character F, defined as Unicode U+0046, is encoded as the sequence of bytes 00 46 on a big endian machine and as the sequence of bytes 46 00 on a little endian machine.

❑ The `UnicodeEncoding` class provides support for both little endian and big endian byte ordering, which makes this class especially useful when converting from the .NET Framework (which is little endian) to exchange data with some mainframes and Unix systems (which are big endian).

❑ The `UTF7Encoding` class, which encodes Unicode characters using the UCS Transformation Format 7-bit form (UTF-7), and supports all Unicode character values and converts them to a 7-bit variable length format.

❑ The `UTF8Encoding` class, which encodes Unicode characters using the UTF-8 encoding, which also supports all Unicode characters. An example for this is provided in the downloadable code for this book.

You can use the `Encoding` class, as used in the example, to convert data to and from Unicode for all code pages that are actually supported by your machine. For instance, this is how you can support the new GB-18030 encoding used in the People's Republic of China. Provided you have installed the proper support files for this encoding on your machine (which you can download from Microsoft China's web site at http://www.microsoft.com/china/windows2000/ downloads/18030.asp), you will then be able to use this encoding in your .NET Framework-based applications through the `Encoding` class.

If we were dealing with a large amount of data, or data that comes from a stream and is only available in sequential blocks, we would probably need to use the `Decoder` and `Encoder` classes to perform the conversion. These classes, unlike the `GetBytes()` and `GetChars()` methods, maintain the state information that is required to support data conversion of data spanning several blocks.

Dealing with Strings

In a real-world application the idea is really to limit the string handling to what is absolutely necessary, as each operation may introduce significant complexity and performance issues. Fortunately, the .NET Framework provides a great deal of help in dealing with this complexity, and enables us as developers to create applications that support international strings in a straightforward manner. However, there are some general truths about operations on international strings, such as that operations done properly on international strings are generally more costly than similar operations that do not care about culture-correctness. Another interesting aspect is that it is always easier to deal with whole strings and not with characters one by one, as international strings may contain combinations of characters that cannot be separated at random without corrupting data.

Before we look into standard string operations, such as uppercasing, lowercasing, and sorting, we need to look at cultures and how they can affect string operations.

The CultureInfo Class

The `CultureInfo` class is the most important class in the `System.Globalization` namespace. It provides culture-specific information, such as culture name, associated language, country/region, calendar, and cultural conventions. This class also provides access to culture-specific instances of other classes that provide additional culture-specific information, such as `DateTimeFormatInfo`, `NumberFormatInfo`, `CompareInfo`, and `TextInfo`. These objects contain the information required for culture-specific operations, such as casing, formatting dates and numbers, and comparing strings. Therefore, by specifying a culture, it is possible to use a set of common preferences for information on strings, and date and number formats that correspond to users' cultural conventions.

Culture Names

The culture names are derived from the RFC 1766 standard (www.ietf.org/rfc/rfc1766.txt). This standard uses the format *language-country/region*, where *language* is a lowercase two-letter (sometimes three-letter) code, derived from the ISO-639-1 standard, and *country/region* is an uppercase two-letter code derived from the ISO 3166 standard. Here are a few examples:

❑ en represents the English language

❑ en-US represents English (United States)

❑ kok-IN represents Konkani (India)

A culture name may or may not contain the country/region information in its name, and it is possible to have cultures whose names are only specified by the language information. For instance, Japanese (as a language) is specified as ja and Japanese as spoken in Japan is specified as ja-JP.

In addition, some culture names have suffixes that specify the script; for example, -Cyrl specifies the Cyrillic script and -Latn specifies the Latin script. Therefore sr-SP-Cyrl indicates Serbian (Cyrillic) (Serbia) and sr-SP-Latn indicates Serbian (Latin) (Serbia). This is different from the MSDN documentation at the time of writing.

The Different Types of Culture

While the .NET Framework implements over 200 cultures, these cultures can be divided into three groups:

❑ The **invariant culture**, which is unique

❑ The **neutral** cultures

❑ The **specific** cultures

Figure 1 shows a subset of the overall culture tree, where only the invariant culture, the neutral English (en) and French (fr) cultures, and the specific French-related cultures are displayed.

Figure 1

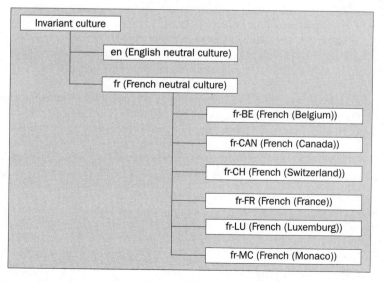

107

The Invariant Culture

The invariant culture is a unique culture that is at the root of the culture tree implemented by the .NET Framework. It is associated with the English language, but not with a country or region, and is a culture that does not exist in the real world. It is a completely culture-insensitive culture.

This may seem quite strange, but there is some logic to it; there are many processes requiring culture-independent results, such as system services. Typical applications of the invariant culture are used for dealing with date and time storage for a web service, and capitalization of file names that are to be passed to the operating system. Storing data in a culture-independent format guarantees a known format that does not change (at least within the same version of the .NET Framework,). When users from different cultures need to access data that is stored using the invariant culture format, the data can be formatted appropriately for the user by converting it to a culture that is appropriate for the specific user. For instance, a date stored using the invariant culture format on the backend can be parsed and formatted on the front-end using a German (Germany) culture for a German user and a Spanish (Mexico) culture for a Mexican user and both will benefit from an appropriate culture on the front-end and a common storage on the backend.

In other cases, such as when used directly for user interface elements, the invariant culture produces results that might be linguistically incorrect, or culturally inappropriate. Therefore, you are recommended to avoid using the invariant culture for any user interface item. In our previous example, displaying the date using the invariant culture for either our German or our Mexican user would be inappropriate.

Neutral Cultures

A neutral culture is a culture that is associated with a language but not with a country or region. As such, a neutral culture is very useful for language-only related operations, but cannot be used for retrieving information, such as date and time formatting, as these are very much country- and region-dependent, and may vary within the same language. For instance, date and time formats differ between the United States and the United Kingdom, although the language can be considered English in both cases.

Names for neutral cultures are specified using the language code format indicated above. For instance, Arabic is specified with `ar`. Neutral cultures cannot be used to perform string operations, such as uppercasing and lowercasing or sorting. To perform these, you need to create a specific culture.

Specific Culture

A specific culture is a culture that provides information for both the language and the country or region. For example, `de` is the neutral German culture and `de-DE` is a specific culture that represents German (Germany). The major difference between a neutral culture and a specific one is that a specific culture provides additional information about the date, time, currency, and number formatting options associated with the specific region or country.

The Two Roles of CultureInfo

An international-aware application needs to handle international data (date, time, currencies, characters that are part of the application data, etc.). In addition, it wants to be localized so that international users can use the application in the easiest, most productive fashion by using a version of the application in their own language. However, the latter point (localization) is not a strict requirement for an international-aware application.

In both cases, the CultureInfo class plays an important role as a provider of cultural preferences. Since these two roles are distinct, even though there are many cases where the same culture is used for both, the .NET Framework implements a mechanism for both roles, which are referred to as the CurrentCulture and the CurrentUICulture.

The CurrentCulture and the CurrentUICulture are set at the thread level for an application, which enables a multithreaded application to use different cultures on different threads. If you do not specify these values, they are inherited from the operating system so that you always have a valid CurrentCulture and CurrentUICulture defined.

CurrentUICulture

The CurrentUICulture value determines how the resources are loaded for a form, and is used for the culture-specific lookup of resource data. This is the culture that determines in which language the form elements are displayed. If it is set to French, the user interface will be in French (provided that the localized resources are available).The sole purpose of the CurrentUICulture value is to indicate the language the resource manager should use to load the resources associated with the form if this one is localizable. You can use either a neutral or a specific culture to set the CurrentUICulture.

CurrentCulture

The CurrentCulture value determines everything else – date formatting, number formatting, string casing, string comparison, and so on. The CurrentCulture value can only be set to **specific cultures**, such as en-US or en-GB, which prevents the problem of identifying the correct currency symbol to use for en.

The two culture settings do not need to have the same value. In the design of your application, it may be important to set them separately. For instance, if you are building an application for the United States but you want the user interface to display menus in Spanish rather than English, you can set the CurrentCulture to en-US so that the number formatting will be correct, and the CurrentUICulture to es so that the localized resources are actually displayed in Spanish. Another interesting aspect is when running a US application that is not localized for Japan. In this case, the CurrentCulture will be set to ja-JP so that the date, time, currency and number formats will be all Japanese, whereas the user interface will remain in English with the CurrentUICulture set to en or en-US.

Setting the CurrentCulture and the CurrentUICulture

First, it should be noted that there are cases where you don't want or need to set these cultures explicitly. For instance, if you are developing a Windows Form application, you usually should avoid setting these values (at least the CurrentCulture one) explicitly, as the operating system provides you with implicit default values that match the current user choice (for CurrentCulture) and settings (for CurrentCulture).

Implicit Values

If the CurrentCulture property is not set explicitly, then a default value is provided by the system, picked up from the GetUserDefaultLCID API in Windows. This default value is affected by changes to Regional Options | Set Locale in Control Panel.

If the CurrentUICulture property is not set explicitly in an application's code, it is set by default when the application starts with the language used for the Windows resources. This default cannot be changed by the user unless they use an MUI (Multilingual User Interface) version of Windows, in which case, an additional option is available in the control panel that lets you change this default value.

Explicit Values

While the default values work in   some cases, there are cases where you will need to set the CurrentUICulture or CurrentCulture explicitly. For instance, if you are developing a server application (such as when using ASP.NET), the default local values are picked up on your server and they are very likely to be different from what your users may expect on their client machines. In that case, setting the values explicitly for the current culture and the current UI culture is necessary.

This is done by setting the culture properties of the current thread to instances of the CultureInfo class you want:

```
using System.Globalization;
using System.Threading;

    . . .
        Thread.CurrentThread.CurrentUICulture = New CultureInfo("en");
        Thread.CurrentThread.CurrentCulture = New CultureInfo("ja-JP");
```

In both samples, the current UI culture will be set to English, whereas the current culture will be set to Japanese.

You now have a better understanding of the cultures and the CultureInfo class, so we can now dig into the actual string handling specifics.

Uppercasing and Lowercasing

It is important to note that operations such as uppercasing, lowercasing, and string comparison are culture-sensitive, and that this impacts on both linguistic correctness and performance. In particular, performance is impacted as potentially more complicated lookup and calculations need to occur behind the scenes so that the correct operation happens for a given culture.

Uppercasing

The `String` class provides the `ToUpper()` method, which uppercases a string. The easiest way to call this method is without any parameters:

```
myString = "This is a string"
myCapStr = myString.ToUpper();
```

This call will actually use the culture that is specified at the current thread level, and use it to perform the capitalization. If the selected culture happens to be en-US, these sample strings would contain:

this is a string
THIS IS A STRING

If the current thread's current culture is set to tr-TR (Turkish, Turkey), then the output will be different, as Turkish uses a different capitalization rule for the "I" character. There are four "I" characters in Turkish and they are matched according to the table below:

Lowercase	Uppercase
i (U+0069)	İ (U+0130)
ı (U+0131)	I (U+0049)

Since the conversion to uppercase for the "i" character is different in Turkish, our sample will have a different string as an output:

this is a string
THİS İS A STRİNG

Another way to call the `String.ToUpper()` method, is to pass a `CultureInfo` parameter to this method. In this case, the passed `CultureInfo` parameter is used instead of the current thread's culture to perform the capitalization operation. This is useful when you want to use several cultures in the same application.

So, for instance, the following code:

111

```
myString = "this is a string";
myCapStr1 = myString.ToUpper(New CultureInfo("en-US"));
myCapStr2 = myString.ToUpper(New CultureInfo("tr-TR"));
```

produces the following results:

this is a string
THIS IS A STRING
THİS İS A STRİNG

Lowercasing

The String class also provides the String.ToLower() method that performs the reverse operation, lowercasing. Just like the ToUpper() method, the ToLower() method either takes a CultureInfo parameter or no parameter, in which case the current thread's culture is used to perform the lowercasing operation.

When Culture-Sensitive Operations are Not Desired

Since both uppercasing and lowercasing operations are culture-sensitive, there are no guarantees that an operation performed using one culture will provide the same results when using another culture, as we have seen in the previous section.

While using culture-sensitive operations is desirable when dealing with user interface strings, so that strings can be displayed properly to the users based on the correct capitalization and lowercasing rules for their cultures, there are cases, such as when dealing with system objects, where this may be a problem. For instance, imagine that you are trying to validate a path; this path name contains some "I" characters and you have two strings, one in uppercase and another in lowercase that are set to the path name. It would be very difficult to actually figure out that these two strings refer to the same file if the two strings do not match, because the current culture has different capitalization rules from the culture that was originally used to produce the path name. In this case, it is important that the conversion rules are always the same, and this is where the invariant culture is useful.

Sorting

There are two ways a string can be sorted: either in a culture-insensitive manner, which only considers the actual code point values of the characters being sorted, or in a culture-sensitive manner that ensures the sorting is performed according to the sorting rules available for the selected culture.

Let's illustrate this with an example. There are two strings: `ciao` and `character`, and we'll first sort these strings using an ordinal sort, which only checks the values of the code points, that is the numeric values associated with the characters:

ciao	character
U+0063	U+0063
U+0069	U+0068
U+0061	U+0061
U+006F	U+0072
	U+0061
	U+0063
	U+0074
	U+0065
	U+0072

We see that the second character in the `ciao` string (i) has a code point value that is higher than the second character of the `character` string (h). Therefore, the ordinal comparison returns that `ciao > character`, as you might expect.

Now, let's assume that we want to use a culture-sensitive sort. If we select the `en-US` (English, United States) culture, the alphabetical rules for this culture indicate that "h" should be sorted before "i", and so the comparison also returns `ciao > character`. However, if we change the culture to use the `cs-CZ` (Czech, Czech Republic) culture, then the rules of the Czech language specify that `ch` is to be treated for comparison and sorting purposes as a single entity that appears after "c". In this case, the comparison between our two strings results in `ciao < character`.

As you can see, using a culture-specific sorting method provides us with a sorting order that closely matches the user's language experience and expectations. As a rule, user interface items, such as listboxes, combo boxes, and other tabular data lists, should use a culture-specific sorting method, so that they match the user's expectations.

So far, we have seen the theory, but you should now want to see how to apply this to .NET.

String.CompareOrdinal()

The `String` class provides the `CompareOrdinal()` method that can be used to compare two strings without considering the current culture. For instance, the following code snippet compares two strings using the `CompareOrdinal()` method and writes the results to the command line:

```
using System;
using System.Globalization;

namespace Wrox.Text.Chapter4
{
  class CompareOrdinalMethod
  {
    [STAThread]
    static void Main(string[] args)
    {
      String firstString = "ciao";
      String secondString = "character";

      int result = String.CompareOrdinal(firstString, secondString);

      if (result < 0)
        Console.WriteLine("\"{0}\" < \"{1}\"",
                          firstString, secondString);
      else if(result == 0)
        Console.WriteLine("\"{0}\" = \"{1}\"",
                          firstString, secondString);
      else
        Console.WriteLine("\"{0}\" > \"{1}\"",
                          firstString, secondString);
    }
  }
}
```

Running this application should result in the following output:

```
"ciao" > "character"
```

In real-world applications, you may want to use the `String.CompareOrdinal()` method to compare strings when you are dealing with system objects (for instance file names) and you don't want the order of the sort to change depending on the culture, such as when you are creating an index or hash table.

String.Compare()

The `Compare()` method implements a culture-sensitive string comparison. There are several overloads for this method that specify whether the comparison should be case-sensitive or not; or in other words, provide a `CultureInfo` object to use instead of the current thread's culture. You can also specify indices and lengths in the strings to be compared so that you effectively compare sub-strings.

Let's look at what the example above might be if we were using the `Compare()` method:

```
using System;
using System.Globalization;
```

```
namespace Wrox.Text.Chapter4
{
  class CompareMethod
  {
    [STAThread]
    static void Main(string[] args)
    {
        string firstString = "ciao";
        string secondString = "character";

        int result = String.Compare(firstString, secondString,
                                    true, new CultureInfo("cs-CZ"));

        if(result < 0)
          Console.WriteLine("\"{0}\" < \"{1}\"",
                              firstString, secondString);
        else if(result == 0)
          Console.WriteLine("\"{0}\" = \"{1}\"",
                              firstString, secondString);
        else
          Console.WriteLine("\"{0}\" > \"{1}\"",
                              firstString, secondString);
    }
  }
}
```

In this case, the comparison would yield:

```
"ciao" < "character"
```

This is because we specified the Czech (Czech Republic) culture to perform the comparison. Note that we passed the Czech (Czech Republic) culture as a parameter to the String.Compare() method, as shown in the section on capitalization and lowercasing above. We also indicated that the comparison should be case-insensitive by specifying the value true for the third parameter passed to the String.Compare() method, which is the IgnoreCase flag for this overload of the Compare() method.

String.CompareTo()

This method is similar to the Compare() method but is not a static method and does not provide any way to specify if the comparison should be case-sensitive or not (it is case-sensitive). The code snippet below implements our comparison using the CompareTo() method:

```
using System;
using System.Globalization;
using System.Threading;

namespace Wrox.Text.Chapter4
{
```

115

```
class CompareToMethod
{
  [STAThread]
  static void Main(string[] args)
  {
    String firstString = "ciao";
    String secondString = "character";

    Thread.CurrentThread.CurrentCulture = new CultureInfo("cs-CZ");
    int result = firstString.CompareTo(secondString);

    if(result < 0)
      Console.WriteLine("\"{0}\" < \"{1}\"",
                        firstString, secondString);
    else if(result == 0)
      Console.WriteLine("\"{0}\" = \"{1}\"",
                        firstString, secondString);
    else
      Console.WriteLine("\"{0}\" > \"{1}\"",
                        firstString, secondString);
  }
}
```

The CompareInfo Class

There are cases, for specific cultures, where the culture-sensitive sorting provided by the Compare() method is not enough for some more advanced ordering.

For instance, Japanese uses two syllabaries named Hiragana and Katakana, which contain characters that are pronounced in identical manners, but are written differently. There are cases, when dealing with Japanese text, where you may want characters that are pronounced the same way to be treated as equal, and cases where they should be treated differently. If you wish to support this functionality in your code, you will need to use another class provided by the .NET Framework – the CompareInfo class.

The CompareInfo class implements a set of methods for culture-sensitive string comparisons. Unlike most other classes in the .NET Framework, an instance of this class cannot be created by using a constructor, but needs to be created using the GetCompareInfo() method. This method accepts several overloads that let you specify an integer that is a Windows LCID identifier, or a string that is a culture identifier (CultureInfo). A list containing Windows LCIDs, which provide alternative sort orders, is available in the MSDN documentation (http://support.microsoft.com/directory/article.asp?ID=KB;EN-US;Q224804&).

In order to create a CompareInfo object for the en-US culture, you can use:

```
CompareInfo ci = CompareInfo.GetCompareInfo(1033);
```

116

or:

```
CompareInfo ci = CompareInfo.GetCompareInfo("en-US");
```

Another way to retrieve a `CompareInfo` object is to get the `CompareInfo` member that is contained in a `CultureInfo` class (in particular, the one in the current culture) with the following syntax:

```
CompareInfo ci = CultureInfo.CurrentCulture.CompareInfo;
```

The most interesting method of this class is `Compare()`, which also provides several overloads. The most interesting ones are those that provide a `CompareOptions` parameter, which can be used to fine-tune the comparison, as with the following overload, for instance, which takes strings as its first two parameters, and a `CompareOptions` as its third:

```
Compare(String string1, String string2, CompareOptions options);
```

The `CompareOptions` enumeration contains the following members that can be combined to customize the comparison options used for the `CompareInfo.Compare()` method:

Member Name	Description
IgnoreCase	Indicates that the string comparison must ignore case. In the case of the en-US culture, if this value is set, then abc and ABC compare equally, whereas they don't otherwise.
IgnoreKanaType	Indicates that the string comparison must ignore the Kana type. The Japanese language uses two syllabaries, **hiragana** and **katakana**, which represent phonetic sounds in the Japanese language. Hiragana is used for native Japanese expressions and words, while katakana is used for words borrowed from other languages, such as computer. The same phonetic sound can be expressed in both hiragana and katakana. If the IgnoreKanaType flag is specified, then the hiragana character for one sound is considered equal to the katakana character for the same sound. In this case, "バナナ" (banana written properly in katakana) is equal to "ばなな" (banana, written using hiragana).
IgnoreNonSpace	Indicates that the string comparison must ignore non-spacing combining characters, such as diacritics. If this value is set, "é" will be equal to "e".

Table continued on following page

117

Member Name	Description
IgnoreSymbols	Indicates that the string comparison must ignore symbols, such as whitespace characters, punctuation, currency symbols, the percent symbol, mathematical symbols, the ampersand, etc. For example, the Kashida used in Arabic is in this category and will be ignored for comparison purposes if this value is set.
IgnoreWidth	Indicates that the string comparison must ignore the character width. For example, Japanese katakana characters can be written as full-width or half-width and, if this value is selected, the katakana characters written as full-width are considered equal to the same characters written in half-width. In this case, "バナナ" equals "バナナ"
None	Indicates the default option settings for string comparisons, which is a comparison that provides the same results as a case-sensitive sort operated with String.Compare().
Ordinal	Indicates that the string comparison must be ordinal. This is equivalent to turning the string comparison into an ordinal string comparison as described at the beginning of the *Sorting* section.
StringSort	Indicates that the string comparison must use the string sort algorithm, where the hyphen and the apostrophe, as well as other non-alphanumeric characters, come before alphanumeric symbols.

Dealing with Characters

Directly dealing with characters, when manipulating international strings, is not a very good idea. There is a lot of complexity that one needs to deal with when doing so. While at first Unicode seems to be an easier model than the code pages systems it has replaced, there is still significant complexity linked to two classes of Unicode characters: **surrogate pairs** and **combining characters**.

The best advice that can be given here is to avoid dealing with single characters altogether and to deal only with strings. However, if you really need to deal with single characters, then the information below should help you. Before we see how to deal with this complexity, it should be noted that Unicode provides information about each character that is defined within the standard. This information can be found online at http://www.unicode.org. It allows us to know which characters are potentially problematic. The .NET Framework exposes information about Unicode characters through the Char class.

Necessary Information about Characters

The Char class provides several methods that are useful in determining the role of a character and its properties. The base method is Char.GetUnicodeCategory(), which indicates the category to which the character belongs.

The following code snippet shows how to retrieve the Unicode category for the character "a":

```
UnicodeCategory uc = Char.GetUnicodeCategory('a');
```

The Char class also provides a series of 'Is' methods that actually loosely match the different Unicode categories. MSDN contains a table that lists all the categories that are available (http://msdn.microsoft.com/library/default.asp?url=/library/en-us/cpref/html/frlrfSystemGlobalizationUnicodeCategoryClassTopic.asp).

Surrogate Pairs

So far, what we have seen from Unicode is not very different in terms of handling characters from existing code pages. Let's now look at the complexity associated with surrogate pairs and combining characters.

Unicode is often thought of as a simple mechanism with all characters defined in 16-bit quantities. However, this is not true. That definition would provide for 65,536 characters, which is not enough to represent all the characters that are available in all the different scripts worldwide. In particular, there are over 85,000 Chinese characters. This means that characters need to be defined on more than 16-bits in order to provide a greater range. In order be able to support these supplemental characters, Unicode defines a mechanism that permits an additional 917,476 characters without having to use 32-bit characters, and while preserving compatibility with the existing set of characters. This mechanism is known as the surrogate pair mechanism.

The Unicode standard defines a surrogate pair as a coded character representation for a single abstract character that consists of a sequence of two code units, where the first unit of the pair is a **high surrogate** and the second is a **low surrogate**. In simple terms, this means that to represent a character value which is higher than can be encoded on 16 bits, we can substitute a pair of 16-bit characters (the high surrogate and the low surrogate) that represent the same value.

119

How Surrogates Work

There is a reserved area of 1,024 characters at the high end of the Unicode code space, from U+D800 through to U+DBFF for high surrogates. There is also a reserved area of 1,024 characters following this, from U+DC00 through to U+DFFF for low surrogates. Combining one high-range value with one low-range value makes a unique surrogate pair. We use two 16-bit Unicode values together and their unique pairing maps at display time to a real-world character. No other characters or symbols are ever assigned inside these two reserved areas. Also, since surrogates have no interpretation except when they occur as part of a surrogate pair, then standing alone, a surrogate is meaningless. Therefore, whenever an application encounters a Unicode value from either one of these reserved areas, it can only be one half of a surrogate pair.

The transformation between a Unicode value of N, which is a value between 0 and 10FFFF (hexadecimal), and a pair of surrogate characters is defined in the following manner. First the high surrogate:

```
(N - 0x10000) / 0x400 + 0xD800;
```

Whereas the low surrogate can be calculated by:

```
(N - 0x10000) % 0x400 + 0xDC00;
```

Let's see an example. If a character has a scalar value of 0x2002F, the matching surrogate pair is as follows, with the high surrogate being 0xD840 ((0x2002F-0x10000)/0x400 + D800), and the low surrogate being 0xDC2F ((0x2002F-0x10000) % 0x400 + 0xDC00) (% is the modulo operator in C#).

Why Support Surrogates

Version 3.1 of the Unicode standard introduced the characters that are represented by surrogates. Here is a list of the ranges that are so defined by the Unicode Standard version 3.2:

Range Name	Range Start	Range End
Old Italic	U+10300	U+1032F
Gothic	U+10330	U+1034F
Deseret	U+10400	U+1044F
Byzantine Musical Symbols	U+1D000	U+1D0FF
Musical Symbols	U+1D100	U+1D1FF
Mathematical Alphanumeric Symbols	U+1D400	U+1D7FF
CJK Unified Ideographs Extension B	U+20000	U+2A6DF

Range Name	Range Start	Range End
CJK Compatibility Ideographs Supplement	U+2F800	U+2FA1F
Tags	U+E0000	U+E007F
Supplementary Private Use Area-A	U+F0000	U+FFFFF
Supplementary Private Use Area-B	U+100000	U+10FFFF

While some of the characters defined here are not used very often, the CJK (China, Japan, and Korea) characters available in the CJK Unified Ideographs Extension B and the CJK Compatibility Ideographs Supplement ranges are essential for the East Asian markets. The Han ideographs used in China, Japan, and Korea are numerous and the original Unicode implementation only captured the most commonly used ideographs; it did not capture all of them. Over time, there have been requests for Unicode support for more of these ideographs and more have been added: first as CJK Extension A, which is within the main Unicode range, and then as CJK Extension B, which is a range that is accessible through surrogate pairs.

Creating such characters with Unicode surrogate pairs ensures that the world remains on the same Unicode encoding, removing the need to move to an even larger one later, which means that we don't need all characters to move to 32-bit, which would be rather expensive in terms of size. There are potentially about a million surrogate pairs that could be assigned via this method. It is not expected that the need for characters will ever outgrow the surrogate pairs range.

Handling Surrogate pairs

To a large extent, the Microsoft .NET Framework provides uniform support for Unicode strings, whether they contain surrogate pairs or not. This means that there are actually only a few cases where you need to worry about surrogate pairs, which are detailed below.

Surrogate pairs are predictable in their form. They are always composed of one high-range value in the first pair member, and one low-range value in the second pair member. Surrogate pairs are also easy to reference. Each pair will always be composed of two 16-bit values. Since pairs always combine in high and low combinations, that provides an easy way to backtrack to the start of a sequence of surrogate pairs. The following sections list cases that typically arise when developing an application and provide information about the level of support that needs to be implemented by developers who are dealing with surrogates.

Displaying Surrogates

Both Windows Forms and Web Forms display surrogates correctly, provided they are using a font that contains glyphs for the characters to be displayed, such as Arial Unicode. Console-based applications do not display surrogates, as the console does not provide any non-proportional font that can display them correctly.

To display surrogates correctly for a Windows Form control, a font must be selected in the form designer, or the font property for a control needs to be changed at run time through code. In the example below, a FontDialog control is used in order to select a font and then assigns the newly selected font to a label that displays the actual surrogate pair. If this font supports surrogates, the control will then display them correctly.

The screenshot below shows a Windows Form based application developed with the Microsoft .NET Framework that displays a set of surrogate characters. No special handling is necessary for display, apart from finding a font that can display characters represented by surrogate pairs.

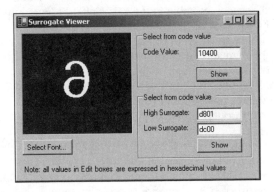

The complete source code for this example can be found in the code download, but the relevant methods are shown below. First the method that deals with the Select Font... button:

```
private void ButtonFont_Click(object sender, System.EventArgs e)
{
    FontDlg.Font = CharDisplay.Font;
    if(System.Windows.Forms.DialogResult.OK == FontDlg.ShowDialog())
        CharDisplay.Font = FontDlg.Font;
}
```

There is nothing complicated in the above class. It just pops up the font dialog and changes the Font property of the CharDisplay item (the box that displays the character) to the selected font. The interesting code is contained in the Display() method below:

```
private void Display(int codepoint)
{
    if(codepoint < 0x10000)
        CharDisplay.Text = "" + (char)codepoint;
    else
        CharDisplay.Text = "" + (char)GetHighSurrogate(codepoint) +
                        (char)GetLowSurrogate(codepoint);
}
```

Here you pass the full code point of the character and if it is not a surrogate pair (code value less than 0x10000) then it just displays it, after converting it to a System.Char and appending it to the end of an empty string to perform implicit conversion to a string. If it is a surrogate, then it calls two methods, GetHighSurrogate() and GetLowSurrogate() and returns the Char of each, appending them to the textbox, where the Windows OS and the supplied font convert them into the required character. The two methods are shown below:

```
private int GetHighSurrogate(int codepoint)
{
  return (codepoint - 0x10000) / 0x400 + 0xD800;
}

private int GetLowSurrogate(int codepoint)
{
  return (codepoint - 0x10000) % 0x400 + 0xDC00;
}
```

As you can see, these just implement the equations shown previously and return the requested high and low surrogates. The reverse of these methods is:

```
private int MakeCodePoint(int high, int low)
{
  return (high - 0xD800) * 0x400 + (low - 0xDC00) + 0x10000;
}
```

The code above just uses the same equations shown previously to retrieve the code value for the high and low surrogates. The event code for the two Show buttons is shown below:

```
private void ButtonCV_Click(object sender, System.EventArgs e)
{
  int ncp = int.Parse(ValueInput.Text,
      System.Globalization.NumberStyles.HexNumber);
  HighInput.Text =
      (ncp < 0x10000) ? "n/a" : GetHighSurrogate(ncp).ToString("X");
  LowInput.Text =
      (ncp < 0x10000) ? "n/a" : GetLowSurrogate(ncp).ToString("X");
  Display(ncp);
}

private void ButtonSP_Click(object sender, System.EventArgs e)
{
  int high = int.Parse(HighInput.Text,
      System.Globalization.NumberStyles.HexNumber);
  int low = int.Parse(LowInput.Text,
      System.Globalization.NumberStyles.HexNumber);

  // check that both high and low surrogates are in correct ranges
  if((high < 0xD800) || (high > 0xDBFF) || (low < 0xDC00) ||
      (low > 0xDFFF))
```

```
        ValueInput.Text = "n/a";
    else
    {
        int ncp = MakeCodePoint(high, low);
        ValueInput.Text = ncp.ToString("X");
        Display(ncp);
    }
}
```

The first method handles the clicking of the first Show button, and the second handles the second. `ButtonCV_Click()` first checks to see if the value entered in the textbox is outside the surrogate pair range. If so, then it enters n/a into the relevant textboxes. If not, then it uses the `GetHighSurrogate()` and `GetLowSurrogate()` methods shown earlier to input the correct values into the textboxes. It then shows this character in the `CharDisplay` label using the `Display()` method.

The second method is simpler and combines the two values in the textboxes together using `MakeCodePoint()` and passes this value to `Display()` before entering it into the previous textbox.

As mentioned earlier, the full code can be found in the code download.

Surrogates Input

Now that we have seen what surrogate pairs are and how to display them, let's see how they can be entered.

Programmatic Input

Programmatically, surrogates are very simple to input as they are defined just like any other Unicode characters and can be input using the same syntax. For instance, the following lines of C# code create a string that contains a character that is represented by a pair of surrogates:

```
String mySurrogatePairString;
mySurrogatePairString = "\uD840\uDC0B";
```

In C#, the \u format is used to express a Unicode character by providing its Unicode code point value. Any Unicode character can be expressed this way, for instance "A" could be expressed as \u0041, and in particular, surrogate pairs can only be expressed in this manner. In this case, as we are setting the string to a surrogate pair, we need to first specify the high surrogate value and then the low surrogate value. This can be used to enter a Japanese string in code on a system that does not provide Japanese input support for instance.

User Input

User input depends on an **Input Method Editor** (IME) that allows a user to input characters directly. An IME is a mechanism provided by Windows for East Asian languages that allows you to enter characters by typing a phonetic value, by drawing the character, or by direct keyboard input. There are different IMEs for Chinese, Japanese, and Korean. If users have installed an appropriate IME, then the surrogate character will be input correctly.

Sorting

No special provision needs to be made for surrogates while sorting, as no linguistically significant sort order is defined for these characters. So, basically, the sort order for surrogate characters is defined as ordinal order, and surrogate pairs will just sort according to the value of the character that they represent.

Combining Characters

Many languages that use either Latin script or other scripts have characters that present diacritic marks. For instance "é" is an "e" with an acute accent. There are two ways to think about such a character. The first one is to consider that this is a character that is always pre-composed, which means the "é" is a character by itself, with its own code point. The other way to think about it is to consider "é" to be an "e" (which we will call a base letter) followed by a non-spacing acute accent. In this case, the, "é" is a **composite character** created by rendering "e" and "ˊ" together. A composed character sequence is typically made up of a base letter, which occupies a single space, and one or more non-spacing marks, which are rendered in the same space as the base letter. In this case, we can have letters that are actually represented as a series of several characters, which provides yet another added complexity when dealing with strings.

The Unicode Standard provides both combining characters and pre-composed characters to retain compatibility with established standards such as Latin 1, which includes many pre-composed characters such as "ü" and "ñ". In the case where such a character is a composite character, the base character comes first, followed by one or more non-spacing marks. If a text element is encoded with more than one non-spacing mark, the order in which the non-spacing marks are stored isn't important if the marks don't interact typographically. If they do, order is important. The Unicode Standard specifies how successive non-spacing characters are applied to a base character.

Dealing with Surrogate Pairs and Combining Characters

While there is no special requirement for handling surrogates and combining characters as far as displaying and sorting is concerned, approaching a string in a naive way by considering that each element represents a character will lead to problems when inserting or deleting characters, or even just traversing the string in order to count the number of actual displayable items.

In well-formed text, a low surrogate can only be preceded by a high surrogate and a high surrogate can only be followed by a low surrogate. The case with combining characters is a little different as it is easy to make an error by deleting the base character and getting the non-spacing marks applied wrongly to the preceding character.

If we are dealing with surrogate pairs, the following string, for instance:

"AB∂c"

is represented in the following manner internally:

0041	0042	D801	DC00	0043
A	B	∂		C

If we are using the following code to retrieve the first three text elements from the string described above, we will not get the appropriate result as we will retrieve the first two characters (AB) and the high surrogate (but not the low surrogate that needs to be associated to the high surrogate to have meaning):

```
string str;
str = "AB\uD801\uHDC00C";
string strFirstThree = str.Substring(0, 3);
```

In order to perform the operation correctly, we need to retrieve additional information on the characters (whether they are surrogates or not). Thus, if we are writing a program that needs to deal with individual characters within a string, we need to make sure that when we delete a character or take a sub-string, we are not breaking a surrogate pair by separating a high surrogate from a low surrogate. The good news is that it is not hard to detect surrogates, as performing range checking will indicate if a character is a surrogate or not. We could definitely do this manually by parsing the string directly and performing tests along the way, but the .NET Framework provides two methods that do all the tedious work.

More importantly, these methods also do the work for combining characters that would need to be taken care of as well if we were to implement code to handle strings manually.

StringInfo.ParseCombiningCharacters()

The StringInfo class provides a method named ParseCombiningCharacters() that can parse a string into text elements. The .NET Framework defines a text element as a unit of text that is displayed as a single character; a **grapheme**. A text element can be a base character, a surrogate pair, or a combining character sequence.

StringInfo.GetTextEnumerator()

The `StringInfo` class provides another method, `GetTextEnumerator()`, which enables you to achieve the same results as are obtained by using the `ParseCombiningCharacters()` method: parsing the text into text elements. The `StringInfo` class provides access to the `TextEnumerator` class via the `StringInfo.GetTextEnumerator()` method.

The `StringWalk` code example in the code download shows how to use either the `ParseCombiningCharacters()` method or the `GetTextElementEnumerator()` method to "walk" a string and retrieve all the text elements contained in the string, including surrogate pairs and combining characters.

Formatting Unicode Strings

The `String.Format()` method lets you format a string by providing format specification in a format string and additional objects. These will be formatted according to the format specifiers. This is often essential for correct formatting of a string with international characters. For instance, we can rewrite:

```
String message = "This is my new " + item;
```

as:

```
String message = String.Format("this is my new {0}", item);
```

While this has an impact in terms of performance, as the `String.Format()` method is more costly than the string concatenation that we used previously, it is good practice as it makes the code much easier to localize into another language. For instance, if we were to port the modified code to Japanese, the only thing we would have to do would be to change the formatting string to: これは私の新しい {0} です and the code would handle Japanese correctly.

Another interesting aspect of the `String.Format()` method is that it can also be used to format numeric values, dates, and times as well as strings. For instance, the following code:

```
string message;
message = String.Format("Date is {0}, value is {1}, word is {2}",
    DateTime.Now, 1234, "car");
```

Produces this output:

```
Date is 18/05/2002 14:24:05, value is 1234, word is car
```

127

Of course, the format specifiers that we have seen earlier for the numeric and the date and time values can be used as well, so if we replace the lines:

```
message = String.Format("Date is {0}, value is {1}, word is {2}",
    DateTime.Now, 1234, "car");
```

with:

```
message = String.Format("Date is {0:d}, value is {1:C}, word is {2}",
    DateTime.Now, 1234, "car");
```

the output is now (if the current culture is set to English (United States)):

```
Date is 5/18/2002, value is $1,234.00, word is car
```

Additionally, a `CultureInfo` (or any other class that implements the `IFormatProvider` interface) can be passed as a parameter for one of the overrides of the `String.Format()` method. If we modified the code to pass the Swedish (Sweden) culture as below:

```
message = String.Format(New CultureInfo("sv-SE"),
    "Date is {0:d}, value is {1:C}, word is {2}", DateTime.Now, 1234,
    "car");
```

we would get the following results:

```
Date is 2002-05-18, value is 1.234,00 kr, word is car
```

Finally, if you are building Console applications, the sequence:

```
message = String.Format("This is a {0}", "car");
Console.WriteLine(message);
```

can be replaced by the following code, which uses the `String.Format()` method internally:

```
Console.WriteLine("This is a {0}", "car");
```

Strings as Resources

When developing international applications, a very common requirement is that the user interface should be localized, so that, for instance, German and Japanese users can use the same application presented in their own language.

A naive approach to localization would be to go and search for all the strings in the source code, replace them with translated versions and recompile the application. This approach would require a tremendous amount of work and is definitely error-prone.

A better approach consists of splitting the code from the user interface elements and storing these in resources that can be used by the code in a straightforward manner, which is independent of the language that the resources are expressed in. This approach makes translation, testing, and shipping of the application much easier and more efficient.

The .NET Framework provides a resource mechanism that implements this approach and offers additional benefits as well.

The .NET Resource Model

The .NET Framework offers a very flexible model for resources that accommodates both strings and objects (any serializable object can be a resource in the .NET Framework) as you can create and use them in different ways. The basic model is as follows.

.resx File

First, you need to create the resources by defining them. This is done in a .resx file, which is an XML file. The way resources are defined is quite simple; a key-value pair is needed to define a resource. For strings, the value is the content of the string, whereas the key is a string that defines the name by which the resource is subsequently referred to in code. Here is an example of the resources definition in a .resx file:

```
<data name="myFirstString">
  <value>Hello, this is the first string</value>
</data>
<data name="mySecondString">
  <value>Hi, this is my second string</value>
</data>
```

Note: if you are only using strings as resources, there is a shortcut that you can use to define your resources. You can put the strings in a text file that has the following format and use the .NET Framework SDK-provided ResXGen tool to generate a corresponding .resx. If you are working with Visual Studio .NET, you just need to add an assembly resource file to your current project and then enter the resources in the data view for this file.

.resources Files

Once the resources are defined, they need to be compiled in order to be used in applications. A .resources file contains a binary representation of the resources defined in the .resx file.

This compilation process is carried out by the `resgen` utility at the command line or directly by the Visual Studio .NET environment when compiling the project. At this stage, the resources are contained in a `.resources` file that is separate from the main assembly and, while this may be a desirable option in some cases, there are many cases where having resources embedded in the main assembly makes more sense.

Embedded Resources

Embedding resources in the main assembly is just an extra step on the command line that can be done by either using the `CSC` (C#) compiler or the `AL` (assembly linker) utility. In Visual Studio .NET, this step will be carried out automatically for an assembly resource file added to a project as its default `BuildAction` property is set to `Embedded Resources`. There are two major advantages of using embedded resources over using loose resources files: deployment simplicity and update scenarios. In terms of deployment, it is always easier to deploy less files and embedding resources in the main assembly enables you to distribute a single file that contains both code and resources. For update scenarios, assemblies are shadow copied, which means that you can actually update your assembly while a user is using it (this is an especially interesting scenario for web applications). However, `.resources` files are not shadow copied and if a user is using the file, then the file is locked and cannot be updated, which makes updates much more complicated.

Now that we have seen how to create resources, let's see how we can use these in code.

Using Resources

In most applications, using resources is simply a matter of constructing a `ResourceManager` and using the methods provided by this class. The `ResourceManager` class contains two methods for retrieving resources, constructors, and also some static methods used to create a file-based resource manager for instance.

In order to retrieve resources, you first need to create an instance of the `ResourceManager` class. Then, retrieving resources is extremely straightforward and done through the `GetString()` and `GetObject()` methods. Both methods take a key name as an input and return a string or an object respectively.

The following example shows how to create a `ResourceManager` and how to retrieve the two string resources that we put in the `.resx` file shown above:

```
using System;
using System.Resources;
using System.Windows.Forms;
using System.Reflection;

namespace ResourcesDemo
{
  class Demo
  {
```

```
    [STAThread]
    static void Main(string[] args)
    {
      ResourceManager rm = new ResourceManager(
          "ResourcesDemo.strings", Assembly.GetExecutingAssembly());
      MessageBox.Show(rm.GetString("myFirstString"));
      MessageBox.Show(rm.GetString("mySecondString"));
    }
  }
}
```

This application will now display the two following message boxes:

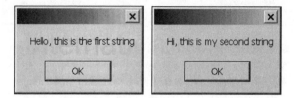

So far, we have seen the use of resources but we have not seen the benefits for localization that were the original reason why we wanted to use resources.

Localization with Resources

The benefit of using resources for the localization of the application above is that we will not touch the code at all. Now that we have implemented resources retrieval through a ResourceManager instance, we only need to provide resources for other languages to get a localized version of our application.

Creating a French version of this application boils down to creating a .resx file that contains the localized strings, compiling the .resx file into a .resources file and embedding the .resources file in a satellite DLL that is an assembly that only contains resources.

The .NET Framework uses a naming convention for these localized resources (explained in the online documentation) that we will follow here.

First, let's create a .resx file named strings.fr.resx (the original one was named strings.resx). We can do this by copying the existing strings.resx and simply translating the strings. So we now have a .resx file that contains the following strings:

```
<data name="myFirstString">
  <value>Salut, ceci est ma première chaîne</value>
</data>
<data name="mySecondString">
  <value>Salut, ceci est ma seconde chaîne</value>
</data>
```

Visual Studio .NET will then automatically generate the appropriate
satellite .resources.dll file and will put it in a fr folder alongside the main
assembly. If you are using C# on the command line, you need to use resgen to
generate the .resources file and then AL to create the satellite DLL.

If we are using the application on a French system, we will see that the application is
now localized.

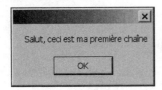
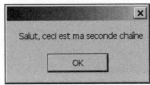

Note that we could simulate this behavior on an English system by setting the current
thread's UICulture to the French culture with the following line of code before
creating the ResourceManager:

```
System.Threading.Thread.CurrentThread.CurrentUICulture =
    new System.Globalization.CultureInfo("fr");
```

The resource model provided by the .NET Framework provides additional benefits
such as a fallback mechanism that are beyond the scope of this book and are described
in the .NET Framework SDK documentation.

Summary

We've seen in this chapter that dealing with international strings and characters is not
always easy. The .NET Framework does a great job of providing a lot of support for
dealing with this complexity but some caution still needs to be applied.

If you only need a couple of points to take away, know when you need to deal with
cultures and culture-sensitive information – essentially when performing user-interface
related operations, such as sorting strings that are to be displayed in a listbox – and
avoid dealing with individual characters as much as possible as this introduces a much
higher level of complexity.

C#

Text Manipulation

Handbook

5

5

Introducing Regular Expressions

Regular expressions, often referred to by their shorthand of **regexes**, are a very powerful way of manipulating and examining string data. A regular expression is a series of characters, special and otherwise, that are transformed into an algorithm against which to match text. Although new to many developers, they have been used extensively in UNIX systems and even in web scripting languages like JavaScript. You may be familiar with wildcard characters such as "%" and "?" in SQL expressions, or "*" in MS DOS. These allow us to do searches without specifying all the possible characters, for example, "del *.txt" would delete all files with the .txt extension. Regular expressions allow for similar expressions, but are much more powerful.

In fact, regular expressions have a simple language of their own that allows us to specify precisely what we are looking to match. In one line we can match patterns of text that would take many lines without regular expressions. However, the downside is that regular expressions can be tricky to create, and are quite cryptic. In this, though, they are not unlike many successful programming languages, such as Perl. Once you become familiar with them, regular expressions are certainly easy enough to use.

The most common sort of problem we can use regular expressions for is data validation. Web Form controls that come with ASP.NET, such as the Regular Expression Validator control, use regular expressions to validate data entered by the user. The control comes with a small number of standard regular expressions to check items such as zip codes, e-mail addresses, and Internet URLs. You'll see in the following chapters how you can validate your own data using your own customized regular expressions, especially since the stock regular expressions provided with the Validator don't quite cover every possible eventuality. Regexes allow you to match against patterns of characters, such as three letters, followed by two numbers, followed by either a letter, or another two numbers. This would take a lot of code without regexes, but is very straightforward to implement with them.

However, it's not just validating data that regular expressions are useful for; you can use them for any situation where you have text-based data you need to manipulate. Let's say you have a string containing HTML tags and you want to extract each tag, and then extract the value of attributes for each tag. Regular expressions make this task easier and take only a few lines of code.

This chapter will gently introduce the .NET aspects of regular expressions, and the regular expression syntax supported. We'll be leaving most of the more advanced features until the next chapter.

System.Text.RegularExpressions

That's enough of theory, so let's move on to practice. The key to regular expression implementation in .NET is the `System.Text.RegularExpressions` namespace, which contains the eight classes listed below:

- ❑ `Regex` – contains your regular expression and has various methods to make use of that regular expression

- ❑ `MatchCollection` – contains all the matches found by a regular expression

- ❑ `Match` – contains all the text matched by a single match

- ❑ `GroupCollection` – contains all the groups in a single match

- ❑ `Group` – contains the details of a single group in a group collection

- ❑ `CaptureCollection` – contains all the `Capture` objects for a single group

- ❑ `Capture` – returns the string matched by a single capture within a group

- ❑ `RegexCompilationInfo` – provides details needed to compile `Regex` into a standalone assembly

Of these, the most important one is the `Regex` class; the other classes provide useful specialized functions, but they are not as commonly used. We'll be looking at the `Regex`, `Match`, and `MatchCollection` classes in this chapter. All this functionality is provided within the `System.dll` assembly.

The Regex Class

The Regex class not only allows us to create regular expressions, but it also provides a number of useful methods for manipulating string data using regular expressions; for example, searching for patterns of characters or doing a sophisticated find and replace. You would create a new Regex object if you had a regular expression that you wanted to use repeatedly on different strings. However, many of the class's methods are static methods; this means that if you are just using the regular expression once, then it's more efficient not to create a Regex object (an instance of its class) to use its functionality, but to simply use the methods as required. So, if you want to use the static Replace() method, you can just write:

```
Regex.Replace(string input,
              String pattern,
              string replacement);
```

You will see that the Regex class supports a number of options, and these alter the way the regular expression syntax works. The more commonly used ones are shown below; we'll be discussing the rest throughout the next two chapters:

RegexOptions Enumeration

The following table shows some of the more commonly used Regex options.

Flag	Description
IgnoreCase	Makes the pattern matching case insensitive. The default is that matches are case sensitive.
RightToLeft	Searches the input string from right to left. The default is from left to right, which suits languages like English that read from left to right but not languages like Arabic or Hebrew that read from right to left.
None	Sets no flags. The default is that none of the flags are set. This means searches are, by default, case sensitive and inspected from left to right.
MultiLine	Specifies that ^ and $ can match the beginning and the end of lines as well as the beginning and end of the string. This means that you can get different matches for each line, separated with a newline character. However, the "." character, which you will read about later in *Matching Different Classes of Characters*, will still not match newline characters.
SingleLine	Specifies that the "." special character matches any character, not any character except a newline. The default is that the "." special character does not match a newline. This is often used with the Multiline option.

Some of the above may only make sense when we have looked at the appropriate regular expression syntax. The default is that none of the flags are set. This means searches are, by default, case sensitive and inspected from left to right.

We can use the `RegexOptions` enumeration to set the flags, for example:

```
RegexOptions.IgnoreCase
```

We either pass this to the regular expression constructor, or as in the case of the static methods, pass it to the method as a parameter:

```
Regex.IsMatch(MyString, "ABC",
              RegexOptions.IgnoreCase | RegexOptions.RightToLeft);
```

To set more than one flag we just "or" each flag together using the "|" character, so in the above example the flag options set are `IgnoreCase` and `RightToLeft`. It is performing a bit-wise operation to return a different value that the method can interpret correctly. To remove all the flags in code, we can use `None`.

Class Constructor

Here we show various ways of creating a `Regex` object and the parameters it takes, especially the `RegexOptions` parameter and how that allows us to specify things like whether the search should be left to right, if it should be case sensitive, and more.

The two main constructors are:

```
Regex(string pattern);
```

```
Regex(string pattern, RegexOptions options);
```

The first parameter is the regular expression for the match. Taking a very simple example, let's consider matching ABC:

```
using System;
using System.Text.RegularExpressions;

namespace Wrox.Text.Chapter5
{
  class ABC
  {
    static void Main(string[] args)
    {
      Regex myRegEx = new Regex("ABC");
      Console.WriteLine(myRegEx.IsMatch("The first three letters of "
        + "the alphabet are ABC"));
    }
  }
}
```

This will output True as the sentence does contain the sequence ABC.

If you wanted to match ABC or abc or any combination of upper or lower case, you could do this by setting the case-insensitive option flag and passing this to the constructor:

```
Regex myRegEx = new Regex("ABC", RegexOptions.IgnoreCase);
Console.WriteLine(myRegEx.IsMatch("Hello abc there"));
```

A further point to note is that by default, the Regex object matches against ASCII text.

IsMatch() Method

The IsMatch() method tests a string to see if there is a match on the regular expression pattern. If a match is found, then the method returns True, otherwise it returns False. The IsMatch() method has a static overload, so we can use it without explicitly creating a Regex object.

The method has four overloads shown below:

```
public bool Regex.IsMatch(string input);
```

```
public bool Regex.IsMatch(string input,
                          int startat);
```

```
public static bool Regex.IsMatch(string input,
                                 string pattern);
```

```
public static bool Regex.IsMatch(string input,
                                 string pattern,
                                 RegexOptions options);
```

The latter two overloads, as you can see, are the static methods, whereas the first two operate on a Regex object instance. The parameters for the latter overloads are all strings, except for the RegexOptions enumeration, which we saw earlier in the *RegexOptions Enumeration* section. The int parameter allows you to specify at what position in the string to begin matching. Therefore, to test if a string contains the words "Wrox Press" we could use IsMatch() like this:

```
string inputString = "Welcome to the publishers, Wrox Press Ltd";

if(Regex.IsMatch(inputString, "wrox press", RegexOptions.IgnoreCase))
{
  Console.WriteLine("Match Found");
}
else
{
  Console.WriteLine("No Match Found");
}
```

139

This will show a match found if the input string contains "wrox press". As we have set the IgnoreCase option, it'll be case insensitive so "Wrox Press" will also be matched. We've used the static method because we are only using the regular expression once, and so there is little need to instantiate a new Regex object. Creating a Regex object is useful where we want to save state: that is, the details of the regular expression, its options, and details of its matches.

Replace() Method

This method, again with a static overload, replaces a matched pattern with the string specified. This method has ten variations in all so we'll just look at the basic ones here, and investigate the more advanced options in the next chapter.

As a static method, it has the following overloaded methods:

```
public static string Regex.Replace(string input,
                                   string pattern,
                                   string replacement);
```

```
public static string Regex.Replace(string input,
                                   string pattern,
                                   string replacement,
                                   RegexOptions options);
```

So, using the static method, if we wanted to replace all instances of "wrox press" with "Wrox Press" we would write:

```
string inputString = "Welcome to the publishers wrox press ltd";
inputString = Regex.Replace(inputString, "wrox press", "Wrox Press");
Console.WriteLine (inputString);
```

With the non-static methods, we have the choice of specifying a maximum number of replacements, and a start index.

```
Public string Replace(string input,
                      string replacement);
```

```
Public string Replace(string input,
                      string replacement,
                      int count);
```

```
Public string Replace(string input,
                      string replacement,
                      int count,
                      int startat);
```

If you want to replace all the matches made while using one of these overloads, then you can pass -1 as the count argument.

So, let's say we have the string "123,456,123, 123,789,123,888" and we want to replace "123" from "456" onwards with xxx, but only a maximum of twice. The code would look like this:

```
string inputString = "123,456,123,123,789,123,888";
Regex regExp = new Regex("123");
inputString = regExp.Replace(inputString, "xxx", 2, 4);

Console.WriteLine(inputString);
```

The output from this will be:

```
123,456,xxx,xxx,789,123,888
```

The first 123 isn't replaced because we passed 4 as the final argument, which means the search for patterns only starts at character index 4; the fifth character, which in this case is the 4 of the 456. The two occurrences of 123 between the 456 and the 789 are replaced with xxx. However, the final 123 isn't replaced because we specified in the third argument that only a maximum of two replacements should be made.

Split()

This splits a string at each point where the matching pattern is found. It returns the results as an array of strings. Again, there are static overloads, as well as ones for Regex instances. The two static methods are:

```
Public static string[] Split(string input,
                             string replacement);
```

```
Public static string[] Split(string input,
                             string pattern,
                             RegexOptions options);
```

Let's say we have a comma-delimited string; to split it we could write the following code:

```
using System;
using System.Text;
using System.Text.RegularExpressions;
using System.Windows.Forms;

namespace Wrox.Text.Chapter5
{
    class Split
    {
        static void Main(string[] args)
        {
            string inputString = "123,ABC,456,DEF,789";
            string[] splitResults;
```

```
        splitResults = Regex.Split(inputString, ",");
        StringBuilder resultsString = new StringBuilder(32);

        foreach (string stringElement in splitResults)
        {
            resultsString.Append(stringElement + "\n");
        }

        MessageBox.Show(resultsString.ToString());
    }
  }
}
```

This code will result in the message box shown below:

The string was split where each comma was found, the comma is not included, and each split string is placed in an array element.

The public non-static methods are similar to those we saw for the `Replace()` method in that they allow us to specify a maximum number of splits, and where the pattern matching should start from:

```
Public string[] Split(string input);
```

```
Public string[] Split(string input,
                       int count);
```

```
Public string[] Split(string input,
                       int count,
                       int startat);
```

If we pass 0 as the argument for `count`, the maximum number of splits, then all the matching splits will be made, the same as the normal default behavior.

The Match and MatchCollection Classes

The `Match` and `MatchCollection` classes allow us to obtain the details of each match made via a regular expression. The `Match` class represents a single match made, whereas the `MatchCollection` class is a collection of `Match` objects, one for each successful match made. We need to use the `Regex` object's `Match()` or `Matches()` methods to retrieve the matches.

Let's look first at the `Regex.Match()` method, which has the following overloaded methods:

```
public Match Match(string input);
```

```
public Match Match(string input,
                   int startat);
```

```
public Match Match(string input,
                   int startat,
                   int length);
```

```
public static Match Match(string input,
                          string pattern);
```

```
public static Match Match(string input,
                          string pattern,
                          RegexOptions options);
```

The first three are instance methods; the last two are static. All of them return a `Match` object as their result, which will contain details of the match made. Note that it's just the first match made, not all matches.

Let's look at a simple example of using the second overload listed above:

```
using System;
using System.Text.RegularExpressions;
using System.Windows.Forms;

namespace Wrox.Text.Chapter5
{
  class MatchMethod
  {
    static void Main(string[] args)
    {
      string inputString = "A sailor went to sea to sea, "
        + "to see what he could see could see.";

      Regex myRegex = new Regex("se.");
      Match matchMade = myRegex.Match(inputString, 20);

      while (matchMade.Success)
      {
        MessageBox.Show(matchMade.Value);
        matchMade = matchMade.NextMatch();
      }
    }
  }
}
```

The input string is a line from a folk song but the repetition of words helps to emphasize the point. The regular expression is "se.". The "." character, as you will learn later, is a wild card character that matches any character. Normally, this regular expression would match every occurrence of see or sea in this string. However, when we used the Regex class's Match() method:

```
Match matchMade = myRegex.Match(inputString, 20);
```

we specified that the match should start from the twenty-first character. Moreover, it will only find the first match, which in this case is the second "sea". However, although we can see in the example that a match will be successful, we often won't know this in practice, and so this is where the Success property of the Match class proves useful. We use the Success property in a while loop, so that while a match succeeds, we keep looping:

```
while (matchMade.Success)
{
  MessageBox.Show(matchMade.Value);
  matchMade = matchMade.NextMatch();
}
```

To get the next match, we use the Match.NextMatch() method. This will search from the point immediately after the last successful match of the Match object. Some of the more useful methods of the Match class are detailed in the following table:

Method	Description
NextMatch()	Returns a new Match with the results for the next match, starting at the position at which the last match ended (at the character beyond the last matched character).
Result()	Returns the expansion of the passed replacement pattern. This is used with groups as shown in the next chapter. It will group the results of all the different regular expression replacement patterns together and return them as a whole.
Synchronized()	Returns a Match instance equivalent to the one supplied that is safe to share between multiple threads in a multithreaded application.

Now for some of the interesting properties:

Property	Description
Captures	Returns a collection of capture objects, one for each capture matched by the capturing group. Groups and captures are covered in the next chapter.

Property	Description
Groups	Returns a collection of group objects, one for each `Regex` group matched by the regular expression.
Index	The position in the input string where the first character of the match was found.
Length	The length of the match.
Success	Returns `True` or `False` depending on whether the match was successful or not.
Value	Gets the matched substring from the input string.

Finally, let's look at the `MatchCollection` class. Using the `Regex.Matches()` method, we can obtain a reference to a `MatchCollection` object; this collection class will contain a `Match` object for each match made by the regular expression. It's especially useful where we are dealing with multiple matches and is a useful alternative to using the `Match.NextMatch()` method. The `MatchCollection` class has two main properties that you will find useful; `Count` and `Item`. `Count` returns the number of items matched, and `Item` allows you to access each particular `Match` object in the collection by its index, or using a `foreach` loop.

To obtain a `MatchCollection` we need to use the `Regex.Matches()` method, which has the following overloads, all of which return a `MatchCollection` object:

```
public MatchCollection Matches(string input);
```

```
public MatchCollection Matches(string input,
                               int startat);
```

```
public static MatchCollection Matches(string input,
                                      string pattern);
```

```
public static MatchCollection Matches(string input,
                                      string pattern,
                                      RegexOptions options);
```

In the example below we use the static `Matches()` method to access the third match made, see:

```
using System;
using System.Text.RegularExpressions;
using System.Windows.Forms;

namespace Wrox.Text.Chapter5
{
```

```
class MatchCollectionClass
{
  static void Main(string[] args)
  {
    string userInputString = "A sailor went to sea to sea, "
      + " to see what he could see could see.";
    MatchCollection matchesMade =
        Regex.Matches(userInputString, "se.");

    if(matchesMade.Count >= 3)
    {
      MessageBox.Show(matchesMade[2].Value);
    }
  }
}
```

We define `matchesMade` as a `MatchCollection` object, then set it to the `MatchCollection` object returned by the `Regex` method `Matches()`. Here we have used the static `Matches()` method, rather than explicitly creating a `Regex` object.

We then check that there are three or more matches made by using the `Count` property, then display the details of the third match, which is item index 2 in the collection.

Regex Tester Example

In the previous section, we touched on what some of the methods of the `Regex` object can do. In this section, we'll be creating an application that will make the creation and testing of regular expressions very easy. Even though it's a simple example, you should find it very useful, and it can be used to test the regular expressions in the later chapters as well. The appearance of the application is shown below:

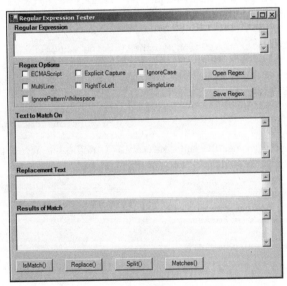

The application allows you to enter regular expressions, set all the options, and then test using the IsMatch(), Replace(), Split(), and Matches() methods described above.

For example, if you enter \d\d\d[a-z] into the regular expression textbox, select the IgnoreCase option, enter the text 456A 321B 789 78AA 444E into the Text to Match On box, and click the Matches() button, you'll see the following:

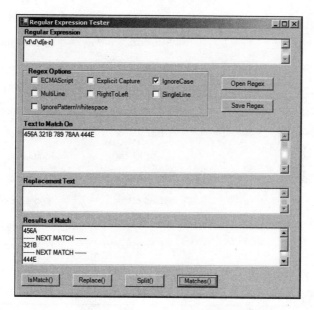

We'll learn about the \d and [a-z] regular expression syntax shortly but you can deduce from the Regular Expression Tester that \d matches a single number character and [a-z] matches any single letter that is in the range a to z. Setting the IgnoreCase flag means lower and upper case characters are matched. We have only covered and will only be covering the Multiline, IgnoreCase, and Singleline options.

We need to create a new Windows Application called RegexTester and change the initial class definition to the following:

```
using System;
using System.ComponentModel;
using System.IO;
using System.Text;
using System.Text.RegularExpressions;
using System.Windows.Forms;
using System.Drawing;

public class RegexTesterForm : System.Windows.Forms.Form
{
```

Here are the controls that need to be added to the form:

147

Name	Control Type	Text
TestRegexButton	Button	IsMatch()
ReplaceButton	Button	Replace()
SplitButton	Button	Split()
MatchesButton	Button	Matches()
OpenRegexButton	Button	Open Regex
SaveRegexButton	Button	Save Regex
OptionsGroup	GroupBox	Regex Options
SingleLineChkBox	CheckBox	SingleLine
RightToLeftChkBox	CheckBox	RightToLeft
MultiLineChkBox	CheckBox	MultiLine
IgnorePatternWhiteSpaceChkBox	CheckBox	IgnorePatternWhiteSpace
IgnoreCaseChkBox	CheckBox	IgnoreCase
ExplicitCaptureChkBox	CheckBox	ExplicitCapture
ECMAScriptChkBox	CheckBox	ECMAScript
openFileDialog1	OpenFileDialog	N/A
saveFileDialog1	SaveFileDialog	N/A

For the following controls, additionally set the Multiline property to True, and the Scrollbars property to Vertical:

Name	Control Type
RegexTextBox	TextBox
InputTextBox	TextBox
ReplacementTextBox	TextBox
ResultsTextBox	TextBox

You can see in the previous screenshot where to add these and the label controls, and what text should be bold. The Open Regex and Save Regex buttons are there for convenience; it's useful to be able to save the more complex regular expressions. We'll start by adding the code to save the regular expression. Double-click on the Save Regex button and change its Click event handler:

148

```
private void SaveRegexButton_Click(object sender, System.EventArgs e)
{
  saveFileDialog1.ShowDialog();
}
```

This shows the Save File dialog, allowing the user to select the drive, directory, and file name for the text file that will hold the regular expression. If the user then clicks OK to save the file, the `FileOk` event fires, so that's where we add the code to save the file. Double-click on `saveFileDialog1` and amend its handler as follows:

```
private void saveFileDialog1_FileOk(object sender,
        System.ComponentModel.CancelEventArgs e)
{
  StreamWriter streamWriterRegex =
      File.CreateText(saveFileDialog1.FileName);
  streamWriterRegex.Write(this.RegexTextBox.Text);
  streamWriterRegex.Close();
}
```

We obtain the file path from the `saveFileDialog.FileName` property just selected by the user, and use the `StreamWriter` class to create a new text file. We use its `Write()` method to save the regular expression to the file.

Opening a regular expression involves a similar method to that for saving one. First, we need to add code to show the open dialog upon pressing the `OpenRegexButton` button:

```
private void OpenRegexButton_Click(object sender,
                                   System.EventArgs e)
{
  openFileDialog1.ShowDialog();
}
```

If the user then clicks the OK button, the `FileOk` event of `openFileDialog1` will fire. We now insert the code to read in the regular expression from the file:

```
private void openFileDialog1_FileOk(object sender,
        System.ComponentModel.CancelEventArgs e)
{
  StreamReader streamReaderRegex =
      File.OpenText(openFileDialog1.FileName);
  this.RegexTextBox.Text = streamReaderRegex.ReadToEnd();
  streamReaderRegex.Close();
}
```

This is similar to the method that saves the regular expression, except this time we use the `StreamReader` object to read in the text, and set the `RegexTextBox.Text` property to its value.

That's the opening and saving of the regular expression dealt with, so now let's see how we can determine which Regex options need to be set, based on which checkboxes have been checked by the user. As this is something all of our Regex testing buttons will need to do, we create a `private` method of the form class called `GetSelectedRegexOptions()` that will be called by each of the other buttons' `Click` events:

```
private RegexOptions GetSelectedRegexOptions()
{
    RegexOptions selectedRegexOptions = RegexOptions.None;

    if(this.IgnoreCaseChkBox.Checked)
        selectedRegexOptions |= RegexOptions.IgnoreCase;

    if(this.ExplicitCaptureChkBox.Checked)
        selectedRegexOptions |= RegexOptions.ExplicitCapture;

    if(this.ECMAScriptChkBox.Checked)
        selectedRegexOptions |= RegexOptions.ECMAScript;

    if(this.IgnorePatternWhitespaceChkBox.Checked)
        selectedRegexOptions |= RegexOptions.IgnorePatternWhitespace;

    if(this.MultiLineChkBox.Checked)
        selectedRegexOptions |= RegexOptions.Multiline;

    if(this.RightToLeftChkBox.Checked)
        selectedRegexOptions |= RegexOptions.RightToLeft;

    if(this.SingleLineChkBox.Checked)
        selectedRegexOptions |= RegexOptions.Singleline;

    return selectedRegexOptions;
}
```

This method is just a long list of `if` statements that check each checkbox. If one is checked then it ORs the `RegexOptions` together.

Taking the top of the code:

```
RegexOptions selectedRegexOptions = RegexOptions.None;

if(this.IgnoreCaseChkBox.Checked)
    selectedRegexOptions |= RegexOptions.IgnoreCase;
```

We define the `selectedRegexOptions` variable as type `RegexOptions`, and this will hold the final tally of options set. We set it initially to `RegexOptions.None`, meaning no options have yet been set.

In the `if` statement, we check to see if the checkbox, `IgnoreCaseChkBox`, has been checked by the user; if it has we then set `selectedRegexOptions` to `IgnoreCase` by using a logical OR assignment operator to set `RegexOptions` to include that option (`|=`). Note that it's a logical OR, not an exclusive OR – it adds to whatever existing options are set; it does not remove them.

The remainder of the function continues in the same manner until all the checkboxes and `Regex` options have been set as requested by the user. We then return the result held in `selectedRegexOptions`.

Each of the buttons has the name of the method used with the regular expression entered in the top box. Let's start with the easiest one, the IsMatch() button. The following code needs to be added to its `Click` event:

```
private void TestRegexButton_Click(object sender,
                                    System.EventArgs e)
{
  try
  {
    RegexOptions selectedRegexOptions =
        this.GetSelectedRegexOptions();
    Regex testRegex = new Regex(this.RegexTextBox.Text,
        selectedRegexOptions);

    if(testRegex.IsMatch(this.InputTextBox.Text))
    {
      this.ResultsTextBox.ForeColor = Color.Black;
      this.ResultsTextBox.Text = "MATCH FOUND";
    }
    else
    {
      this.ResultsTextBox.Text = "NO MATCH FOUND";
      this.ResultsTextBox.ForeColor = Color.Red;
    }
  }

  catch (ArgumentException ex)
  {
    this.ResultsTextBox.ForeColor = Color.Red;
    this.ResultsTextBox.Text =
        "There was an error in your regular expression:\r\n"
        + ex.Message;
  }
}
```

The code is placed inside a `try...catch` block; this is particularly useful in this case because if we make a mistake in our regular expression syntax, the `Catch` clause will grab the `ArgumentException`, and will then write it out to `ResultsTextBox`. The error message usually gives enough detail to hint at where the regular expression syntax is wrong.

At the start of the `try` clause, we create a new variable to hold the `RegexOptions` enumeration and initialize it to the user-selected options with our `GetSelectedRegexOptions()` method created earlier.

Then we use the `IsMatch()` method to check to see if any match is made using the regular expression on the text in the `InputTextBox` textbox. If a match has been found, then `True` is returned, and we set `ResultsTextBox` to "MATCH FOUND" in black letters. If no match is found, then "NO MATCH FOUND" is output in red letters.

Let's now turn to the Replace() button and the code for its `Click` event:

```
private void ReplaceButton_Click(object sender, System.EventArgs e)
{
  try
  {
    RegexOptions selectedRegexOptions =
        this.GetSelectedRegexOptions();
    Regex replaceRegex = new Regex(this.RegexTextBox.Text,
        selectedRegexOptions);

    this.ResultsTextBox.ForeColor = Color.Black;
    this.ResultsTextBox.Text = replaceRegex.Replace(
        this.InputTextBox.Text, this.ReplacementTextBox.Text);
  }

  catch (ArgumentException ex)
  {
    this.ResultsTextBox.ForeColor = Color.Red;
    this.ResultsTextBox.Text = "There was an error in "
        + "your regular expression:\r\n" + ex.Message;
  }
}
```

Again, we have a `try...catch` block that will capture any errors in our regular expression syntax and write them to `ResultsTextBox`. Inside the `try` clause, we obtain the `RegexOptions` and then create a new `Regex` object using the regular expression in the `RegexTextBox` textbox. However, we then use the `Replace()` method, which replaces the matches made by the regular expression on the text in `InputTextBox` with the text inside `ReplacementTextBox` and displays the results in the `ResultsTextBox` textbox.

The next button to describe is the Split() button, and its `Click` event handling code is as follows:

```
private void SplitButton_Click(object sender, System.EventArgs e)
{
  try
  {
    RegexOptions selectedRegexOptions =
        this.GetSelectedRegexOptions();
```

```
        Regex splitRegex = new Regex(this.RegexTextBox.Text,
            selectedRegexOptions);

        String[] splitResults;
        splitResults = splitRegex.Split(this.InputTextBox.Text);
        StringBuilder resultsString = new
            StringBuilder(this.InputTextBox.Text.Length);

        foreach (String stringElement in splitResults)
            resultsString.Append(stringElement + Environment.NewLine);

        this.ResultsTextBox.ForeColor = Color.Black;
        this.ResultsTextBox.Text = resultsString.ToString();
    }

    catch (ArgumentException ex)
    {
        this.ResultsTextBox.ForeColor = Color.Red;
        this.ResultsTextBox.Text = "There was an error in "
            + "your regular expression:\r\n" + ex.Message;
    }
}
```

Our `try...catch` block is as with the previous methods – it captures any errors in the regular expression. We then get the selected `RegexOptions` and use them with the regular expression string to create a new `Regex` object.

We declare an array called `splitResults` that will hold the results, if any, returned by the `Split()` method; it returns each split data item as a string in a string array. We then execute the `Split()` method on the `Regex` object, and store the results in the `splitResults` array.

Having got the results in the array, we now need to loop through each array element using a `foreach` loop, and append the results to the `resultsString` `StringBuilder` object: This was initialized to the size of the string being split, to decrease memory allocations.

```
        foreach (String stringElement in splitResults)
            resultsString.Append(stringElement + Environment.NewLine);
```

Finally, we write out the results to the `ResultsTextBox` textbox:

```
        this.ResultsTextBox.Text = resultsString.ToString();
```

The final button we need to cover here is the Matches() button, and its event code is as follows:

153

```
private void MatchesButton_Click(object sender, System.EventArgs e)
{
  try
  {
    RegexOptions selectedRegexOptions = GetSelectedRegexOptions();
    Regex matchesRegex = new Regex(this.RegexTextBox.Text,
        selectedRegexOptions);

    MatchCollection matchesFound;
    matchesFound = matchesRegex.Matches(this.InputTextBox.Text);

    String nextMatch = "------- NEXT MATCH -------\r\n";
    StringBuilder resultsString = new StringBuilder(64);

    foreach (Match matchMade in matchesFound)
        resultsString.Append(matchMade.Value
            + (Environment.NewLine + nextMatch));

    this.ResultsTextBox.ForeColor = Color.Black;
    this.ResultsTextBox.Text = resultsString.ToString();
  }

  catch (ArgumentException ex)
  {
    this.ResultsTextBox.ForeColor = Color.Red;
    this.ResultsTextBox.Text = "There was an error in "
        + "your regular expressions:\r\n" + ex.Message;
  }
}
```

We start, as with the previous click events, with a try...catch block to capture any regular expression exceptions while creating a new Regex object. However, we now want to obtain the text of each match made by the regular expression. To do this we need to use the MatchCollection and Match objects to hold the text of each of these matches. The variable matchesFound is set to the MatchCollection object returned by the Matches() method. This collection object contains Match objects, one for each match made. We loop through this collection using a foreach loop, where each Match.Value property is appended to the resultsString StringBuilder object, along with a string to indicate the match boundaries. We have grouped together Environment.NewLine and nextMatch because, if you remember, this increases the chance that the string will be cached and so won't need a separate string object created just to be marked ready for disposal at garbage collection immediately after the contents are placed in the StringBuilder object.

Finally, the code writes the results to the ResultsTextBox textbox.

Fundamental Regular Expression Syntax

So far, with only two short exceptions, we have only used the Regex methods with plain character matches for our regular expression, for example, matching the actual characters "ABC". However, this is nothing more than we can do with the String class and its similar methods. If we just want to match actual characters then it's much more efficient to use the String class's methods; the Regex methods are more powerful but also consume greater processing power.

Where regular expressions show their power is not when matching specific characters, but patterns of types of character instead. For example, whitespace characters, letters, numbers, punctuation, and ranges of letters or numbers.

Matching Different Classes of Characters

Shown below are the special character classes in regular expression syntax. These groups replace one single character. For instance, a \d will match any digit.

Character Class	Characters it Matches	Example
\d	Any digit from 0 to 9	\d\d matches 72, but not aa or 7a.
\D	Any character that is not a numerical digit	\D\D\D matches abc, but not 123.
\w	Any word character, as in A-Z, a-z, 0-9, and the underscore character _	\w\w\w\w matches Ab_2, but not £$%* or Ab_@.
\W	Any non-word character	\W matches @, but not the letter a.
\s	Any whitespace character; includes tab, newline, carriage return, form feed, and vertical tab	Matches all traditional whitespace characters, as defined in HTML, XML, and other standards.
\S	Any non-whitespace character	Every character bar whitespace: A%&g3:, etc.
.	Any character	"." matches any single character, except a newline character.
[...]	Any one of the characters between the brackets	[abc] will match a single character a, or b, or c, but nothing else. [a-z] will match any single character in the range a to z.

Table continued on following page

155

Character Class	Characters it Matches	Example
[^...]	Any character, except one of those inside the brackets	[^abc] will match any character except a or b or c, but A or B or C could be matched by this pattern. [^a-z] will match any character which is not in the range a to z, but all uppercase letters could be matched by this pattern.

Let's demonstrate this. To match a telephone number in the format 1-800-888-5474, the regular expression could be:

```
\d-\d\d\d-\d\d\d-\d\d\d\d
```

Any \d will match any character in the digit class and the "-" matches a dash. To test it works in code use the following:

```
Console.WriteLine(Regex.IsMatch("1-800-888-5474",
    @"\d-\d\d\d-\d\d\d-\d\d\d\d"));
```

You'll notice that there is an @ character inserted before the regular expression string. This is because C# recognizes certain escape characters in strings, like \n for newline and would report an error when it came across the \d character. Without the quoted string literal character, you would have to insert an extra \ character before every regular expression escape character. Try this and you'll see a message box with True displayed to show that it's valid. If you change the string to be tested to this:

```
Console.WriteLine(Regex.IsMatch("X-800-888-5474",
    @"\d-\d\d\d-\d\d\d-\d\d\d\d"));
```

False will be displayed. You can, of course, also test this regular expression in our new Regex Tester application. To match a date, presented as "Oct 31 2002", our regular expression would be:

```
[a-zA-Z][a-zA-Z][a-zA-Z] \d\d \d\d\d\d
```

[a-zA-Z] will match any character from lowercase a to lowercase z, and uppercase A to uppercase Z. Therefore, what we are saying is match any pattern consisting of exactly three letters that are in the range a-z or A-Z, followed by one space, followed by exactly two digits, followed by another space, and ending with exactly four digits.

A good practice in this situation is to use the IgnoreCase option to make the match case insensitive and just have [a-z] or [A-Z].

If we wanted to allow dashes between date digits as well as spaces, such as "Oct-31-2002", we'd change our regular expression to:

```
[a-z][a-z][a-z][ -]\d\d[ -]\d\d\d\d
```

Something you're probably starting to notice is there is a lot of repetition of characters. In the regular expression above, we have three instances of [a-z], two of \d in the middle, and at the end, four \d special characters. To help us in this situation, regular expression syntax has special repetition characters and these are the topic of a later section, *Specifying Repetition*.

> **An alternative to using the @ character when we use Regex in our code is to add an extra \ in front of all the Regex syntax that starts with a \ so that C# doesn't think it's a string escape character, but realizes it's a Regex character. So \d becomes \\d and \s becomes \\s and so on. The same applies to Regex syntax we see later in the book.**

Specifying Match Position

Now we will look at the regular expression language aspects that allow us to specify where the match should start, end, or occur between. For example, we can use ^ to specify the match must start at the beginning of the string, or \b for word boundaries. The regular expressions seen so far would allow any characters in the string before and after the matched characters.

The position characters allow us to specify where in a string the pattern should be found. This is called **anchoring** the pattern. By anchoring, we mean that (at least) one end of the regular expression is fixed to a point in the string to be matched. Therefore, anchors stop the normal behavior of searching all the string for any match.

There are seven special position characters and these are shown in the table below:

Position Character	Description
^	The following pattern must be at the start of the string, or if it's a multi-line string, at the beginning of a line. For multi-line text (a string that contains carriage returns), we need to set the Multiline flag.
$	The preceding pattern must be at the end of the string, or if it's a multi-line string then at the end of a line.

Table continued on following page

Position Character	Description
\A	The proceeding pattern must be at the start of the string; the multi-line flag is ignored.
\z	The preceding pattern must be at the end of the string; the multi-line flag is ignored.
\Z	The proceeding pattern must be at the end of the string or before a newline at the end of the string.
\b	This matches a word boundary, essentially the point between a word character and a non-word character. Remember a word character is any of [a-zA-Z0-9_]. The start of a word.
\B	Match a position that is not a word boundary; not the start of a word.

If we are using regular expressions to perform validation of user input, then we'll often want to make sure that only the data we want is there and there is nothing before or after the data. For example, "1234 4567 1234 1232" is a valid credit card number. However, if "XXXX1234 4567 1234 1232" is entered then the input is invalid. To solve the problem we can use a "^" (caret) character at the start of the regular expression to ensure the card number is the first thing in the string and the $ character to ensure that the pattern is also the end of the string. By adding these characters, we ensure that the card number pattern is the first, last, and only thing in the string. So, our regular expression for a credit card becomes:

```
^\d\d\d\d \d\d\d\d \d\d\d\d \d\d\d\d$
```

It's with the "^" and "$" special characters that the setting of the Multiline option becomes important. If the Multiline option is set, then "^" matches the position following a \r or \n (Cr/Lf) character as well as the position at the very beginning of the string, and "$" matches the position preceding \r or \n, as well as the position at the very end of the string.

If the Multiline option is not set then "^" only matches the position at the beginning of a string, and $ only matches the position at the end of a string, up to the first \r or \n. Repetition characters were mentioned earlier with regards to the telephone matching example in the last section; now we will describe them.

Specifying Repetition

Repetition characters not only make our regular expressions more compact, they also allow us to specify how often a character or, as we'll see shortly, group of characters occurs. Let's start by looking at the basic repetition characters available.

Repetition Character	Meaning	Example
{n}	Match n of the previous item	x{2} matches xx, but not x or xxx
{n,}	Match n or more of the previous item	x{2,} matches two or more xs, that is xx, xxx, xxxx, xxxxx, ...
{n,m}	Match at least n and at most m of the preceding item, if n is 0, that makes the character optional	x{2,4} matches xx, xxx, and xxxx, but not x or xxxxx
?	Match the previous item zero or one times, essentially making it optional	x? matches x or nothing.
+	Match the previous item one or more times	x+ matches x, or xx, or any number of xs greater than zero
*	Match the previous item zero or more times	x* matches nothing, x, xx, or any number of xs

After learning from this table, and the earlier section on anchoring regular expressions, let's change the telephone and date regular expressions we saw earlier. First, the telephone regular expression can be changed from:

```
\d-\d\d\d-\d\d\d-\d\d\d\d
```

to:

```
^\d-\d{3}-\d{3}-\d{4}$
```

The updated regular expression will match exactly the same pattern, reading 1 digit, followed by a dash, followed by 3 digits, followed by a dash, followed by 3 digits, followed by a dash, and finally followed by 4 digits. It will also anchor it so that there can be no other characters either side of this pattern.

Let's also update our short date matching expression from:

```
[a-zA-Z][a-zA-Z][a-zA-Z][ -]\d\d[ -]\d\d\d\d
```

to:

```
^[a-zA-Z]{3}[ -]\d\d[ -]\d{4}$
```

We haven't changed the \d\d in the middle to \d{2} as it would add an extra character and so lengthen the expression rather than shortening it, which would be pointless.

Even more useful than the shorthand of {n} are the "?", "+", and "*" special repetition characters. Let's say we wanted to match a 16-digit credit card number. When users enter credit card numbers, they sometimes enter the whole number with no spaces, and sometimes they split it up into groups of four digits with spaces between the groups as it's printed on the card itself. This could present a problem as it would mean either stripping out spaces using a Replace() before performing the regular expression pattern match, or having two regular expressions to match each situation – as follows:

```
\d{16}
```

and:

```
\d{4} \d{4} \d{4} \d{4}
```

Using the "?" repetition character, which matches the previous character zero or one times, we can combine the two regular expressions like this:

```
^\d{4} ?\d{4} ?\d{4} ?\d{4}$
```

Now the "?" following the space after the digits means the space must appear zero or one times. Additionally, we only match if the pattern fills the entire string by anchoring at both ends.

Greedy and Lazy Expressions

The quantifiers we have looked at so far have all been what is termed **greedy**; in other words the regular expression engine will do its very best to match as many characters as it can, as long as the rest of the expression is possible. Think of it like this: When the regex engine comes across one of these repetition characters, it will move from the left to the right as far as that particular component of the regular expression will allow it to. For instance, \d*3 will match numbers until there are no more numbers grouped together to match against. Once it has grabbed as much as possible, the engine will attempt to match the 3. If it cannot, and it will not be able to immediately as it has already matched all the numbers, then it will remove one character from the previous match and try again, and it will repeatedly do this until a match can be made, where it will continue. This means that where there is a quantitative decision to be made, the engine will take as much as it can first and grudgingly release one character at a time if a later character cannot be matched. You can see how this works in Figure 1. It uses the \d*3 regex, and attempts to match against the string "123456789fgfd".

Figure 1

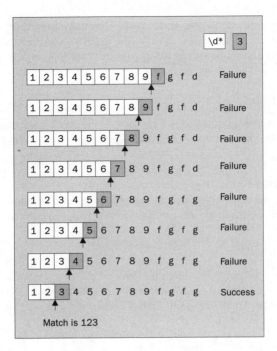

Each of the points where a decision can be made is placed on an internal stack that the Regex engine uses. This means that on failure, the engine returns to the last decision point and makes the next decision available to it. In Figure 1, this was to attempt to match one less digit. If all options have been considered, it is popped off the stack and the previous decision is returned to. If there are no more decisions on the stack, then it knows that there is no match and the IsMatch() method returns False.

The best way to demonstrate this is with an example. Let's use a different example, one to match ISBNs; publishers and individuals often use different ISBN forms. What is the same is that there are always ten digits and the last digit can be an "X" (the last digit is a check digit, with eleven possibilities). To allow for the different forms, we will permit any number of "-" or whitespace characters to separate the number at any point in the sequence. So for a particular book we could use 1-861008-23-6 or 1-86100-823-6, for instance. One regular expression that could be used is the following:

```
^(\d[- ]*){9}[\dxX]$
```

This is quite straightforward if you break it up. This says that at the start there must be one digit. It then says there can be zero or more hyphens or any whitespace characters. It then repeats this sequence a further eight times (as {9} is a shorthand for repeating the sequence a further eight times), and the brackets represent a group (groups are covered in the next chapter). At the last character, it states there can be one of a digit, an "x", or an "X". We will use the following ISBN to match against:

```
1-861-0008  236
```

If you look closely at the sequence, you can see that there are too many digits there; an extra zero has been added. There is only one greedy quantifier used in this example, but let's look at how the regular expression matches this. This is best illustrated in a numbered list:

1. 1 is matched.

2. "-" is matched, but there is also another choice of matching whitespace that could have been made here, so this position is placed on the stack.

3. 8 is matched.

4. "-" was not found. The engine moves to the next decision and no whitespace is found, which as the "*" character is used, is deemed valid and so matches. There are no further decisions to be made, and so nothing extra is left on the stack.

5. 6 is matched.

6. "-" was not found. The engine moves to the next decision and no whitespace is found, which as the "*" character is used, is deemed valid and so matches. There are no further decisions to be made, and so nothing extra is left on the stack.

7. 1 is matched.

8. "-" is matched, but there is also another choice of matching the whitespace that could have been made here, so this position is placed on the stack.

9. 0 is matched.

10. "-" was not found. The engine moves to the next decision and no whitespace is found, which as the "*" character is used, is deemed valid and so matches. There are no further decisions to be made, and so nothing extra is left on the stack.

11. 0 is matched.

12. "-" was not found. The engine moves to the next decision and no whitespace is found, which as the "*" character is used, is deemed valid and so matches. There are no further decisions to be made, and so nothing extra is left on the stack.

13. 0 is matched.

14. "-" was not found. The engine moves to the next decision and no whitespace is found, which as the "*" character is used, is deemed valid and so matches. There are no further decisions to be made, and so nothing extra is left on the stack.

15. 8 is matched.

16. This case is different from the previous case. "-" was not found, so it moves on to the next choice, zero or more whitespace characters. It tries to grab as much as possible, which in this case is two space characters. It then passes control to the next instruction and sticks on the stack the decision to match 2 whitespace characters.

17. 2 is matched.

18. "-" was not found. The engine moves to the next decision and no whitespace is found, which as the "*" character is used, is deemed valid and so matches. There are no further decisions to be made, and so nothing extra is left on the stack.

19. 3 is matched, but there was also a choice of x or X, so this decision point is placed on the stack.

Now, it finds that it should be at the end of the string, but there is still another character, so it has to walk back through its decisions, selecting a different one for each to see if it can match. In this case, there are four decision points to return to and try again: those at positions 2, 8, 16, and 19 in the above list. It returns to the last decision point at point 19 and tries to see if either "x", or "X" can be matched instead. As the number is 3, they cannot and so this decision point is removed from the stack.

It now moves to position 16, where it tries to match one less whitespace character – one space. It succeeds and so starts moving forwards again. There are still more decisions possible, though, as there could be no whitespace characters so this point is left on the stack. However, the engine wants to match a digit and cannot, so it fails and returns to the last point (16). It attempts the match with no whitespace characters and it will remove this decision from the stack, as there are no more decisions that could be made. It fails again as there is a space character at the next position, when the regex engine still wants a digit.

It now returns to the next decision point in the stack, which is at point 8. "-" was matched here, but the other decision wasn't attempted so it tries that. However, there are no whitespace characters there, it is still a "-", and so this match fails. It removes this point from the stack, and moves to the last decision point at point 2. It attempts to do the same with this character, but fails again. There are no more decisions to return to in the stack, so the match fails.

This is a very long and convoluted way of determining failure. However, because the engine has to make decisions at various points in the expression, it is actually essential for this kind of regex engine. However, there are ways of improving the regular expression to reduce the number of decision points to which it has to return. This has to be considered because the regex engine starts again from the last decision point, and in some choices of string and regex, it can work its way to the end again before discovering failure and having to work back once more. Alternatively, it can still succeed without matching everything expected. Thankfully, there are ways of stopping wildcards from being greedy.

To perform a non-greedy, or **lazy**, match with the wildcard characters, we simply use the quantifiers we have seen so far but add "?" after them. The difference is that with the non-greedy repetition the regex engine will always favor as few matches as possible. Another example will help make this clearer.

Let's imagine we want to match a single line of a text file. In this file we have the lines:

```
This is the first line.
This the second line.
The final line.
```

We want each match to capture just one whole line. Therefore, we are looking for one or more whitespace or non-whitespace characters. We want it to start at the beginning of a line and end at the end of a line. Our first attempt at a regular expression might be this:

```
^[\w\W]+$
```

Let's try this with our Regular Expression Tester, with the MultiLine option checked:

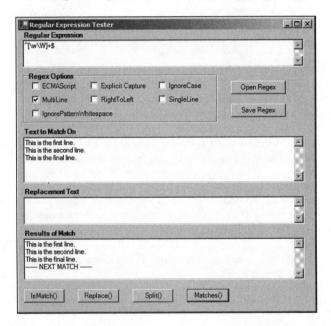

The Matches() button will show what substrings are actually matched. When we click the Matches() button, we see that there is just one match, the whole string. We wanted the match to start at the beginning of a line and end at the end of a line, but it only found one match.

The problem is that the Regex engine is greedy. Moreover, the match it first made is valid; it starts at the beginning of a line, has one or more word or non-word characters in it, and ends at the end of the string. The problem is that it matched too much; it matched all the lines in between as well. In this case, the Multiline option is irrelevant. The problem is with our greedy repetition character, "+". The solution is to use a non-greedy repetition instruction, in this case, "+?". If you change the regular expression to:

```
^[\w\W]+?$
```

and hit the Matches() button again, you'll see this time that each line is contained within one match:

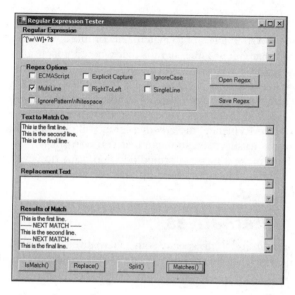

Now the regex engine only matches as many characters as it needs to for a successful match. This means that it starts at the first line, matches all the characters until it hits the end of the line, and then stops matching. The \W character can match against a newline character, because the MultiLine option states it. So, as the "$" character follows, it stops.

There are no hard and fast rules governing when you should use lazy matching, but it is often quite clear from what your characters are asking for. By looking at what your instruction will and won't match, you can decide if you want it to be greedy or not. If you are using the "." character with a wildcard, you will often want to use the non-greedy version as it would otherwise match all of the rest of the string before it moves on to the next regex instruction. A greedy instruction will discover how many it can match and then count down if a failure occurs later, whereas a lazy match will try with as few as possible until a later instruction fails, when it tries again with another occurrence. If the regex engine reaches a character it cannot match while using a lazy wildcard, or it reaches the end of the string while it was attempting to increase the number of characters to match against, then it will fail and so step back through the decision stack.

Greediness and laziness will need to be applied at different times; you will want to take into account how far through the string the lazy character would match, how large the string is likely to be in total, and how many repeated characters you are likely to have. Let's show another example, the ISBN example used earlier. We'll change the regex to:

```
^(\d[-\s]*?){9}[\dxX]$
```

We'll use the same string as before:

```
1-861-0008  236
```

Here it will match 0 and then attempt to match zero or more whitespace characters. The difference in the matching routine here is that when it gets to the point where there are two whitespace characters, it will attempt to match against one character first, but this will fail because the next character wants to match a digit. This means that when it does match two spaces, then it leaves nothing on the stack as there are no more than two whitespace characters there and so there are no more decisions that can be made. In terms of performance, the greedy search will often be faster matching a string, but its eagerness to succeed can mean that you don't match what you expect to. You should be able to make a more informed decision now, however, by considering how these operators work when you build up your expression.

Specifying Alternatives

You've seen how we can use [] to specify some alternatives. However, it only matches against single characters. The alternation character (|) allows you to provide broader choices.

Let's say you wanted to match "Paul" or "John" with a regular expression. Without the alternation character you'd need two regular expressions and therefore two different comparisons, but with this character, you can write just one:

```
Paul|John
```

The alternation character becomes even more useful when coupled with grouping, which we look at in detail in the next chapter. With all alternation decisions, the engine will attempt to match the first choice first, and step through each from left to right.

Special Characters

In the previous sections, you have seen many regular expression characters. You've seen that if you want to match any word character then you'd use \w, or if you wanted to match the previous character one or more times then you'd use "+". However, you may want to match an actual + sign rather than indicating zero or more characters. Alternatively, you may want to match characters that cannot be typed in; for example, non-standard characters and characters such as tab or line feed. Thankfully, there are escape sequences that can be used to specify these characters. "\" is the character indicating that what follows is an escape sequence of characters. What follows indicates what character each escape sequence represents, so \t represents a tab. A list of these is shown in the following table:

Escape Sequence	Description
\\	Matches actual the "\" character
\.	Matches "." character
*	Matches "*" character
\+	Matches "+" character
\?	Matches "?" character
|	Matches "|" character
\(	Matches "(" character
\)	Matches ")" character
\{	Matches "{" character
\}	Matches "}" character
\[	Matches "[" character
\^	Matches "^" character
\$	Matches "$" character
\n	Matches newline
\r	Matches carriage return
\t	Matches tab
\v	Matches vertical tab
\f	Matches form feed
\nnn	Matches ASCII character specified by octal number nnn; so \103 matches an uppercase C

Escape Sequence	Description
\xnn	Matches ASCII character specified by hexadecimal number nn; so \x43 matches C
\unnnn	Matches the Unicode character specified by the four hexadecimal digits represented by nnnn
\cV	Matches a control character; for example, \cV matches *Ctrl+V*

Let's say we have the string, "The price is $1.95 and it is available now", and want to match the "$" and replace it with a "£". The dollar must be escaped; otherwise, it is interpreted as meaning the pattern must be at the end of the string:

```
string myString = "The price is $1.95 and it is available now";
Console.WriteLine(Regex.Replace(myString, @"\$", "£"));
```

Another example is a string that only contains a URL, which you want to split into its separate parts, for example, www.subdomain.domain.com into:

```
www
subdomain
domain
com
```

You need to split the input string at each point there is a "." character. However the "." is part of the regular expression syntax and therefore you need to tell the Regex parser that you mean a literal ".", and not the regular expression syntax version. You escape it by simply adding a "\" in front of it; this means your regular expression would be: "\.".

Summary

In this chapter, we have covered the basics of regular expression syntax and how regular expressions are implemented in the .NET Framework. Specifically, you learned about the following:

❑ In .NET, regular expression functionality is provided via the System.Text.RegularExpressions namespace, and is contained within System.dll.

❑ The most important class is the Regex class. This allows you to create and use regular expressions to test for patterns of characters, and to search, replace, and split strings. The class has a number of static methods that remove the need to create a Regex object if you just want to use a regular expression only once in the code.

❏ Regular expression syntax allows you to specify not just to match actual characters, but also specify to match a type of character, for example, digits, letters, and whitespace.

❏ The number of times a character should be matched can be specified with the repetition characters.

❏ The alternation character "|" is a logical OR statement in that it allows one or other of the patterns to be matched.

❏ When you want to specify characters that can't be typed in using the keyboard, or when you want to match a character that is normally part of regular expression syntax, you can use one of the special character escapes.

In the next chapter, we look at the more advanced aspects of regular expression syntax. We also look at the trickier aspects of the .NET regular expression support and cover the other classes in the `System.Text.RegularExpressions` namespace.

C#

Text Manipulation

Handbook

6

6

Advanced Regex Concepts

In this chapter, we'll be covering the more advanced regular expression syntax we left out of the previous chapter. We'll also be looking at other .NET Framework classes that deal with regular expressions, like the `Group` and `GroupCollection` classes. We'll give examples of the more tricky aspects of regular expressions: groups, using groups in substitutions, and backreferences.

Groups, Substitutions, and Backreferences

In this section, we'll look at the .NET `Group` and `GroupCollection` classes, substitutions, and backreferences. It's no coincidence that we're discussing these all in the same section, as they are all related. Groups allow us to specify that a pattern of characters should be considered as a distinct item. One example of where we might do this is when matching someone's whole name, where although the whole match should be of the whole name, we want to split the match up into first name and last name. Using the `Group` and `GroupCollection` classes we can then access the first and last name parts of the match separately.

Substitutions and backreferences allow us to use the characters matched by a group. Substitutions allow the group to be used in replacement operations as part of the text that replaces the pattern. Let's say we wanted to replace all instances where someone had typed in a word twice accidentally, for example, "and and", with just one word. We can place one of the matched words in a group, and then replace the whole match with just the group ("and and" becomes "and"). We'll see how this works shortly when we look at substitutions.

Backreferences allow us to reuse the pattern matched by a group later in the regular expression, that is, reference a previously matched group. For example, if we want to match the opening and closing tag of an HTML element we obviously want to match the opening tag first, for example, <p>, and then match the same close tag (</p>). However, we don't know in advance what the start tag will be, so we can't specify the close tag's contents unless we use backreferences. So, in our example, let's say for our input string we had the following HTML string:

```
<P>some text</P><H2>some heading</H2>
```

In our simple example an HTML opening tag consists of a letter followed optionally by a number (obviously real HTML has more complex tags but this will do for out simple example). To match the start tag we could use the regular expression:

```
<[a-zA-Z]\d?>
```

This will produce two matches in our input string: <P> and <H2>.

So, for the first match the closing tag must be </P> and for the second it must be </H2>. The important bits are the "P" and the "H2", as it's these that must be matched in the closing tag, so we need to group them in the start tag matching pattern:

```
<([a-zA-Z]\d?)>
```

The brackets specify the grouping of the pattern. So, for each match there is now one group, and in the example the group will contain "P" and "H2".

So, in our closing tag we just need to match "</" and ">" with whatever the contents of the first group were inside, which will be: </P> and </H2>.

So the full regular expression would be:

```
<([a-zA-Z]\d?)>[^<]*</\1>
```

This matches the opening tag, making sure the tag type is captured within a regex group. Then any characters are matched so long as they are not a "<" character, that is we've not hit a new opening or closing tag. We tell the closing tag to match "<\", then the contents of group1 (the \1 specifies group1), and finally ">".

Simple Groups

In the following sections, we explain the grouping characters that can be used in regular expressions.

Capturing: ( )

This groups together the characters matched by the pattern inside the brackets. It's a capturing group, which means that the characters matched by the pattern become part of the final match, unless the ExplicitCapture option is set, which would mean that, by default, the characters are not part of the match.

As an example, let's look at the following input string: ABC1 DEF2 XY. A regular expression that matches three characters A to Z and then one digit would look like:

```
([A-Z]{3})\d
```

This will produce the following two matches:

```
1st Match = ABC1
2nd Match = DEF2
```

Each match will have one group:

```
1st match's 1st group = ABC
2nd match's 1st group = DEF
```

With back referencing we can access the group via its number within the regular expression and via .NET using the Group and GroupCollection classes. If the ExplicitCapture option is set then the contents captured by the groups will not be available.

Non-Capturing: (?:)

This groups together the characters matched by the pattern inside the brackets. It's a non-capturing group, which means that the characters matched by the pattern will not be captured as a group, though it will form part of the final match results. It's basically exactly the same as the group type above but with the ExplicitCapture option set.

As an example, let's look at the following input string: 1A BB SA 1 C. The regular expression that matches a digit **or** a letter from A - Z, followed by any word character looks like:

```
(?:\d|[A-Z])\w
```

This regular expression will produce three matches:

```
1st Match = 1A
2nd Match = BB
3rd Match = SA
```

However, there will be no groups captured.

Capturing-By-Name: (?<name>)

This groups together the characters matched by the pattern inside the brackets and gives the group the name specified between the angle brackets. Within the regular expression we can use the name for backreferencing, instead of having to use a number. It's a capturing group, even if the ExplicitCapture option is set, which means that the characters matched within the group are available for backreferencing or accessible from the Group class, as we'll see shortly.

Consider the following input string:

Characters in Seinfeld include Jerry Seinfeld, Elaine Benes, Cosmo Kramer and George Costanza

The regular expression to match their first and last names and capture the last name in a group called lastName is:

```
\b[A-Z][a-z]+ (?<lastName>[A-Z][a-z]+)\b
```

This produces four matches:

```
1st match = Jerry Seinfeld
2nd match = Elaine Benes
3rd match = Cosmo Kramer
4th match = George Costanza
```

There is one group in each match, the lastName group:

```
1st match lastName group = Seinfeld
2nd match lastName group = Benes
3rd match lastName group = Kramer
4th match lastName group = Costanza
```

The groups will be captured regardless of whether the ExplicitCapture option is set or not.

Comparing Simple Groups

The easiest group to use from those explained above is the capturing group. By simply placing part of our regular expression inside brackets, we can tell the regex engine to treat the pattern as a distinct entity. This can be especially useful when used with the alternation character "|". For example, if we wanted to match an individual's title, for example, Mr, Mrs, Miss, Ms, Dr, and then their last name, we could use the following expression:

```
(Mr|Mrs|Miss|Ms|Dr) [A-Z][a-z]*
```

Within the brackets we have five possible matches that can be made, either Mr or Mrs or Miss or Ms or Dr. The pattern inside the brackets requires only that we match one of these. Following the group is a space, then a capital letter, and then zero or more lower case letters. So, using our Regular Expression Tester program from the previous chapter, we will see the following:

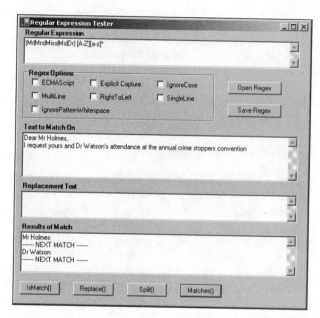

When the Matches() button is clicked, the two matching patterns will be found:

```
Mr Holmes
Dr Watson
```

Contrast this with the same regular expression *without* a group:

```
Mr|Mrs|Miss|Ms|Dr [A-Z][a-z]*
```

The problem here is this will seek to match Mr or Mrs or Miss or Ms. In addition, it will match Dr followed by the last name. Therefore, if we alter the regular expression in the Regular Expression Tester and click Matches() again, we'll get the following matches:

```
Mr
Dr Watson
```

By adding the brackets, we are telling the regex engine to treat the alternatives as one group and therefore to match any single one of them. Notice that with the capturing groups, the pattern matched by the group becomes part of the final match. Indeed, we'll see shortly that we can access the individual matches made by a group. As you learned in the last chapter, this is referred to as a greedy match as it "hungrily" consumes the characters and stores them. However, we can specify that we don't want to capture the group. In our example, we needed to use the group so that our alternation would work; we did not have any particular interest in the results of the group as such, only as part of the whole match. In this case, we can use the non-capturing, or non-greedy, group (?:).

If we change our last name example to include a non-capturing group we will get the following:

```
(?:Mr|Mrs|Miss|Ms|Dr) [A-Z][a-z]*
```

If we test this in our Regular Expression Tester, we now get exactly the same match as we first got (Mr Holmes and Dr Watson) but the regex engine doesn't save the specific characters matched by the group for use later, as we'll see shortly when we look at getting group information. An alternative to using a non-capturing group is to set the ExplicitCapture option; this makes all groups non-capturing by default.

We would want to use non-capturing groups for one of two reasons. Firstly efficiency; capturing groups require extra work and resources so we should not capture data that we don't need or use. Secondly, we may be interested in the results of some of the capturing groups and not others. The unnecessary information from groups we are not interested in just confuses matters, so it's better to make them non-capturing rather than having to alter our code to ignore them.

One final change we could make to the expression is to allow an optional period after the title, that is, "Mr." as well as "Mr", etc. Remember that the "." character has special significance in Regex syntax and means match any character, therefore we must tell the Regex parser that we mean a literal "." and not the regex syntax one. We do this as follows:

```
(?:Mr|Mrs|Miss|Ms|Dr)\.? [A-Z][a-z]*
```

The \. characters tell the Regex parser that we mean a literal "." and the "?" makes it optional, meaning that the "." should appear zero or one times.

The final group we discussed was a named capturing group – (?<name>). This allows us to reference previously matched groups using the group name. At this stage, it's not that useful, so we will leave its discussion until later in the chapter when we explain backreferences.

176

The Group and GroupCollection Classes

The .NET Framework allows us to access the captured characters within a group. It provides the Group class, which represents a single group within a match, and the GroupCollection class, which contains Group objects, one for every group in a successful match.

To obtain a collection of all the groups in a single match, we can use the Groups property of the Match class. This returns a GroupCollection object, so we can obtain each of the individual groups inside each match.

Let's imagine we have the following regular expression:

```
(\d\d)\s([A-Z][A-Z])
```

This will match two digits, followed by a whitespace character, and then by two uppercased letters. We have added brackets around the two digits, giving our first capturing group, and around the two [A-Z] blocks to give the second capturing group. Note that as always if we use the regular expression in code we must escape any character with a "\" in front, so \d becomes \\d and \s becomes \\s. Alternatively, as you saw in the previous chapter, you can use the @ symbol to explicitly quote the string. If we have the input string "12 AB 34 CD 56 EF" then we would get the following matches:

```
12 AB
34 CD
56 EF
```

Within each of these matches are the two groups. So, for example, in the first match the groups are 12 and AB. These can be accessed because each Match object contains the Groups property; this returns a GroupCollection object:

```
Regex matchRegex = new Regex(@"(\d\d)\s([A-Z][A-Z])");
Match matchMade = matchRegex.Match("12 AB 34 CD 56 EF");
GroupCollection matchGroups = matchMade.Groups;
```

Now the matchGroups collection will hold a Group object for each regex group inside our regular expression. We can access each group using its index; however, note that the first group in the group collection is always the whole match. Therefore, even if no groups at all are defined, the GroupCollection will have at least one Group object in it, as demonstrated by the following code:

```
Console.WriteLine(matchGroups[0].Value);
Console.WriteLine(matchGroups[1].Value);
Console.WriteLine(matchGroups[2].Value);
```

For the first match (12 AB), it would retrieve the following:

```
12 AB
12
AB
```

For the second match (34 CD) it would retrieve:

```
34 CD
34
CD
```

Remember we said earlier that we can give names to groups using the regular expression syntax (?<name>). Well, if we do that, we can access the groups using the name as well as the index. Let's change the regular expression to:

```
(?<numberGroup>\\d\\d)\\s(?<letterGroup>[A-Z][A-Z])
```

Now, we can access the groups using their index and name:

```
Console.WriteLine(matchGroups[1].Value);                // 12
Console.WriteLine(matchGroups["numberGroup"].Value);    // 12
Console.WriteLine(matchGroups[2].Value);                // AB
Console.WriteLine(matchGroups["letterGroup"].Value);    // AB
```

> **Regular expression group names are case sensitive, so `letterGroup` and `LetterGroup` are not the same.**

Note what happens if we use a non-capturing group:

```
(?:\d\d)\s([A-Z][A-Z])
```

Now matchGroups(1).Value will be AB for the first match because the characters captured by the first group are not stored for later reference, either in code using the GroupCollection class or for backreferences or substitutions as we'll see shortly.

Let's alter our regular expression tester and add a button that when clicked shows what groups are matched in a regular expression. First, we need to open the Regular Expression Tester project, and then add a button to the form named GroupsButton. Our form should look like the following:

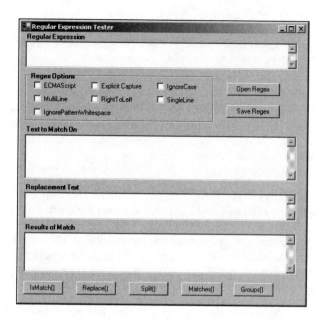

Now we need to add the code for the Click event of the new GroupsButton button:

```
private void GroupsButton_Click(object sender, System.EventArgs e)
{
  try
  {
    RegexOptions selectedRegexOptions = GetSelectedRegexOptions();
    Regex matchesRegex = new Regex(this.RegexTextBox.Text,
                                   selectedRegexOptions);
    MatchCollection matchesFound;
    matchesFound = matchesRegex.Matches(this.InputTextBox.Text);
    StringBuilder resultsString = new StringBuilder(64);
    GroupCollection matchGroups;

    foreach(Match matchMade in matchesFound)
    {
      matchGroups = matchMade.Groups;
      foreach(Group matchGroup in matchGroups)
          resultsString.Append(" (" + matchGroup.Value + ")");
      resultsString.Append(Environment.NewLine + Environment.NewLine);
      resultsString.Append("------- NEXT MATCH -------\r\n");
    }

    this.ResultsTextBox.ForeColor = System.Drawing.Color.Black;
    this.ResultsTextBox.Text = resultsString.ToString();

  }

  catch(ArgumentException ex)
  {
```

179

```
        this.ResultsTextBox.ForeColor = System.Drawing.Color.Red;
        this.ResultsTextBox.Text = "There was an error in your "
            + "regular expression:\r\n" + ex.Message;
    }
}
```

Much of the code is very similar to the code we saw for the Matches() button. The main change is the insertion of the foreach loop that iterates through each group inside a match:

```
foreach(Group matchGroup in matchGroups)
    resultsString.Append(" (" + matchGroup.Value + ")");
```

First, we define variables to hold the details of an individual group and a collection of groups. Then for each match made, we execute an inner foreach loop that iterates through each group inside a match. We set matchGroups to the GroupCollection object returned by the Groups property of the Match object. Then we loop through each group (remember that even with no groups defined, the whole match will be the first item in the group collection). We add the value of each group to the results string for display in the Results of Match textbox.

Let's create a regular expression that matches title and last name, but only returns the last name as a captured group:

```
(?:Mr|Mrs|Miss|Ms|Dr) ([A-Z][a-z]*)
```

With our Regular Expression Tester, we get:

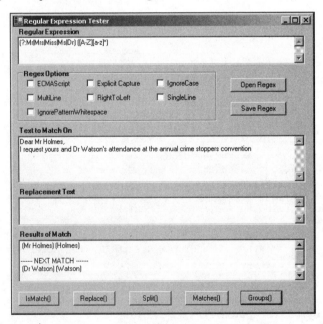

We can see from the results that the `GroupCollection` for each match contains the whole match in the first group, and then the individual group matches, just the last name in this case. We needed the title part to be in a group because of the use of the alternation characters, but we are not interested in the characters it captures, only the characters captured for the last name, which is the second group. Therefore, we made the alternation group a non-capturing group by using the `?:` characters after the opening bracket.

An alternative to using non-capturing groups is to specify that by default all groups should be non-capturing using the `ExplicitCapture` option. We can do this in our Regular Expression Tester by selecting the relevant checkbox and clicking the `Groups()` button. This time, none of the groups are matched; only the whole match is displayed. When the option `ExplicitCapture` is set, we need to specify when we want to capture a group by giving it a name. Let's do this by changing our regular expression to:

```
(Mr|Mrs|Miss|Ms|Dr) (?<lastName>[A-Z][a-z]*)
```

Now we get the results we want; the second group is captured even though the `ExplicitCapture` is set because we have explicitly told it to capture that group by naming it.

Substitutions

We saw the `Replace()` method of the `Regex` class in the last chapter. This does a global search and replace on the input string, whenever a match is made, and its text is replaced with the text we specify. However, there are times when we want to use some of the matched text of a regular expression in our replacement. Let's say we have a list of names and want to replace all titles and last names with titles and "X", such that "Mr Washington" becomes "Mr X". We've seen that the regular expression to match title and last name is:

```
(Mr|Mrs|Miss|Ms|Dr) [A-Z][a-z]*
```

The problem is we don't know what the title will be so we can't simply use code like the following, as this would result in all the titles being changed to `Mr X`:

```
string userInputString = "Dr Watson, Mr Holmes, and Mrs Smith";
userInputString = Regex.Replace(userInputString,
    "(Mr|Mrs|Miss|Ms|Dr) [A-Z][a-z]*", "Mr X");
Console.WriteLine(userInputString);
```

Clearly what we want to do is use whatever text has been captured by the first title-matching group, and substitute that into the replacement text. We can do this with the `$\groupNumber` syntax, where `groupNumber` is the position the group appears in the regular expression pattern. We need to add it to our replacement text, so the code becomes:

181

```
string userInputString = "Dr Watson, Mr Holmes, and Mrs Smith";
userInputString = Regex.Replace(userInputString,
    "(Mr|Mrs|Miss|Ms|Dr) [A-Z][a-z]*", "$1 X");
Console.WriteLine(userInputString);
```

We can use our Regular Expression Tester to demonstrate this, as shown below where the `Replace()` button is used:

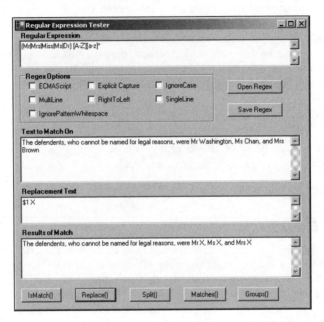

As we can see from the above screenshot, $ followed by a number indicates the group number that should be used in the replacement text, in this case the first group. There are a number of additional substitution characters available, as shown in the table below:

Character	Description
$*group*	Substitutes with the group number specified by *group*
${*name*}	Substitutes the last substring matched by a (?<*name*>) group
$$	Substitutes a literal $ character
$&	Substitutes the entire match
$`	Substitutes all the text of the input string before the match
$'	Substitutes all the text of the input string after the match
$+	Substitutes the last group captured
$_	Substitutes the entire input string

We have already seen the $group used in our previous example. However, we could also have used $+ as the last group captured, since in our example the only group captured in the match was also the first group, our title group.

An alternative to using group numbers is to give the group a name and substitute using that group name. Our regular expression could be:

```
(?<title>Mr|Mrs|Miss|Ms|Dr) [A-Z][a-z]*
```

and our replacement string would be:

```
${title} X
```

Remember that regular expressions and the replacement text are case sensitive, so if we name our group `title`, then using `Title` as the name in the replacement pattern won't work. No errors will be thrown, but we'll see something like this:

```
The defendants, who can't be named for legal reasons, were ${Title} X,
${Title} X, and ${Title} X.
```

The regex engine could find no group called `Title` so instead it assumed we want to replace with the text {Title}.

Backreferences

Within our regular expression, backreferences allow us to match the same characters as a previous group. A common example is matching repeated words. The syntax for matching a previous group is \groupNumber or \k<groupName>. However, as always we must remember when using it in code that we need to add a "\" in front, so it becomes \\k<groupName>.

Let's say we want to replace all repeated words with just the one original word. We could use the following regular expression:

```
(\b[a-zA-Z]+\b)\s\1
```

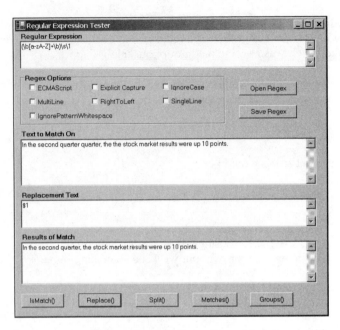

This will match one or more letters, bounded on either side by a word boundary, all of which is inside a capturing group. Then we match a whitespace character and, using a backreference, we match whatever the first group matched. In the Regular Expression Tester, the replacement text is simply $1; we substitute the match for the text matched for in the first group. By clicking the Replace() button, we correct the two double-word problems in the sentence.

Instead of a number, we could have given the group a name and backreferenced it by name, which does the same thing in this case:

```
(?<firstWord>\b[a-zA-Z]+\b)\s\k<firstWord>
```

Something to be aware of with backreferences is how they could be confused when specifying octal numbers. \1 to \9 will always be treated as backreferences. Any number with a leading "0", for example, \040, will be treated as an octal number referring to an ASCII character, as we saw in the previous chapter. If there is no leading zero then it will be treated as a backreference, so long as there is a matching group to backreference. If we have eleven groups then \11 will match the eleventh group; if we had only ten groups, then \11 would be treated as an octal number indicating an ASCII character.

Advanced Groups

We've seen the three basic and more common groups: capturing, non-capturing, and capturing-by-name. However, there are a number of advanced groups that we need to discuss.

Positive Look-Ahead Assertion: (?=)

This specifies that the pattern in the brackets must be found to the right of the assertion. The pattern will not form part of the final match. For example, let's consider the following input string:

```
The languages were Java, C#.NET, VB.NET, C, JScript.NET, Pascal
```

We could use the following regular expression on this input string:

```
\S+(?=\.NET)
```

We would then get these results:

```
C#
VB
JScript
```

Negative Look-Ahead Assertion: (?!)

This specifies that the pattern must not be found immediately to the right of the assertion. As before, the pattern will not form part of the final match. Let's consider the following input string:

```
123A 456c 789 111C
```

We could use the following regular expression on this input string:

```
\d{3}(?![A-Z])
```

We would then get these results as they are not followed by a capital letter:

```
456
789
```

Positive Look-Behind Assertion: (?<=)

This specifies that the pattern in the brackets must be found to the left of the assertion. The pattern will not form part of the final match. Let's consider the following input string:

```
New Mexico, West Virginia, Washington, New England
```

We could use the following regular expression on this input string:

```
(?<=New )([A-Z][a-z]+)
```

185

We would then get these results:

```
Mexico
England
```

Negative Look-Behind Assertion: (?<!)

This specifies that the pattern must not be found immediately to the left of the assertion. As before, the pattern will not form part of the final match. Let's consider the following input string:

```
123A 456F 789C 111A
```

We could use the following regular expression on this input string:

```
(?<!1)\d{2}[A-Z]
```

We would then get these results:

```
56F
89C
```

Non-Backtracking: (?>)

This prevents the regex engine from backtracking in an attempt to match in the event of a failure, and is also known as a greedy sub-expression. Let's say we want to match all words ending in "ing". Let's use the following as our input string:

```
He was very trusting
```

To get the entire text we would use the following regular expression:

```
.*ing
```

However, if we turn off backtracking we will find no matches:

```
(?>.*)ing
```

Comparing Advanced Groups

Strictly speaking, these are assertions rather than groups; they assert (insist) that a pattern must exist at a specific place. The patterns that the assertion groups match do not form part of the final match, and so they cannot be used in backreferencing.

The first two advanced groups described match a pattern to the right of the assertion; they look ahead to see if the pattern exists. The positive look-ahead needs the existence of the pattern for the whole match to be successful. Conversely, the negative look-ahead checks to see the pattern does not exist, and if it does then no match can be made, and the whole match fails.

So, let's use our Regular Expression Tester with the following input string:

```
A1 B 2 C D3 E4
```

We can use a positive look-ahead assertion such as this:

```
[A-Z](?=\d)
```

This will produce the following matches:

```
A
D
E
```

Note that even though the assertion's pattern (here just \d) must be matched, it does not form part of the final match results. We can change the regular expression to a negative look-ahead assertion:

```
[A-Z](?!\d)
```

Now the matches will be:

```
B
C
```

In other words, a match will only be made when there is no following digit.

The next two groups are identical assertions, except they look to the immediate left of the assertion (look behind themselves) for the matching pattern. Again, a positive one asserts the pattern must exist for a successful whole match and the negative one asserts that the pattern must not exist for a successful match.

So, let's use the same input string as for the look-ahead examples, but change to a positive look-behind assertion:

```
(?<=[A-Z])\d
```

This will match any digits where they are immediately preceded by a letter in the range A to Z, producing the following matches:

```
1
3
4
```

The same thing but with a negative look-behind assertion is:

```
(?<![A-Z])\d
```

This matches any digit that it is not preceded by a character in the range A to Z and produces:

```
2
```

The final group is the non-backtracking group, which is perhaps the least obvious to understand. The regex engine will do its best to make a match. Let's demonstrate this with an example that has been simplified to make it easier to understand. Let's say we want to match a URL ending in .com; we could create a regular expression like this:

```
www\.(.*)\.com
```

This matches www, followed by a period character, then one or more of any characters inside a capturing group, followed by another period, and then finally by com. We can use the Regular Expression Tester to test this.

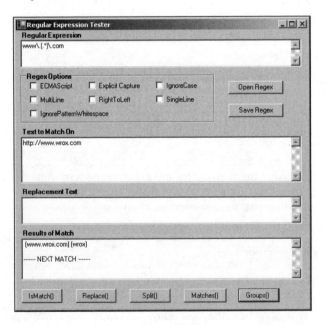

In the screenshot, the Groups() button has been clicked and we can see that the first group, containing ".*", has matched wrox. Intuitively, the "." should match any character, while the "*" should match one or more of any character, so you may be interested to discover why the group has not also matched the .com part.

To make a successful match the whole regular expression has to be matched; the regex engine cannot just ignore the .com part. Like a results-only dating agency, the regex engine is very keen to make a match. Therefore, what it does is backtrack until it can make a match; let's see how it is thinking.

Its first attempt might be:

Regular Expression	Match characters	Match Made?
www.	www.	Yes
(.*)	wrox.com	Yes
.com		No

It failed on the first pass because the group (.*) has matched all the remaining characters and so .com cannot be matched. On the next pass, the regex engine backtracks a character:

Regular Expression	Match characters	Match Made?
www.	www.	Yes
(.*)	wrox.co	Yes
.com	m	No

That's still not enough for a whole match. Now, the regex engine keeps backtracking a character until finally it makes a match:

Regular Expression	Match characters	Match Made?
www.	www.	Yes
(.*)	wrox	Yes
.com	.com	Yes

All this backtracking is hard work and inefficient. The non-backtracking group allows us to turn off backtracking and increases efficiency. Let's change our regular expression to the non-backtracking group and try it in the Regular Expression Tester to see what happens:

```
www\.(?>.*)\.com
```

What we find now is that no matches are made. The problem is the regex engine tests just the first option (where .* matches everything including .com) and as that fails, and backtracking is turned off for the group, then no match can be made. In this circumstance, we need to change our regular expression to:

```
www\.(?>[^.]*)\.com
```

This successfully matches because we look for any character until a period character is found. That way the .com bit isn't matched by the brackets. It's a more efficient regular expression as it removes the need for backtracking. However, it won't match sub-domains like www.domain.subdomain.com. Also, note that the non-backtracking group is also a non-capturing group – its value is not captured and made available for later use.

Making Decisions in Regular Expressions

We saw simple decision making with the alternation character "|" earlier in this chapter. However, regular expressions provide two further advanced decision-making instructions, as discussed now.

Expression alternations can have either of the following general syntaxes:

```
(?(expression)yes|no)
```

```
(?(?=expression)yes|no)
```

If expression is matched, then matching the yes regular expression will be attempted. Otherwise, the no regular expression is attempted. The no regular expression is optional. It is important to note that expression, the pattern that makes the decision, is zero width, which means the yes or no regexes will commence matching from the same place as expression.

Let's look at the following input string as an example:

```
1A CB 3A 5C 3B
```

Consider the following regular expression:

```
(?(\d)\dA|[A-Z]B)
```

Using this regular expression, we get these results:

```
1A
CB
3A
```

Name alternations have the following general syntax:

```
(?(name)yes|no)
```

If the name regular expression in the group is matched then matching the yes regular expression is attempted. Otherwise, matching the no regular expression is attempted. The no regular expression is optional.

Let's demonstrate this with the following input string:

```
77-77A 69-AA 57-B
```

We'll use the following regular expression:

```
(\d7)?-(?(1)\d\d[A-Z]|[A-Z][A-Z])
```

This will produce these matches:

```
77-77A
-AA
```

The decision-making regular expression syntax can be quite confusing if we forget that matching of the yes or no regular expressions starts from the same place as the regex pattern that did the test. Let's take the example regex:

```
(?(\d)A|B)
```

and try it with the input string:

```
1A CB 3A 5C 3B
```

Using the Regular Expression Tester you will see the following:

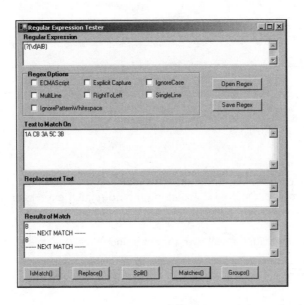

Given `1A` and `3A` are there, why have they not been matched? Well, the reason is that, although the pattern that decides the `yes` or no test (`\d`) is successful, our `yes` regular expression (here simply an actual `A` character) does not match. The `yes` test starts in the same place as the decision test, that is with the digit and, as `A` is clearly not a digit, the `yes` regex fails even though the decision making regex was successful. To make our regex work in the above example, we need to change it to this:

```
( ? (\d) \dA | B)
```

Now the results are:

```
1A
B
3A
B
```

The important thing is that the `yes` regular expression must at least match the same pattern as the decision making regex or else it will fail. It does not have to be the same, just so long as it matches the same pattern. For example, this would work for our example too:

```
( ? (\d) \wA | B)
```

This is because `\w` will match a word character and word characters include digits.

Setting Options within a Regex

The regex syntax allows us to change the regex options within a group. For example, let's say we want to set a group to be case insensitive:

```
(?i:[a-z])
```

Now the [a-z] will also match A-Z regardless of the global options set when we created the regex. To remove an option, we simply use the "-" sign. For example, to make it case sensitive we would use:

```
(?-i:[a-z])
```

There are five options we can set inline, as shown in the following table.

RegexOption	Flag	Description
ExplicitCapture	n	This specifies that the only valid captures are explicitly named or numbered groups of the form
IgnoreCase	i	This specifies case-insensitive matching
IgnorePatternWhitespace	x	This specifies that unescaped whitespace is excluded from the pattern and enables comments following a # sign
MultiLine	m	This specifies multiline mode, which changes the meaning of the ^ and $ characters
SingleLine	s	This specifies that the only valid captures are explicitly named or numbered groups of the form

We can set as many of the options at once as we wish, for example:

```
(?n-i:[a-z])
```

This sets the group to ExplicitCapture and case-sensitive.

Rules of the Regex Engine

We've now covered all the regex syntax for this book. We'll finish off by looking at some rules of how the regex engine does its matching. To make life easier for us there are some basic rules to remember:

Rule 1: The regex engine will start matching as soon as possible in the input string. It will look one character at a time until it finds the start of a match.

```
Input string = 123 ABC 456 DEF
Regex = [A-Z]*
```

This will start matching at the ABC.

Rule 2: Having found the start of a match, the regex engine will continue to match until it hits a character that is not permitted by the pattern.

```
Input string = 123 ABC 456 DEF
Regex = [A-Z]*
```

The first match will start at ABC and stop when it hits the space, which is not permitted by this pattern.

Rule 3: The regex engine is very greedy – it's looking to make as big a match as the pattern allows.

```
Input String = 'Dr Watson's watch'
Regex = '.*'
```

The match made is the whole string. The regex pattern says match a single quote, followed by any characters, and then ending with another single quote. So 'Dr Watson' also matches; there is no need for the regex engine to continue and match the other characters, it already has a pattern that matches. However, the regex engine continues (see Rule 2 – the match continues until an invalid character is hit) and finds that it can also match:

```
s watch'
```

Let's see how things change if we make the "*" a non-greedy quantifier by adding a "?" after it:

```
Input String = 'Dr Watson's watch'
Regex = '.*?'
```

Now in this case the match is only:

```
'Dr Watson'
```

The regex engine has got to the second ' and now, having sufficient characters for a match, has stopped. That is, it's non-greedy, it has enough for a match and does not try to grab any more.

Rule 4: The regex engine is keen to find a match and will backtrack if necessary to make a match.

```
Input string = 'Hello world' said K & R.
Regex = '.*'
```

This will match:

```
'Hello World'
```

However, it wouldn't if it wasn't for backtracking. We saw in Rule 3 that the regex engine is looking for the biggest match it can make. The .* says match any character zero or more times. So, while the "'" after world is enough for a match, the regex engine wants more and continues looking while Rule 2 does not apply (so long as a character that does not match is not found). The regex engine continues right until it hits the end of the input string in this case, as the "." character matches all of the characters. However, it has a problem: the pattern specifies that there must be a "'" character at the end of the pattern, but, as it has gobbled up all the characters with the .*, it means no "'" can be matched on. So the regex engine, ever keen to make a match, backtracks a character at a time until it gets back to the "'" after world; now it has its match.

We can see what happens if we disable back tracking by using a non backtracking group:

```
Input string = 'Hello world' said K & R.
Regex = '(?>.*)'
```

Now this time no match is made because the .* has matched all the characters right to the end, and because we have told it not to backtrack, it can't go back and make a match based on 'Hello World'.

Rule 5: The regex engine, given a choice, will always take the first option.
When we use the "|" character to give alternatives, the regex engine will try to match the first one, if that doesn't match then the second, then the third, and so on.

```
Input string = 1234 123 3456
Regex = (\d{2}|\d{3}|\d{4})
```

This produces the following matches:

```
12
34
12
34
56
```

We can see that, even though it could choose to match 1234 or 123 or 3456 as complete matches, it has simply gone for the first of the alternatives and matches two digits each time.

It's handy to keep the five rules in mind, as often the regex does things that seem surprising.

Summary

In this chapter, we looked at:

- ❏ How regular expression syntax allows us to group a pattern
- ❏ How we can use groups in the .NET Framework and access their values using the `Group` class
- ❏ How groups can be used inside the substitution part of a `Replace()` method
- ❏ How we can use previously matched groups inside the regular expression itself

In the next chapter, we'll be using the regular expression syntax learned so far to create a number of useful real-world examples.

C#

Text Manipulation

Handbook

7

7

Regular Expression Patterns

In this chapter, we'll be taking a detailed look at many practical examples of regular expression patterns. Not only will it give you a library of useful patterns, but it will also help you see how regular expressions are assembled. This should be a useful guide for learning how to construct regular expressions, as well as providing you with a set of useful regular expressions for manipulating common data.

Validating Characters

We start with some basic and commonly used regular expressions to check whether a string contains any invalid characters. Our first set of methods look at the validation of sequences of letters, numbers, and spaces:

Pattern	Description
[^a-zA-Z\\d]	Checks that the text does **not** contain letters of the alphabet, numbers, or spaces
[^a-zA-Z\\d]	Checks that the text does **not** contain letters of the alphabet or numbers
[^a-zA-Z]	Checks that the text does **not** contain letters of the alphabet or spaces

These are useful where you have user input and what to make sure it only contains the characters you want. Using each of the regular expressions above is very similar; for example, to test that variable userInputString contains characters other than those of the alphabet, numbers, and spaces:

```
if (Regex.IsMatch(userInputString, "[^a-zA-Z\\d ]"))
{
  // Invalid Chars found
}
else
{
   //Valid chars only found
}
```

It is normally advisable, however, to match only on what is present, rather than on what is not. It is easier attempting to match on characters that are or should be there, rather than on those that are not. However, these patterns can be useful to match invalid characters if a previous match failed, for instance. In the following simple matches, we will be matching negatively as in the case used above.

Validating Numbers

In this section, we look at various methods for validating different types of number.

Numbers Only

We start with a simple regular expression to check that the passed string contains only numerical characters:

Pattern	Description
[^\\d.]	Checks if the string contains characters other than numbers or a decimal point

For this pattern, anything that's not a digit or decimal place is considered invalid. Note that normally the "." is a special regex character meaning match any character and if we wanted to match an actual "." we'd need to escape it like this: "\.". However, this is not necessary when using the square brackets to specify which characters to match.

We can test to see if invalid characters exist in userInputString with the following code:

```
if (Regex.IsMatch(userInputString, "[^\\d.]"))
{
   // Invalid Chars found
}
else
{
   //Valid chars only found
}
```

Integer Numbers Only

Our next regular expression checks for integers:

```
^((\+|-)\d)?\d*$
```

Unlike the simple character matching expressions we have seen previously, this one matches a specific pattern. It specifies that the string may optionally start with a "+" or "-" sign, but that if it does, then it must be then followed by at least one digit, then followed by zero or more digits. The "$" at the end ensures that no other characters are allowed after the last digit. Note that because "+" is part of the regular expression language we had to escape it in the first group, \+, to tell the regex engine that we mean an actual "+", and not the regex syntax "+".

The following would be valid:

```
+1
234
-2445234
```

whereas, these would not:

```
++123
ABC
1.23
1234C
```

Previously if a match was found, it meant invalid characters were present. This time if a match is found it means the input string is valid. It makes more sense to check for the string being valid rather than invalid as happened previously, because you are not just checking for the existence of certain characters, but also specifying that the characters must be in a specific order, so +123 is valid but 123+ is not. The code to use the expression is therefore:

```
if (Regex.IsMatch(userInputString, "^((\\+|-)\\d)?\\d*$"))
{
    // Input string valid
}
else
{
    // Invalid input string
}
```

Floating-Point Numbers

Assume you want to check for positive or negative floating-point numbers:

```
^(?:\+|-)?\d+(?:\.\d+)?$
```

As a floating-point number can be identical to an integer (1 is a valid integer and floating-point number), the regular expression will be valid for both integers and floating-point numbers.

This time the regular expression specifies that digits, minus signs, and decimal points are to be permitted. The `^(?:\+|-)?` specifies that the characters must start at beginning of the string, (our valid number can't be in the middle of other characters. It also specifies, in a non-capturing group, that we can start with a "+" or a "-". We need to put the "+" and "-" check in a group, because of the "|", which matches either the regex pattern on the left, our "+" sign, or the regex pattern on the right, our minus sign. If we don't put the "\+|-" in a group, we will get erroneous results – the pattern will look for either just a "+" sign or a "-" sign with a number following it. As we are not interested in the results of the capture, a non-capturing group has been used – an alternative is to set the `ExplictCapture` option when using the `Regex` object.

Next, we specify that one or more digits can follow using the `\d+`. This matches one or more digits before the decimal point. Finally we have `(\.\d+)?$`, the part of the regular expression that matches a decimal point and any numbers following it. It matches a literal period character; remember that this character is part of the regex language and so we need to escape it when it's the actual character we want to match. We then match one or more digits. Finally, as there is a "?" after the group, it means the group must be matched zero or more times. Essentially it makes the group optional, which allows numbers with no decimal point to be matched successfully:

```
if (Regex.IsMatch(userInputString, "^(?:\\+|-)?\\d+(?:\\.\\d+)?$"))
{
  // Input string valid
}
else
{
  // Invalid input string
}
```

Validating a Telephone Number

So far, the data being checked has been simple. However, telephone numbers are more of a challenge to validate. The problems are:

- Phone numbers differ from country to country

- There are different ways of entering a valid number, for example, adding the national or international code, or not

One way to clarify what we expect in terms of the format of the telephone number is to split the telephone number input into separate boxes, for example, one box labeled for the international dialing code, one for the area code, one for the number itself, and one for the extension number (if applicable).

An alternative, which we look at here, is to use regular expressions to match variations of international phone numbers. We need to specify more than just the valid characters – we also need to specify the format of the data. For example, all of the following are valid:

```
+1 (123) 123 4567
+1123123 456
+44 (123) 123 4567
+44 (123) 123 4567 ext 123
+44 20 7893 4567
```

> *You can find more information on world telephone numbering systems at* http://phonebooth.interocitor.net/wtng/.

The variations that our regular expression needs to deal with (optionally separated by spaces) are:

Number	Format
The international number	"+" followed by 1 to 3 digits (optional)
The local area code	2 to 5 digits, sometimes in parentheses (compulsory)
The actual subscriber number	3 to 10 digits, sometimes with spaces (compulsory)
An extension number	2 to 5 digits, preceded by x, xtn, extn, pax, pbx, or extension, and sometimes in parentheses

Obviously there will be countries where this won't work, which is something that you will need to deal with based on where your customers and partners are. The following regular expression is rather complex compared to the last one:

```
^(\+\d{1,3} ?)?(\(\d{1,5}\)|\d{1,5}) ?\d{3} ?\d{0,7}
( (x|xtn|ext|extn|extension)? \.? ?\d{1,5})?$
```

We will need to set the case-insensitive option with this, as well as the explicit capture option. Although complex, if we break it down, it's quite straightforward. In fact, its length meant it had to be split across two lines; make sure you type it in on one line.

We'll start with the pattern that matches an international dialing code:

```
(\+\d{1,3} ?)?
```

So far, we're matching a plus sign (\+) followed by 1 to 3 digits (\d{1,3}) and an optional space (?). Remember that since the "+" character is a special character, we add a "\" character in front of it to specify that we mean an actual "+" character. The characters are wrapped inside parentheses to specify a group of characters. We allow an optional space, and match this entire group of characters zero or one times – as indicated by the "?" character after the closing parenthesis of the group.

Next, let's look at the pattern to match an area code:

```
(\(\d{1,5}\)|\d{1,5})
```

This pattern is contained in parentheses, which designate it as a group of characters, and matches either 1 to 5 digits in parentheses ((\d{1,5})) or just 1 to 5 digits (\d{1,5}). Again, since the parenthesis characters are special characters in regular expression syntax and we want to match actual parentheses, we need the "\" character in front of them. Also note the use of the pipe symbol (|), which means "OR" or "match either of these two patterns".

Next, we match the subscriber number:

```
?\d{3} ?\d{0,7}
```

Note that there is a space before the first "?" – this space and question mark mean, "match zero or one space". This is followed by three or four digits (\d{3}), as although there are always three digits in the US, there are often four in the UK. Then, another "zero or one space", and finally between zero and seven digits (\d{0,7}).

Finally, we add the part to cope with an optional extension number:

```
( (x|xtn|ext|extn|extension)? \.? ?\d{1,5})?$
```

This group is optional, since its parentheses are followed by a question mark. The group itself checks for a space, optionally followed by one of x, ext, xtn, extn, and extension, followed by zero or one periods (note the \ characters, since "." is a special character in regular expression syntax), followed by zero or one space, followed by between two and five digits.

Putting these four patterns together, we can construct the entire regular expression, apart from the surrounding syntax: recall that the regular expression starts with "^" and ends with "$". The "^" character specifies that the pattern must be matched at the beginning of the string, and the "$" character specifies the pattern must be matched at the end of the string. This means that our string must match the pattern completely – it can contain no other characters before or after the pattern that is matched.

Therefore, with the regular expression explained, we can now show it in use, remembering of course that we need to add an extra "\" in front of the existing ones:

```
if (Regex.IsMatch(userInputString,
                  "^(\\+\\d{1,3} ?)?(\\(\\d{1,5}\\)|" +
                  "\\d{1,5}) ?\\d{3} ?\\d{0,7}" +
                  "( (x|xtn|ext|extn|extension)? \\.? ?\\d{1,5})?$",
                  RegexOptions.IgnoreCase |
                  RegexOptions.ExplicitCapture))
{
  MessageBox.Show("Valid");
}
else
{
  MessageBox.Show("Invalid");
}
```

Note in this case that it is important to set the IgnoreCase option; otherwise, our regular expression could fail to match the ext parts.

> **As explained in Chapter 5, an alternative to using "\" as an escape character is to prefix the regular expression with the "@" character.**

Validating a Postal Code

We just about managed to check worldwide telephone numbers, but to do the same for postal codes would be something of a major challenge. Instead, we'll create a method that only checks for US Zip codes and UK postcodes. If we needed to check for other countries, then the code would need modifying. You may find that checking more than one or two postal codes in one regex begins to get unmanageable, and it may well be easier to have an individual regex for each country's postal code you need to check. For this purpose though, we will combine the regular expression for the UK and the US:

```
^(\d{5}(-\d{4})?|[a-z][a-z]?\d\d? ?\d[a-z][a-z])$
```

This is actually in two parts: the first part, which checks for zip codes and the second part, which checks UK post codes. We'll start by looking at the zip code part.

Zip codes can be represented in one of two formats – as five digits (12345), or five digits followed by a dash and four digits (12345-1234). The Zip code regular expression to match these is:

```
\d{5}(-\d{4})?
```

This matches five digits, followed by an optional non-capturing group that matches a dash followed by four digits.

For a regular expression that covers UK post codes, let's consider their various formats. UK postcode formats are one or two letters followed by either one or two digits, followed by an optional space, followed by a digit, and then two letters. Additionally, some central London postcodes look like this: SE2V 3ER, with a letter at the end of the first part. Currently it is only some of those starting with SE, WC, and W, but that may change. Valid examples of UK postcode include: CH3 9DR, PR29 1XX, M27 1AE, WC1V 2ER, and C27 3AH.

Based on this, our pattern is:

```
([a-z][a-z]?\d\d?|[a-z]{2}\d[a-z]) ?\d[a-z][a-z]
```

These two patterns are combined using the | character to "match one or the other" and grouped using parentheses. We then add the "^" character at the start and "$" character at the end of the pattern to be sure that the only information in the string is the postal code. Although postal codes should be upper case, it is still valid for them to be lower case, so we have also set the case-insensitive option when we use the regular expression:

```
^(\d{5}(-\d{4})?|([a-z][a-z]?\d\d?|[a-z]{2}\d[a-z]) ?\d[a-z][a-z])$
```

Using the regular expression is much the same as it was with the previous examples. Again we must use the extra "\" character when using a string:

```
if (Regex.IsMatch(userInputString,
            "^(\\d{5}(-\\d{4})?|([a-z][a-z]" +
            "\\d\\d?|[a-z]{2}\\d[a-z]) ?" +
            "\\d[a-z][a-z])$",
            RegexOptions.IgnoreCase |
            RegexOptions.ExplicitCapture))
{
  MessageBox.Show("Valid");
}
else
{
  MessageBox.Show("Invalid");
}
```

Validating an E-mail Address

Before we start working on a regular expression to match e-mail addresses, we need to look at the types of valid e-mail addresses we can have:

❑   someone@mailserver.com

❑   someone@mailserver.info

❑   someone.something@mailserver.com

❑   someone.something@subdomain.mailserver.com

❑   someone@mailserver.co.uk

❑   someone@subdomain.mailserver.co.uk

❑   someone.something@mailserver.co.uk

❑   someone@mailserver.org.uk

❑   some.one@subdomain.mailserver.org.uk

Also, if you examine the SMTP RFC (http://www.ietf.org/rfc/rfc0821.txt), we can have:

❑   someone@123.113.209.32

❑   """Paul Wilton"""@somedomain.com

That's quite a list and contains many variations we need to cope with, so we would be best breaking it down. Firstly, there are a couple of things to note about the two immediately above. The latter two versions are not often used, but are provided for. In fact, the RFC is ambiguous and suggests that the IP address version of the e-mail should be written as: someone@[123.113.209.32]. However, the RFC also allows domain names to be provided on either side, so we shall use the more commonly used form shown above. Regarding the latter version, only a few e-mail servers actually support this form. However, we shall cover it for completeness. We need to break up the e-mail address into separate parts, and we will concern ourselves with the part after the "@" symbol first.

Validating an IP Address

This is the simplest and so is the one we will cover first. An e-mail address can either have a domain name or an IP address following the "@" symbol. An IP address consists of a *dotted quad* notation of four 8-bit numbers written in decimal form, separated by dots. There are no leading zeroes used. Regular expressions are a text pattern matching language, so we cannot test for ranges of numbers and have to specify instead exactly how they appear. As they are repeated, let's deal first with how to match just one of the numbers:

```
(1??\d{1,2}|2[0-4]\d|25[0-5])
```

The first option covers the largest number of possibilities. It defines a lazy optional 1, followed by one or two digits. This allows every number from 0 to 199. A lazy wildcard is chosen, as there are more numbers that don't begin with a 1, than those that do, so it makes sense to attempt to match against those first. Then the alternation character is reached, which defines that we can have 2, followed by any number from 0-4, followed by any number: 200-249. The last group specifies that we can have 25, followed by any number from 0-5. It is then wrapped in a group to allow us to anchor the whole expression by specifying either that it is a whole expression, or that it is surrounded by periods, which is covered now.

207

Making this part of an IP address is trivial. The expression looks as follows:

```
^((1??\d{1,2}|2[0-4]\d|25[0-5])\.){3}(1??\d{1,2}|2[0-4]\d|25[0-5])$
```

The first thing it does is specify the start of the string, and then it adds an extra group bracket as it is going to check for a repetition of the pattern. The pattern is the same as the above, with a period following it. This matches fine. However, if you wanted to pull out the components of the IP address, then you couldn't do it. You would have to remove the repetition to do so. In addition, "\." would have to be contained within a non-capturing group. If this were part of a larger expression, the "^" and "$" would be removed.

This matches an IP address fine, but you may also want to exclude certain addresses like those starting with 10, 127, or 192.168 for private address ranges. It would depend on the nature of the application.

Validating a Domain Name

Everything has become more complicated since Unicode domain names have been allowed. However, the e-mail RFC still doesn't allow these so we shall stick with the traditional definition of how a domain can be described using ASCII. A domain name consists of a dot-separated list of words with the last word being between 2 and 4 characters long. It was often the case that if a two letter country word was used, then there would be at least two parts to the domain name before it – a grouping domain (.co, .ac, etc.) and a specific domain name before it. However, with the advent of the .tv names, this is no longer the case. We could make this very specific and provide for the allowed top-level domains (TLDs), but that would make the regular expression very large and it would be more productive to perform a DNS lookup instead.

Each part of a domain name has certain rules it must follow. It can contain any letter, or number, or a hyphen, but it must start with a letter. The exception is that, at any point in the domain name, you can use "#", followed by a number, which represents the ASCII code for that letter, or in Unicode, the 16-bit Unicode value. Knowing this, let's begin to build up our regular expression, firstly with the name part, assuming that we have the IgnoreCase option set:

```
([a-z]|#\d+)([a-z0-9-]|#\d+)*([a-z0-9]|#\d+)
```

This breaks the domain into three parts. In all parts there is the option of using the #nn notation, so we won't mention them there. The RFC doesn't specify how many digits can be contained here, so neither shall we. The first part must only contain an ASCII letter; the second must contain zero or more of a letter, number, or hyphen, and the third must contain either a letter or number. The top-level domain has more restrictions, as shown:

```
[a-z]{2,4}
```

This restricts us to a 2, 3, or 4-letter top-level domain. So, putting it all together, with the periods:

```
^(([a-z]|#\d+?)([a-z0-9-]|#\d+?)*([a-z0-9]|#\d+?)\.)+([a-z]{2,4})$
```

Again, the domain name is anchored at the beginning and end of the string. The first thing is to add an extra group to allow one or more "name." portions, and then a 2 to 4 letter domain name anchored at the end in its own group. We have also made most of the wildcards lazy. Because much of the pattern is similar, it makes sense to do this as otherwise it would require too much backtracking. However, we have left the second group with a greedy wildcard; it will match as much as it can, up until it reaches a character that does not match. Then it will only backtrack one position to attempt the third group match. This is more resource-efficient than a lazy match is in this case, as it could be constantly going forward to attempt the match. One backtrack per name is an acceptable amount of extra processing.

Validating a Person's Address

Now we can attempt to validate the part before the "@" sign. The RFC specifies that it can contain any ASCII character with a code in the range from 33 to 126. We are assuming that we are matching against ASCII only, and so we can assume that there are only 128 characters that the engine will match against. This being the case, it is simpler to just exclude the required values:

```
[^<>()\[\]\\.,;:@"\x00-\x20\x7F]+
```

Using this we are saying that we allow any number of characters, as long as none of them are those contained within the square brackets. The "[", "]", and "\" characters have to be escaped. However, the RFC allows for other kinds of matches. You can escape any of the previous characters using a "\" character. This means that carriage returns are also permitted in the person's address. However, it is highly unlikely that anyone would use this version of the regular expression, so we won't use the SingleLine option here. However, we do need to allow for the other excluded characters, so we need to add an | match of:

```
\\.
```

Additionally, there is yet another form that can be used for a mailbox name, and that is a quoted string. This takes the form of any string, including spaces, surrounded by three double quote characters. The string can contain anything except carriage returns, line feeds, double quotes, or backslashes. So the regular expression looks as follows:

```
"""[^\x0A\x0D"\\]+"""
```

You can escape characters in the quoted string, though by using backslash. However, as we have decided not to allow carriage returns, the only character we need to escape is "\":

```
"""([^\x0A\x0D"\\]|\\\\)+"""
```

Our full regular expression for the mailbox name would therefore be:

```
^(([^<>()\[\]\\.,;:@"\x00-\x20\x7F]|
\\.)+|("""([^\x0A\x0D"\\]|\\\\)+"""))$
```

This should obviously be all on one line, and the entire string must match.

Validating the Complete Address

Now we have seen all the previous sections, we can build up a regular expression for the entire e-mail address. First, everything up to and including the "@" sign:

```
^(([^<>()\[\]\\.,;:@"\x00-\x20\x7F]|
\\.)+|("""([^\x0A\x0D"\\]|\\\\)+"""))@
```

That was straightforward. Now for the domain or IP address part. First the domain name:

```
^(([^<>()\[\]\\.,;:@"\x00-\x20\x7F]|\\.)+|
("""([^\x0A\x0D"\\]|\\\\)+"""))@(([a-z]|#\d+?)([a-z0-9-]|#\d+?)*
([a-z0-9]|#\d+?)\.)+([a-z]{2,4})
```

This matches the traditional style of e-mail addresses. However, we want to allow for IP addresses as well, and this is quite easily done. If we click the ExplicitCapture option, then add the named groups as indicated below, then it will match the person and the domain name (or IP address):

```
^(?<person>([^<>()\[\]\\.,;:@"\x00-\x20\x7F]|\\.)+|
("""([^\x0A\x0D"\\]|\\\\)+"""))@(?<domain>(([a-z]|#\d+?)
([a-z0-9-]|#\d+?)*([a-z0-9]|#\d+?)\.)+([a-z]{2,4})|((1??\d{1,2}|
2[0-4]\d|25[0-5])\.){3}(1??\d{1,2}|2[0-4]\d|25[0-5])))$
```

This is a rather long expression, but it is provided as part of an enumeration in the code download. This will match against any kind of e-mail address, except those with carriage returns escaped. Test it in the Regular Expression Tester and you should see that it works fine. We have to put the choice between the domain name and the IP address in a group of its own so that either matches to the end of the string.

Analyzing an SMTP Log File

This section contains an example of analyzing a system file. In this example we are going to use regular expressions to extract information from an SMTP log file – to be more precise, from IIS's SMTP log file. For the example to work, the log file's extended properties are:

- ❏ date-time
- ❏ c-ip
- ❏ cs-username
- ❏ cs-method
- ❏ cs-uri-query
- ❏ sc-bytes
- ❏ cs-bytes
- ❏ time-taken

These properties are set from the General tab of the SMTP virtual server properties – either from IIS, or if you have Exchange 2000 installed, then from the exchange manager:

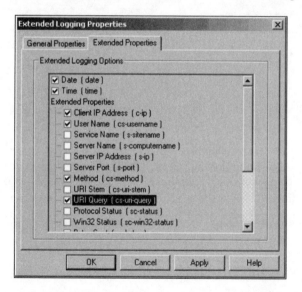

The program allows the user to select a log file and then it displays a list of the SMTP sessions and the actions taken, and highlights in red any potentially dubious sessions (attacks by a hacker, for example):

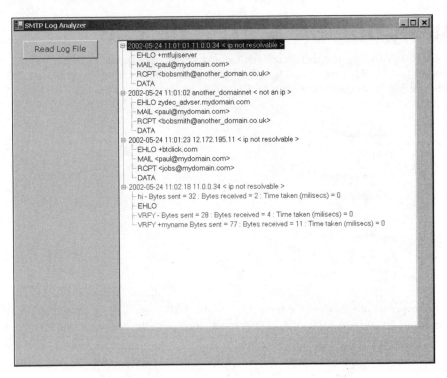

Most SMTP sessions consist of:

```
HELO or EHLO
MAIL
RCPT
DATA
QUIT
```

Therefore, those sessions are not logged in red. Those logged in red are sessions that include an SMTP command other than those, or where the time taken or the bytes sent or received are of an unusual size.

Our first task is to analyze the log files ourselves and see how the information is structured; a sample from a log file is shown below:

```
#Software: Microsoft Internet Information Services 5.0
#Version: 1.0
#Date: 2002-05-24 11:01:01
#Fields: date time c-ip cs-username cs-method cs-uri-query sc-bytes
cs-bytes time-taken
2002-05-24 11:01:01 11.0.0.34 mtfujiserver EHLO +mtfujiserver 331 17
170
2002-05-24 11:01:01 11.0.0.34 mtfujiserver MAIL
+FROM:+<paul@mydomain.com> 42 30 40
```

```
2002-05-24 11:01:01 11.0.0.34 mtfujiserver RCPT
+TO:+<bobsmith@another_domain.co.uk> 32 30 0
2002-05-24 11:01:01 11.0.0.34 mtfujiserver DATA
+<000001c20312$8844cc60$0400000a@mtfujiserver> 129 501 370
2002-05-24 11:01:02 - OutboundConnectionResponse -
220+another_domainnet+Mail+Service+ESMTP+(oceanus.uk.another_domain.ne
t) 54 0 781
2002-05-24 11:01:02 another_domainnet OutboundConnectionCommand EHLO
zydec_advser.mydomain.com 4 0 781
2002-05-24 11:01:02 another_domainnet OutboundConnectionResponse -
250-oceanus.uk.another_domain.net+Hello+host113-113-204-18.in-
addr.btopenworld.com+[213.123.214.118] 92 0 821
2002-05-24 11:01:02 another_domainnet OutboundConnectionCommand MAIL
FROM:<paul@mydomain.com> 4 0 821
2002-05-24 11:01:02 another_domainnet OutboundConnectionResponse -
250+<paul@mydomain.com>+is+syntactically+correct 48 0 851
2002-05-24 11:01:02 another_domainnet OutboundConnectionCommand RCPT
TO:<bobsmith@another_domain.co.uk> 4 0 861
2002-05-24 11:01:04 11.0.0.34 mtfujiserver QUIT mtfujiserver 74 4 0
2002-05-24 11:01:23 12.172.195.11 btclick.com EHLO +btclick.com 336 16
30
2002-05-24 11:01:23 12.172.195.11 btclick.com MAIL
+FROM:<paul@mydomain.com> 42 38 0
2002-05-24 11:01:23 12.172.195.11 btclick.com RCPT
+TO:<jobs@mydomain.com> 30 27 0
2002-05-24 11:01:23 12.172.195.11 btclick.com DATA
+<000101c20312$955140a0$0400000a@mtfujiserver> 129 664 311
2002-05-24 11:01:26 12.172.195.11 btclick.com QUIT btclick.com 74 4 0
2002-05-24 11:01:43 another_domainnet OutboundConnectionResponse -
250+<bobsmith@another_domain.co.uk>+verified 34 0 41389
2002-05-24 11:01:43 another_domainnet OutboundConnectionCommand DATA -
4 0 41399
2002-05-24 11:01:43 another_domainnet OutboundConnectionResponse -
354+Enter+message,+ending+with+"."+on+a+line+by+itself 54 0 41419
2002-05-24 11:01:43 another_domainnet OutboundConnectionResponse -
250+OK+id=17BCpT-000G0E-00 26 0 41519
2002-05-24 11:01:43 another_domainnet OutboundConnectionCommand QUIT -
4 0 41529
2002-05-24 11:01:43 another_domainnet OutboundConnectionResponse -
221+oceanus.uk.another_domain.net+closing+connection 43 0 41549
2002-05-24 11:02:18 11.0.0.34 - hi - 32 2 0
2002-05-24 11:02:22 11.0.0.34 - EHLO - 331 4 0
2002-05-24 11:02:26 11.0.0.34 - VRFY - 28 4 0
2002-05-24 11:02:31 11.0.0.34 - VRFY +myname 77 11 0
2002-05-24 11:02:36 11.0.0.34 - QUIT - 77 11 4186
```

The first thing to notice is that each individual command is on a single line. Above, it doesn't look that way, but that is due to the width constraints of a book; each line starts with a date. We can also see that each element of data (date, time, client-ip, and so on) is delimited by a space. Getting the data from an individual line should be quite easy. The tricky part is making sure all the information for each session goes together – it's particularly tricky because the server, as in the log above, can have numerous concurrent sessions. This means that we don't have a nice ordering of the lines into separate sessions; for example, the top of the log starts with a standard SMTP session sending an e-mail:

```
2002-05-24 11:01:01 11.0.0.34 mtfujiserver EHLO +mtfujiserver 331 17
170
2002-05-24 11:01:01 11.0.0.34 mtfujiserver MAIL
+FROM:+<paul@mydomain.com> 42 30 40
2002-05-24 11:01:01 11.0.0.34 mtfujiserver RCPT
+TO:+<bobsmith@another_domain.co.uk> 32 30 0
2002-05-24 11:01:01 11.0.0.34 mtfujiserver DATA
+<000001c20312$8844cc60$0400000a@mtfujiserver> 129 501 370
```

However, instead of a QUIT command line at this point, the log now contains data for another quite separate concurrent session:

```
2002-05-24 11:01:02 - OutboundConnectionResponse -
220+another_domainnet+Mail+Service+ESMTP+(oceanus.uk.another_domain.ne
t) 54 0 781
```

This continues for a few more lines before the final line from the first session suddenly appears:

```
2002-05-24 11:01:04 11.0.0.34 mtfujiserver QUIT mtfujiserver 74 4 0
```

This means our regular expression has to match the individual lines and data in a line, and somehow ensure the lines of a single session are contained within one match. Now it may well be possible to write such an expression but it would be fiendishly complex, span a number of lines, and be very difficult to maintain. Sometimes with regular expressions we need to know when to limit complexity – otherwise we'll end up with two pages of regular expression so complex that it makes mapping the Human Genome seem like a trivial task.

Instead, what we'll do is capture each line in a match and within that put each item of data in its own group. It means we'll have to use code to put the sessions together, but that will be much easier than using a regex – and almost certainly more efficient:

```
^(?<date>[^ #]+) (?<time>[^ ]+) (?<clientAddress>[^ -]+)
(?<clientName>[^ ]+) (?<method>[^ -]+) (?<uriQuery>[^ ]+)
(?<sentBytes>[\d]+) (?<receivedBytes>[\d]+) (?<timeTaken>[\d]+)
```

The limits of the page's width mean the single regex line has wrapped on to three lines. We have nine groups in our regular expression, each with a name indicating the data the group will hold. While it's not necessary to give the groups names, it will make our code easier to create and understand later on. Note that at the end of the first two lines there is a space character.

The regex is broken down in the table opposite. This table shows what happens when it is matched against an example log line of:

```
2002-05-24 11:01:01 11.0.0.34 mtfujiserver EHLO +mtfujiserver 331 17 170
```

214

Regular Expression	Description	What it matches
`^`	We will specify the `MultiLine` option in our code later on; this means the `^` matches the beginning of each line. Without the option set, it only matches the beginning of the input string.	Start of each new line
`(?<date>[^ #]+)`	This is a capturing group, named `date`, whose pattern is one or more space or hash (#) characters. The "#" character denotes a remarks line in the log so our code will ignore those. The space is the delimiter between log data fields. As it's a named group, it will always capture the group even if `ExplicitCapture` option is set.	2002-05-24
`(?<time>[^ ]+)`	This group, named `time`, matches one or more characters that are not a space.	11:01:01
`(?<clientAddress>[^ -]+)`	The `clientAddress` group matches one or more characters that are not a space or "-". When there is no data, IIS inserts a "-". We are not interested in logs with no client address as this indicates information received, rather than an SMTP command.	11.0.0.34
`(?<clientName>[^ ]+)`	The `clientName` group matches one or more characters that are not spaces.	mtfujiserver
`(?<method>[^ -]+)`	The `method` group matches one or more characters that are not a space or a "-" sign.	EHLO
`(?<uriQuery>[^ ]+)`	The `uriQuery` group matches one or more characters that are not a space.	+mtfujiserver
`(?<sentBytes>[\d]+)`	The `sentBytes` group matches one or more digits.	331
`(?<receivedBytes>[\d]+)`	The `receivedBytes` group matches one or more digits.	17
`(?<timeTaken>[\d]+)`	The `timeTaken` group matches one or more digits.	170

Now we have seen the regex, let's create a new Windows project that will use the regular expression to analyze the log.

Open Visual Studio .NET and create a new Windows project called SMTPLogAnalyze. Add a button, an open file dialog box, and a tree view control as shown below. The button is named cmdReadLogFile, and the open file dialog box and tree view control have their default names of OpenFileDialog1 and TreeView1.

At the start, the code looks as follows:

```
using System;
using System.Drawing;
using System.ComponentModel;
using System.Windows.Forms;
using System.Data;
using System.Collections;
using System.Text.RegularExpressions;
using System.IO;
using System.Net;

namespace CSharpSMTPLogAnalyser
{
    public class frmSMTPLogAnalyzer : System.Windows.Forms.Form
    {
```

Let's start examining the code proper by adding the code to the cmdReadLogFile.Click event, which shows the open file dialog to allow the user to pick the log file to be analyzed:

```
private void cmdReadLogFile_Click(object sender, System.EventArgs e)
{
    OpenFileDialog1.ShowDialog();
}
```

Now we need to add the code for the OpenFileDialog1.FileOk event; this code reads in the file and analyzes it. There's a lot of code so we'll examine it in stages. We'll start with the code that reads in the log file:

```
private void OpenFileDialog1_FileOk(object sender,
        System.ComponentModel.CancelEventArgs e)
{
    try
    {
        // Clear any pre-existing details;
        TreeView1.Nodes.Clear();

        // Create a hashtable object to hold details of sessions;
        Hashtable ipIndex = new Hashtable();
```

```
// read in the file to be analysed; need to make a temporary
// copy of the file because IIS locks the latest log entry;
String logFileText;
String filePath = OpenFileDialog1.FileName;
String tempFile = Path.GetTempFileName();

File.Copy(filePath, tempFile, true);
StreamReader streamReaderRegex =
        File.OpenText(tempFile);
logFileText = streamReaderRegex.ReadToEnd();

streamReaderRegex.Close();
File.Delete(tempFile);
```

The code, placed inside the start of a try...catch statement, first clears TreeView1, and then creates a new Hashtable object. This object will be used later to store details of SMTP sessions and where they are located in the TreeView's nodes.

Next, we obtain the file name of the log file the user selected and we get a temporary file name. We can't read in the IIS log file directly because if it's today's log file and IIS is using it, then it will be locked – any attempts to open it will cause an error. The easiest way around this, and the one chosen here, is to make a temporary copy of the log file, read in its information, and then delete the temporary file.

We use the File object's shared Copy() method to do the copying, and we then open the temporary file using StreamReader and File. Using the StreamReader, we read to the end of the file, close it, and finally delete the temporary file.

We now need to create our regular expression to make the matches on each log line and capture its data in specific named groups:

```
// get the individual log lines and data within them;
Regex logLinesRegex = new Regex("^(?<date>[^ #]+) (?<time>[^ ]+) " +
                      "(?<clientAddress>[^ -]+) " +
                      "(?<clientName>[^ ]+) " +
                      "(?<method>[^ -]+) " +
                      "(?<uriQuery>[^ ]+) " +
                      "(?<sentBytes>[\\d]+) " +
                      "(?<receivedBytes>[\\d]+) " +
                      "(?<timeTaken>[\\d]+)",
                      RegexOptions.Multiline);

Regex getEmailAddressDataRegex = new Regex("<[^>]+>",
    RegexOptions.Compiled);

MatchCollection logLineMatches; .

string clientAddress;
string clientHostName = "";
string method;
```

```
string uriQuery;
TreeNode logNode;
Boolean suspectSession = false;

logLineMatches = logLinesRegex.Matches(logFileText);
```

We now have our log data, with each match containing one line from the log and each group within that match containing the data we need. What we have to do now is loop through each of these matches, extract the data, and append it to the `TreeView` control's nodes. However, this is made trickier because we want to make sure all the lines from a single session are placed under the correct node for that session. Because there can be concurrent SMTP sessions, and the lines in a log for a single session run sequentially, there may be other sessions in between. Our code needs to take account of this and does so by keeping track of each session, via the client IP address, in the `ipIndex Hashtable` object created earlier. Each time a new session is found, the code makes a note of the index of the node in the `TreeView` control's `Nodes` property. Then until the session ends in the log we keep adding new log lines to the same node.

Continuing with the code, we have a `foreach` loop that will loop through each match in the `logLinesMatches MatchCollection` object:

```
// Go through each line matched in the log;
foreach (Match logLineMatch in logLineMatches)
{
    // Obtain the data in uriQuery, method and clientaddress;
    uriQuery = logLineMatch.Groups["uriQuery"].Value;
    method = logLineMatch.Groups["method"].Value;
    clientAddress = logLineMatch.Groups["clientAddress"].Value;
```

At the top of the loop, we obtain the values for the `uriQuery`, `method`, and `clientAddress` for that log line. All these details are in groups within the regex match; as we gave the groups names we can easily extract them by name, rather than having to remember which order the groups are in. This is something that is easy to get wrong when there are as many groups as there are here.

Next comes the code that attempts to pull out the abnormal SMTP sessions. It does this based on whether the SMTP session contains commands that are less common, or if the session was unusually large or took a particularly long time. The checks are fairly simple and could easily be made more sophisticated if the program was developed further:

```
// If the SMTP method is ! mail, rcpt, helo, ehlo || data
// or if the time taken is more than a minute
// or the sent bytes are more than 1mb;
// or the received bytes more than a 1mb;
// then this might be a suspect line;
if (method != "MAIL" && method != "RCPT" && method != "HELO" &&
        method != "EHLO" && method != "DATA" ||
    ( Int32.Parse(logLineMatch.Groups["timeTaken"].Value) > 60000
```

```
        ||
        Int32.Parse(logLineMatch.Groups["sentBytes"].Value) > 1048576
        ||
        Int32.Parse(logLineMatch.Groups["receivedBytes"].Value) > 1048576))
   {
       uriQuery = uriQuery + " Bytes sent = " +
           logLineMatch.Groups["sentBytes"].Value;

       uriQuery = uriQuery + " : Bytes received = " +
           logLineMatch.Groups["receivedBytes"].Value;

       uriQuery = uriQuery +" : Time taken (milisecs) = " +
           logLineMatch.Groups["timeTaken"].Value;

       suspectSession = true;
   }
   else
   {
       suspectSession = false;
   }
```

If the session is potentially suspect, then we add additional information to the
uriQuery data to help the user work out why the session was dubious. We also then
set the Boolean variable suspectSession to true. Later the code will check this
variable and highlight the suspect session in red.

If the line contains either a MAIL (send mail from) or RCPT (send mail to recipient)
command then it would be useful to extract the e-mail address involved and display it
in the analysis. This is the task for the next few lines:

```
   // if (the mail || rcpt methods are used) {
   // extract the e-mail address the mail is;
   // being sent to or from;
   if (method == "MAIL" || method == "RCPT")
   {
       uriQuery = getEmailAddressDataRegex.Match(uriQuery).Value;
   }
   else if (uriQuery == "-" || method == "DATA")
   {
       uriQuery = "";
   }
```

We have the data we need, so it is now time to add the new node to the TreeView.
There are three possibilities for the new node:

- ❑   It's a new session

- ❑   It's the QUIT command of an existing session

- ❑   It's another line in an existing session

In the following `if` statement the code checks to see if there is an existing session node. If there is, then it checks for the SMTP QUIT command. If it is the QUIT command, then it doesn't need to add the log line, as all sessions must have a QUIT command – even if the session has timed out. Instead, we simply remove the IP address from the `ipIndex`, which contains all the open sessions so far in the log. If it wasn't a QUIT command then the code needs to discover the index of the top-level node for that session, then add a new node under it with the latest log line and its details. Note if the `suspectSession` variable is `True`, then we must highlight the current log line in red and the line for the session node as well. The code to do all this is shown below:

```
// Has this IP been found before?;
if (ipIndex.ContainsKey(clientAddress))
{
    // if (QUIT method found) { current session has ended for that IP
    // and we need to remove details of its node from the session index;
    if (method == "QUIT")
    {
        ipIndex.Remove(clientAddress);
    }
    else
    {
        // only add the line if the method was ! empty
        // IIS indicates no data with a minus sign;
        if (method != "-")
        {
            TreeView1.Nodes[Int32.Parse(
                ipIndex[clientAddress].ToString())].Nodes.Add(method +
                " " + uriQuery);

            // if (this is one of the lines noted as being suspect)
            // make the line and the session line appear in red;
            // and add extra data for info
            if (suspectSession)
            {
                TreeView1.Nodes[Int32.Parse(
                    ipIndex[clientAddress].ToString())].LastNode.ForeColor
                    = Color.Red;
                TreeView1.Nodes[
                    Int32.Parse(ipIndex[clientAddress].ToString())].ForeColor
                    = Color.Red;
            }
        }
    }
}
```

The other alternative is that this is a new session, in which case we try to obtain the name of the server using DNS, or failing that to simply add the session's IP address to the `ipIndex`, then add a new top-level node to the `TreeView` control, and then add to this the node details of the log line:

```
else
{
  // This is a new session - create a new top level node;
  // and record session's location in tree;
  logNode = new TreeNode();
  try
  {
    clientHostName = " <" +
        Dns.GetHostByAddress(clientAddress).HostName + ">";
  }
  catch (Exception ex)
  {
    if (ex is System.FormatException)
    {
      clientHostName = " < not an ip >";
    }
    else if (ex is System.Net.Sockets.SocketException)
    {
      clientHostName = " < ip not resolvable >";
    }
  }

  logNode.Text = logLineMatch.Groups["date"].Value + " " +
                 logLineMatch.Groups["time"].Value + " " +
                 clientAddress +
                 clientHostName;

  logNode.Nodes.Add(method + " " + uriQuery);
  TreeView1.Nodes.Add(logNode);
  ipIndex.Add(clientAddress, TreeView1.GetNodeCount(false) - 1);

  // Display suspect sessions in red;
  if (suspectSession)
  {
    TreeView1.Nodes[Int32.Parse(ipIndex[
        clientAddress].ToString())].LastNode.ForeColor = Color.Red;

    TreeView1.Nodes[Int32.Parse(ipIndex[
        clientAddress].ToString())].ForeColor = Color.Red;
  }
}
```

We then complete the code by closing the if and foreach statements, supplying a
catch block for the try block we started with, and closing the
OpenFileDialog1_FileOk() method, the form, and the namespace:

```
      }
    }
    catch (Exception ex)
    {
      MessageBox.Show("Error occurred - " + ex.Message);
    }
```

221

```
        }
      }
    }
  }
```

This can be now be used to analyze all of your SMTP log files.

HTML Tags

In this section, you'll see how to match HTML tags. We'll start by creating a regular expression that will spot if a string contains any HTML open or close tags. This can be useful when obtaining input from a user in a web page if we want to avoid them inserting their own HTML tags, such as for images, links, or JavaScript. We may want to take it further and allow some HTML tags, for example formatting tags, but for now we'll just look for any kind of tag.

The second regular expression we'll look at is not for data validation, but instead for splitting an HTML file into its component tags and attributes. We'll be creating an example that creates a tree view of a web page's HTML.

As always with creating regular expressions, the first task is to work out what patterns and variations of patterns we will need to match; for HTML it is those shown below:

```
<tag>Text to retain</tag>
<tag>
<tag tagattribute1="somevalue">
<tag tagattribute1="somevalue" tagattribute2="somevalue">
<tag tagattribute1="somevalue">Text to retain</tag>
<tag tagattribute1=somevalue>Text to retain</tag>
<tag tagattribute1='somevalue' tagattribute2='somevalue'>
  Text to retain
</tag>
<tag></tag>
<tag attribute1="somevalue" attribute2="somevalue></tag>
```

Let's start by looking at how to match these tags inside an input string.

Removing HTML from User Input

The regular expression that will match either a start or end HTML tag is this:

```
(<[a-z]+[^>]*>)|(</[a-z\d]+>)
```

In fact, it's two regular expressions with the alternation character allowing the pattern to match one or the other pattern. The pattern on the left:

```
(<[a-z]+[^>]*>)
```

matches an HTML start tag. It looks for a "<" followed by one or more characters from a to z, then zero or more of any character so long as it's not the close tag character ">". You might be wondering why we can't have the following expression:

```
(<[^>]+>)
```

This will match any HTML start tag; however, it will also match where a "less than" character is used and there is no HTML, for example:

```
The value was < 22,000 but always > 10,000
```

This would provide a false match. Often with regular expressions, it's as much about defining what you don't want to match, as defining what you do want to match. Insisting the "<" should be followed by a to z reduces the chances of a false match.

The second part of the regular expression that matches the close tag is this:

```
(</[a-z\d]+>)
```

Close tags don't have attributes, so our regular expression can be simplified. It matches a "<" followed by a "/" and then a through z, or a number, occurring one or more times. Finally it matches the ">" character.

We can use the regular expression to see if there is a match, meaning that the user has inserted HTML in the input:

```
if (Regex.IsMatch(userInputString,
                "(<[a-z]+[^>]*>)|(</[a-z\\d]+>)",
                RegexOptions.IgnoreCase |
                RegexOptions.ExplicitCapture))
{
    MessageBox.Show("HTML FOUND");
}
else
{
    MessageBox.Show("HTML NOT FOUND");
}
```

We could also use the `Replace()` method to simply remove all the offending tags and just leave the plain text.

Extracting All HTML Tags

In this section, we look at how regular expressions can help to extract quite detailed information from an HTML page. In the example, we'll build a `TreeView` control that gives a detailed overview of a web page and its tags. However, the regex itself could prove useful in any situation where we would want to analyze specific components of an HTML page.

The regular expression to extract HTML tags and their attributes is far more complex:

```
<(?<outertag>[a-z]+[\d]?)(?<attributes> [^>]*)*>
(?<innerhtml>(<(?<innertag>[a-z]+[\d]?)[^>]*>.*?</\k<innertag>>|
<[a-z]+[\d]?[^>]*>|(?>[^<]*))*(?=</\k<outertag>>))?
```

The aim of the regular expression is to split each tag and its content into a single match, but within that match there is one group that matches the HTML tag type and a second one that matches the attributes of that tag. Let's examine the following HTML:

```
<p>
    Welcome to Wrox
</p>
<img src="ThePlane.jpg" width="149">
<hr>
<p align="left">my text</p>
```

This will produce the following matches and groups:

Full Match	Group 1: outertag	Group 2: attributes	Group 3: innerhtml
`<p>  Welcome to Wrox`	P		Welcome to Wrox
`<img src="ThePlane.jpg" width="149">`	Img	src="ThePlane.jpg" width="149"	
`<hr>`	Hr		
`<p align="left">my text`	P	align="left"	my text

One of the biggest problems we have to deal with is that of nested tags, for example:

```
<p>
    <p>some text<img src="myimg.jpg">
    <a href="somepage.htm">click here</a></p>
</p>
```

The problem we have is forcing the regular expression to work out which is the correct closing tag. In this case the closing tag for the first <p> is actually the very last </p> tag. We will need to work out a way of dealing with this. We'll see that the technique we use is to *consume* the HTML inside the outer tag; that way the regular expression engine has no choice but to match the last </p> tag as well.

We'll need to set the following options for the regular expression to work:

- ❑ IgnoreCase
- ❑ ExplicitCapture
- ❑ SingleLine

We are not concerned about the case of the HTML, hence the IgnoreCase option. In addition, we are only concerned with the contents of four of the groups, so for convenience and efficiency we set the ExplicitCapture option so only the named groups will have their matches stored. The SingleLine option allows the "." character to match newlines, as the HTML for one tag may well be on multiple lines.

The regular expression is very large, so let's split it down, firstly taking the regular expression pattern that matches the first opening tag:

```
<(?<outertag>[a-z]+[\d]?)(?<attributes> [^>]*)*>
```

This matches tags like <p> and <img src="ThePlane.jpg" width="149">

First, it matches the "<" of an HTML tag, then it attempts to match a group named outertag. This group will match the tag type, such as h1, p, and img. We'll be using this group for the results initially, and to match the closing tag type. Next is the attributes group; this matches any HTML tag attributes, for example src="myfile.jpg". Again, by putting it in its own group, it can easily be accessed in Visual Basic .NET code from the match results.

Some singleton tags only have an open tag, for example the <img> tag, and so the pattern matched so far is all that's needed. The majority of elements have a close tag, however, so we need the remainder of the pattern:

```
(?<innerhtml>(<(?<innertag>[a-z]+[\d]?)[^>]*>.*?</\k<innertag>>|
<[a-z]+[\d]? [^>]*>|(?>[^<]*))*(?=</\k<outertag>>))?
```

This will be analyzed shortly, but it matches any HTML open and close pairs, or any single HTML tag, or any plain text followed by a close tag, matching the outer open tag we matched above.

The outer group is the innerHTML group; this matches all the content inside the outer open tag and final close tag. So if our HTML were the following:

```
<p>
   <p>some text<img src="myimg.jpg">
   <a href="somepage.htm">click here</a></p>
</p>
```

then the innerhtml group would match this:

```
<p>some text<img src="myimg.jpg">
<a href="somepage.htm">click here</a></p>
```

225

The `innerhtml` group will only perform a match if the outer close tag exists, although the outer close tag is not captured either in the group or in the match itself.

Let's break the group down. Inside the `innerhtml` group is another non-capturing group, non-capturing because we use the `ExplicitCapture` option. Inside this group are three separate patterns, each split by the "`|`" character, which is the regular expression's equivalent of the logical OR. The three groups and what they match are shown below:

Regular expression	Description	Example match
`(?<innertag>[a-z]+[\d]?)` `[^>]*>.*?</\k<innertag>`	This matches an open HTML tag, the contents between it and its close tag, as well as this closing HTML tag	`<p align=left>` `some text` `</p>`
`<[a-z]+[\d]?[^>]*>`	This matches a single HTML open tag with no closing tag	`<img>`
`(?>[^<]*)`	This matches anything other than HTML tags	`Some plain` `text`

Remember that the "`|`" will first try to match the expression on the left, and then, if there is no match for that, the expression on the right. We use this to our advantage because it means our pattern will first look for an HTML open tag with a subsequent close tag, such as `<p>some text</p>`. If there is no match for that, then it will look for a single HTML tag with no matching close tag, such as `<img src="image.gif">`. If there is still no match, then it simply looks for anything, matching plain text or newline characters.

Let's start with the first regular expression in the table:

```
(?<innertag>[a-z]+[\d]?)[^>]*>.*?</\k<innertag>
```

This is very similar to the regular expression that matches the outer HTML tag. First, we create an explicitly capturing group called `innertag` that will capture the start tag. We'll use it later in the pattern to match a close tag of the same type.

Then, as we have seen before, we match one or more letters from a through z, followed by an optional number, so that tags like `h1` and `h2` are matched. Following the `innertag` group, we have a non-greedy match, that will look for zero or more characters of any type, including the newline character, because we have the `SingleLine` option set. We're using a non-greedy version of "`*`" because we want to limit what the regular expression engine matches. There's a danger it will match everything it can, including things we don't want it to, such as the rest of the string, when there are more HTML tags to match separately.

Finally, at the end we match a close tag of the same type as the open tag:

```
</\k<innertag>>
```

The next item in the table, described here, is the regular expression that matches a single open tag:

```
<[a-z]+[\d]?[^>]*>
```

This is almost identical to the pattern for the `innertag` group we saw above, except we don't need to capture any further groups, as there is no close tag to match.

The final regular expression in the table is as follow:

```
(?>[^<]*)
```

This simply matches anything the previous matches didn't match, except a "<" character. This will capture any text in between the tags.

We've looked at the `innerhtml` group; all that's left is this:

```
)*(?=</\k<outertag>>))?
```

After the `innerhtml` group is an "*", which tells the regex engine to match the contents of the group zero or more times. So if our HTML was this:

```
<p>
  <h1><img>some text<p>more text</p></h1>
</p>
```

the first `<p>` tag is matched by the outer tag matching pattern, and all of the `innerhtml`; the `<h1>` tag, the `<img>` tag, the text, the inner `<p>` tag, and its text, will all be matched by the `innerhtml` group. Without the "*", only the `<h1>` tag would be matched.

At the very end of our regular expression is the pattern to match the close tag of the same type as the outer HTML tag:

```
<(?<outertag>[a-z]+[\d]?)(?<attributes> [^>]*)*>
(?<innerhtml>(<(?<innertag>[a-z]+[\d]?)[^>]*>.*?</\k<innertag>>|
<[a-z]+[\d]?[^>]*>|(?>[^<]*))*(?=</\k<outertag>>))?
```

In the next section, we turn this regular expression into a useful example of C# code.

HTML Extraction Example

We're going to create a new application in .NET so that we can use some of these new concepts just covered. We'll be loading an HTML page and then using the regular expression above to split the HTML up into its individual tags and display the results in a TreeView.

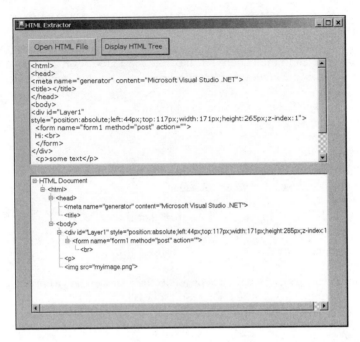

Start up Visual Studio .NET and start a new Windows application called HTMLExtractor. We need to create a form with the controls as shown in the previous screenshot.

The relevant properties for the individual controls are shown in the table below:

Control Type	Properties
Button	Name = cmdOpenHTML
	Text = Open HTML File
Button	Name = cmdDisplayHTML
	Text = Display HTML Tree
Form	Name = frmHTMLExtractor
OpenFileDialog	Name=OpenFileDialog1
	Filter = Web Pages|*.htm;*.html;

228

Control Type	Properties
TextBox	Name=txtInputText
	MultiLine= True
	ScrollBars = Vertical
TreeView	Name = HTMLTreeView

Firstly, at the top of the form class we need to inform the compiler that we'll be using the System.Text.RegularExpressions and System.IO namespaces:

```
using System;
using System.Drawing;
using System.Collections;
using System.ComponentModel;
using System.Windows.Forms;
using System.Data;
using System.Text.RegularExpressions;
using System.IO;

namespace CSharpHTMLExtractor
{
```

Within the frmHTMLExtractor class, we now need to declare two variables; the first containing our Regex object, and the second a variable that keeps a count of how many matches have been made:

```
public class frmHTMLExtractor : System.Windows.Forms.Form
{
  Int32 intMatchesMade = 0;
  Regex extractHTMLRegex =
      new Regex("<(?<outertag>[a-z]+[\\d]?)(?<attributes> [^>]*)*>" +
"(?<innerhtml>(<(?<innertag>[a-z]+[\\d]?)[^>]*>.*?</\\k<innertag>>|" +
      "<[a-z]+[\\d]?[^>]*>|(?>[^<]*))*(?=</\\k<outertag>>))?",
      RegexOptions.IgnoreCase |
      RegexOptions.Compiled |
      RegexOptions.ExplicitCapture |
      RegexOptions.Singleline);
```

We have set the three options IgnoreCase, ExplicitCapture, and SingleLine necessary for the regular expression to match correctly. Also, by setting the Compiled option, we tell the regex engine to convert the regular expression into something more approaching how the computer uses the pattern, as opposed to the more 'human-friendly' syntax. If you remove the Compiled option, you'll see a noticeable increase (about 50%) in the time taken to analyze a web page.

Let's now add the code to read in an HTML file; first the button-click code:

229

```
private void cmdOpenHTML_Click(object sender, System.EventArgs e)
{
  OpenFileDialog1.ShowDialog();
}
```

Using the `OpenFileDialog1.ShowDialog()` method, the code obtains the name of the HTML file to be analyzed. Now the code for the `OpenFileDialog1.FileOk` event:

```
private void OpenFileDialog1_FileOk(object sender,
    System.ComponentModel.CancelEventArgs e)
{
  String filePath = OpenFileDialog1.FileName;
  StreamReader streamReaderRegex = File.OpenText(filePath);
  this.txtInputText.Text = streamReaderRegex.ReadToEnd();
  streamReaderRegex.Close();
}
```

This uses the `System.IO.StreamReader` class to read in the selected file and sets the `Text` property of the `txtInputText` box to the contents of the file. Next, we need to add code to the `cmdDisplayHTML` button's click event; this event starts the matching and tree creation:

```
private void cmdDisplayHTML_Click(object sender, System.EventArgs e)
{
  intMatchesMade = 0;
  HTMLTreeView.Nodes.Clear();
  HTMLTreeView.Nodes.Add(populateTagNode(this.txtInputText.Text,
    "HTML Document"));
  HTMLTreeView.ExpandAll();
  MessageBox.Show("Completed " + intMatchesMade + " matches");
}
```

We reset the `MatchesMade` variable, which counts how many HTML tags have been found, and then clear the `TreeView` control ready for the new HTML. We then add a new tree node to the tree, a value that is returned by the `populateTagNode()` method, which is shown below:

```
private  TreeNode populateTagNode(String sInputString,
    String sTitleText)
{

  TreeNode htmlTagNode = new TreeNode();

  try
  {
    MatchCollection matchesFound;

    TreeNode htmlSubTagNode;
    String sTag;
    matchesFound = extractHTMLRegex.Matches(sInputString);
```

```
    htmlTagNode.Text = sTitleText;

    foreach (Match matchMade in matchesFound)
    {
      intMatchesMade = intMatchesMade + 1;
      sTag = "<" + matchMade.Groups[1].Value +
          matchMade.Groups[2].Value + ">";
      htmlSubTagNode = populateTagNode(matchMade.Groups[3].Value,
          sTag);
      htmlTagNode.Nodes.Add(htmlSubTagNode);
    }
  }

  catch (ArgumentException ex)
  {
    MessageBox.Show("The following error occurred "
        + "\r\n" + ex.Message);
  }

  return htmlTagNode;
}
```

The method is a recursive one; it keeps extracting nested HTML tags by obtaining the outer tags, and then keeps calling itself to obtain the inner tags. The easiest way to understand the code is with an example:

```
<html>
<body>
  <p>some text</p>
  <img src="myimage.png">
</body>
</html>
```

When the above HTML is matched there will be only one match, the whole HTML. However in the first group will be the <html> tag, the second its attributes, if it had any, and the third group will contain the entire HTML between the opening and closing <html> tags. The function creates a TreeNode with the title of html.

Next, the method calls itself, but this time passing not the whole HTML input string, but only the HTML in the third group – the HTML between the outer start and close tags. This will be split, and this time there is again just one match, the body tag. Again, a TreeNode is created and the populateTagNode() method is called again, but with just the HTML inside the <body> tag. This time there are two matches, the <p> tag, and the <img> tag. If the nesting were deeper, then the populateTagNode() method would be called repeatedly until the entire HTML had been extracted, and a node created for each tag. The application is currently very simple, but it could be expanded for other uses. For example, it could check for missing close tags, or it could be used for displaying poorly formatted HTML.

Summary

In this chapter, we have used all the knowledge gained in the previous two chapters and put it into practice. You have seen a range of regular expressions, from simple ones for data validation, to more complex ones for validating e-mail addresses and to multi-line expressions that can analyze log files or an HTML page.

You've seen that the way to approach regular expressions is to first look at the data against which we are planning to match. Often when you look at some data, you can instantly spot the pattern; for example, you can guess what `person@somedomain.com` is without much further instruction. With regexes, you need to replicate how you spot the pattern by working out how you see it, and then by working out what information you use to recognize it. Having worked this out, you then need to work out all of the combinations of valid patterns, and importantly, which patterns you don't want to match. We've seen that if we do this preparation, and then construct the regular expression in stages, it is not as difficult as it might first appear.

Throughout the entire book, you have learned both how text is stored, and how various tools can be used to assist in the construction, matching, appending, and replacing of strings. You should now be knowledgeable enough to manipulate text confidently in all your applications. The following appendices provide a quick reference to the methods of the `String` and `StringBuilder` classes, as well as for the various characters used in regex patterns. We hope you find this book useful in your future projects.

C#

Text Manipulation

Handbook

Appendix A

The String Class

This appendix contains all the constructors, properties, and methods of the `String` class. You can find more details in Chapter 2.

Constructors

Here you can see the various overloads for the construction of a new `String` object instance:

Constructor	Description
`String(char[] charArray)`	Creates a new string with the contents of a character array `charArray`.
`String(char c, int count)`	Creates a new string consisting of the specified character, `x`, repeated count number of times.
`String(char[] charArray, int pos, int count)`	Creates a new string consisting of a substring defined within character string `charArray`, defined by starting position pos and count number of characters.

Properties

Below are the properties of this class:

Property	Description
Empty	Read-only **static** constant representing the empty string.
Chars(int index)	Returns the character within the string at position index.
Length	Returns the number of characters in the string.

Methods

This table contains all the methods and overloads of these methods for the String class. The table also indicates whether the method is an instance method, or static:

Method	Access Level	Description
Clone()	Instance	Returns a reference to the String object. This is counter to how Clone() is normally implemented on objects, but is appropriate as System.String is immutable and so shouldn't need a copy made.
Compare(string s1, string s2)	Static	Performs a case-sensitive comparison of the two given strings according to the current culture.
Compare(string s1, string s2, bool ignoreCase)	Static	Performs a comparison of the two given strings according to the current culture. If ignoreCase is true, a case-insensitive comparison is performed.
Compare(string s1, string s2, bool ignoreCase, CultureInfo culture)	Static	Performs a comparison of the two given strings according to the provided culture settings. If ignoreCase is true, a case-insensitive comparison is performed.

Method	Access Level	Description

Compare(string s1,
     int index1,
     string s2,
     int index2,
     int length)
	Static	Performs a case-sensitive comparison of two substrings defined by the given parameters.

Compare(string s1,
     int index1,
     string s2,
     int index2,
     int length,
     bool ignoreCase)
	Static	Performs a comparison of two substrings defined by the given parameters. If ignoreCase is true, a case-insensitive comparison is performed.

Compare(string s1,
     int index1,
     string s2,
     int index2,
     int length,
     bool ignoreCase,
     CultureInfo culture)
	Static	Performs a comparison of two substrings defined by the given parameters and according to the provided culture settings. If ignoreCase is true, a case-insensitive comparison is performed.

CompareOrdinal(string s1, string s2)	Static	Performs a comparison of the two given strings without regard to their cultures.

CompareOrdinal(string s1,
     int index1,
     string s2,
     int index2,
     int length)
	Static	Compares the two given sub-strings without regard to their cultures.

CompareTo(object obj)	Instance	Performs a case-sensitive, culturally aware comparison of the given object with the instance string.
CompareTo(string s)	Instance	Performs a case-sensitive, culturally aware comparison of the given string with the instance string.
Concat(object obj)	Static	Creates a string representation of the given object.
Concat(ParamArray objects)	Static	Creates a string based on the concatenation of the objects in the given array.
Concat(ParamArray strings)	Static	Creates a string based on the concatenation of the strings in the given array.

Table continued on following page

Method	Access Level	Description
Concat(object obj1, object obj2)	Static	Creates a string based on the concatenation of the two given objects.
Concat(string s1, string s2)	Static	Creates a string based on the concatenation of the two given strings.

Concat(object obj1,
      object obj2,
      object obj3)
	Static	Creates a string based on the concatenation of the three given objects.

Concat(string s1,
      string s2,
      string s3)
	Static	Creates a string based on the concatenation of the three given strings.

Concat(string s1,
      string s2,
      string s3,
      string s4)
	Static	Creates a string based on the concatenation of the four given strings.

Copy(string s)	Static	Returns a new string with the same value as the given string.

CopyTo(int sourceIndex,
      char[] dest,
      int destIndex,
      int count)
	Instance	Copies a sub-string from the instance string to the given destination string.

EndsWith(string s)	Instance	Returns true if the instance string ends with the given string.
Equals(string s)	Instance	Returns true if the instance string has the same value as the given object.
Equals(string s1, string s2)	Static	Returns true if the two provided strings have the same value.
Format(string format, object arg)	Static	Returns a string consisting of the format specification replaced by the given argument.
Format(string format, ParamArray args)	Instance	Returns a string consisting of the format specification replaced by the argument array.

Method	Access Level	Description

Format (
    IFormatProvider provider,
    string format,
    ParamArray args)
	Instance	Returns a string consisting of the format specification replaced by the argument array according to the given format provider.

Format(string format,
       object arg1,
       object arg2)
	Instance	Returns a string consisting of the format specification replaced by the given two arguments.

Format(string format,
       object arg1,
       object arg2,
       object arg3)
	Static	Returns a string consisting of the format specification replaced by the given three arguments.

GetEnumerator()	Instance	Returns an object that can be used to iterate through the characters in the string.
GetHashCode()	Instance	Returns the unique hash code for the string instance.
GetType()	Instance	Returns the type of the string instance.
GetTypeCode()	Instance	Returns the type code for the string class.
IndexOf(char c)	Instance	Returns the index of the first occurrence of the given character.
IndexOf(string s)	Instance	Returns the index of the first occurrence of the given string.
IndexOf(char c, int startPos)	Instance	Returns the index of the first occurrence of the given character starting at the given position.
IndexOf(string s, int startPos)	Instance	Returns the index of the first occurrence of the given string starting at the given position.

IndexOf(char c,
       int startPos,
       int count)
	Instance	Returns the index of the first occurrence of the given character starting at the given position and searching for count characters.

Table continued on following page

Method	Access Level	Description

IndexOf(string s,
      int startPos,
      int count)
	Instance	Returns the index of the first occurrence of the given string starting at the given position and searching for count characters.

IndexOfAny(char[] chars)	Instance	Returns the index of the first occurrence of any character in the given array.
IndexOfAny(char[] chars, int startPos)	Instance	Returns the index of the first occurrence of any character in the given array starting at the given position.

IndexOfAny(char[] chars,
      int startPos,
      int count)
	Instance	Returns the index of the first occurrence of any character in the given array starting at the given position and searching for count characters.

Insert(int startPos, string s)	Instance	Inserts the given string into the instance string at the given position.
Intern(string s)	Instance	Returns a reference to the given string. If the string is not interned, this method will intern it.
IsInterned(string s)	Instance	Returns a reference to the given string if it is in the intern pool. Otherwise Nothing.
Join(string separator, string[] arrStr)	Instance	Returns a string consisting of the strings in the given array concatenated together and with the given separator between each element.

Join(string separator,
    string[] arrStr,
    int startIndex,
    int count)
	Instance	Returns a string consisting of the strings in the given array concatenated together and with the given separator between each element. Only a number of count array elements are used and first string to use is startIndex.

LastIndexOf(char c)	Instance	Returns the index of the last occurrence of the given character.

240

Method	Access Level	Description
LastIndexOf(string s)	Instance	Returns the index of the last occurrence of the given string.
LastIndexOf(char c, int startPos)	Instance	Returns the index of the last occurrence of the given character starting at the given position.
LastIndexOf(string s, int startPos)	Instance	Returns the index of the last occurrence of the given string starting at the given position.
LastIndexOf(char c, int startPos, int count)	Instance	Returns the index of the last occurrence of the given character starting at the given position and searching for count characters.
LastIndexOf(string s, int startPos, int count)	Instance	Returns the index of the last occurrence of the given string starting at the given position and searching for count characters.
LastIndexOfAny(char[] chars)	Instance	Returns the index of the last occurrence of any character in the given array.
LastIndexOfAny(char[] chars, int startPos)	Instance	Returns the index of the last occurrence of any character in the given array starting at the given position.
LastIndexOfAny(char[] chars, int startPos, int count)	Instance	Returns the index of the last occurrence of any character in the given array starting at the given position and searching for count characters.
PadLeft(int totalWidth)	Instance	Adds to the left the required number of spaces to the instance string to make it totalWidth.
PadLeft(int totalWidth, char c)	Instance	Adds to the left the required number of the given character to the instance string to make it totalWidth.

Table continued on following page

Method	Access Level	Description
`PadRight(int totalWidth)`	Instance	Adds to the right the required number of spaces to the instance string to make it `totalWidth`.
`PadRight(int totalWidth, char c)`	Instance	Adds to the right the required number of the given character to the instance string to make it `totalWidth`.
`Remove(int startPos, int count)`	Instance	Starting at `startPos`, removes count characters.
`Replace(char oldChar, char newChar)`	Instance	Replaces all occurrences of `oldChar` with `newChar` in the instance string.
`Replace(string oldString, string newString)`	Instance	Replaces all occurrences of `oldString` with `newString` in the instance string.
`Split(ParamArray separators)`	Instance	Splits the instance string according to the given character separators.
`Split(ParamArray separators, int maxElements)`	Instance	Splits the instance string according to the given character separators. Returns up to `maxElements`.
`StartsWith(string s)`	Instance	Returns `true` if the instance string starts with the given string.
`SubString(int startPos)`	Instance	Returns a sub-string starting at the given position.
`SubString(int startPos, int length)`	Instance	Returns a sub-string starting at the given position and for given length.
`ToCharArray()`	Instance	Returns a character array with the character values in the string instance.
`ToCharArray(int startPos, int length)`	Instance	Returns a character array with the character values in the string instance starting from `startPos` of `length` characters.
`ToLower()`	Instance	Returns a lowercase copy of the instance string.
`ToLower(CultureInfo culture)`	Instance	Returns a lowercase copy of the instance string according to the given culture settings.

Method	Access Level	Description
`ToString()`	Instance	Returns a reference to the instance string.
`ToString(` `  IFormatProvider format)`	Instance	Returns a reference to the instance string.
`ToUpper()`	Instance	Returns an uppercase copy of the instance string.
`ToUpper(CultureInfo culture)`	Instance	Returns an uppercase copy of the instance string, according to the given culture settings.
`Trim()`	Instance	Removes all leading and trailing whitespace characters in the string instance.
`Trim(ParamArray chars)`	Instance	Removes all leading and trailing specified characters in the string instance.
`TrimEnd(ParamArray chars)`	Instance	Removes all trailing specified characters in the string instance. If none are specified, whitespace characters are removed.
`TrimStart(ParamArray chars)`	Instance	Removes all leading specified characters in the string instance. If none are specified, whitespace characters are removed.

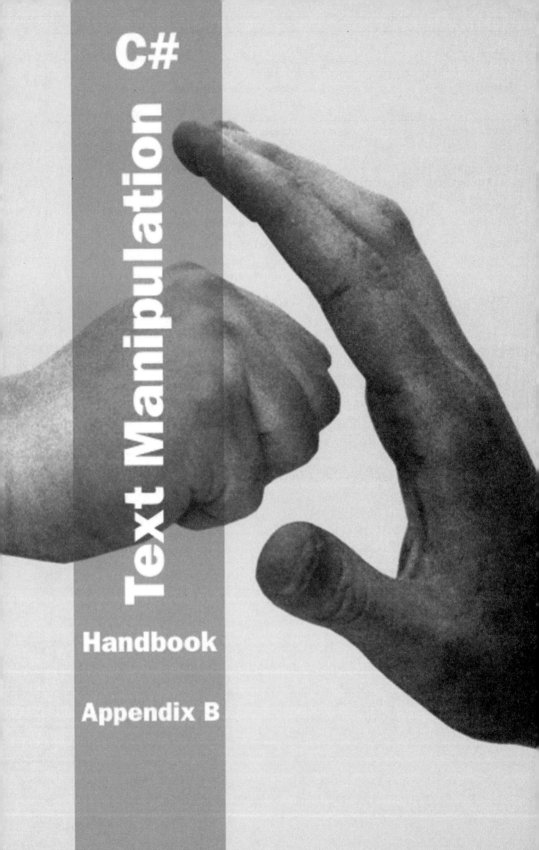

C#

Text Manipulation

Handbook

Appendix B

The StringBuilder Class

In this appendix are listed all of the constructors, properties, and methods for the StringBuilder class. More details can be found in Chapter 2.

Constructors

Below are the constructors invoked on creation of a new StringBuilder object:

Constructor	Description
StringBuilder()	Creates a new StringBuilder object with an initial length of zero characters and default capacity of 16 characters.
StringBuilder(int capacity)	Creates a new StringBuilder object with an initial length of zero characters and given initial capacity.
StringBuilder(string s)	Creates a new StringBuilder object with string value of s.
StringBuilder(int capacity, int maxCapacity)	Creates a new StringBuilder object with an initial length of zero characters and given initial capacity. The capacity is defined not to grow larger than maxCapacity.

Table continued on following page

Constructor	Description
StringBuilder(string s, int capacity)	Creates a new StringBuilder object with string value of s, and given initial capacity.

StringBuilder(string s,
       int startPos,
       int length,
       int capacity)
	Creates a new StringBuilder object with a value of the given sub-string of s defined by startPos and length.

Properties

Here are the properties of any StringBuilder instance:

Property	Description
Capacity	The number of characters currently allocated for the instance. Not necessarily the same value as the Length property.
Chars(int index)	Gets or sets the character within the string at the position index.
Length	The number of characters in the string. Can be set smaller than the current string value to truncate it.
MaxCapacity	The maximum number of characters that can be allocated for this instance.

Methods

Below are all the methods of a StringBuilder instance. There are no static methods:

Method	Description
Append(type)	Appends the string representation of the given value. There is an overload for each .NET primitive type. For brevity, they are not all listed here.
Append(char value, int count)	Appends the given character value count times.

Append(char charArray(),
     int startPos,
     int count)
	Appends a substring of a Char() array, defined by the given parameters.

Method	Description

Append(string s,
        int startPos,
        int count)
	Appends a sub-string of s, defined by the given parameters.

AppendFormat(
    string specification,
    object value)
	Appends a formatted string defined by the given specification and value.

AppendFormat(
    string specification,
    ParamArray values)
	Appends a formatted string defined by the given specification and values.

AppendFormat(
    IFormatProvider provider,
    string specification,
    object value)
	Appends a formatted string defined by the given specification and value and according to the given format provider.

AppendFormat(
    string specification,
    object value1,
    object value2)
	Appends a formatted string defined by the given specification and values.

AppendFormat(
    string specification,
    object value1,
    object value2,
    object value3)
	Appends a formatted string defined by the given specification and values.

EnsureCapacity(int capacity)	If the current capacity is less than the given capacity, memory is allocated to increase memory to the given capacity.
Equals(StringBuilder sb)	Returns true if current instance and given StringBuilder have the same value.
GetHashCode()	Returns a unique hash code for the StringBuilder instance.
GetType()	Returns the type of the StringBuilder instance.
Insert(int position, <type>)	Inserts at the given position the value provided as the second parameter. There is an overload for each .NET primitive type. For brevity, they are not all listed here.

Insert(int position,
        string s,
        int count)
	Inserts s at the given position, count number of times.

Table continued on following page

Method	Description

`Insert(int position,`
`        char[] charArray,`
`        int startPos,`
`        int count)`
	Inserts a sub-string of the given `Char` array, defined by the given parameters, at the given position.

`Remove(int startPos,` `       int count)`	Removes count characters starting at `startPos`.
`Replace(char oldChar,` `        char newChar)`	Replaces all occurrences of `oldChar` with `newChar` in the instance string.
`Replace(string oldString,` `        string newString)`	Replaces all occurrences of `oldString` with `newString` in the instance string.

`Replace(char oldChar,`
`        char newChar,`
`        int startPos,`
`        int count)`
	Replaces all occurrences of `oldChar` with `newChar` in the instance string between positions `startPos` and count - 1.

`Replace(string oldString,`
`        string newString,`
`        int startPos,`
`        int count)`
	Replaces all occurrences of `oldString` with `newString` in the instance string between positions `startPos` and count - 1.

`ToString()`	Returns a `String` object whose value is the same as that contained within the `StringBuilder` instance.
`ToString(int startPos,` `         int count)`	Returns a `String` object whose value is the substring of contents of a `StringBuilder` instance, defined by the given parameters.

C#

Text Manipulation

Handbook

Appendix C

C

Regular Expression Syntax

In this appendix we include details of the various characters that can be used inside a regular expression to match text. This can be used as a quick reference if you need to decipher an existing regular expression.

Matching Characters

Character Class	Characters it Matches	Example
\d	Any digit from 0 to 9	\d\d matches 72, but not aa or 7a.
\D	Any character that is not a numerical digit	\D\D\D matches abc, but not 123.
\w	Any word character, as in A-Z, a-z, 0-9, and the underscore character _	\w\w\w\w matches Ab_2, but not £$%* or Ab_@.
\W	Any non-word character	\W matches @, but not the letter a.
\s	Any whitespace character, includes tab, newline, carriage return, form feed, and vertical tab	Matches all traditional whitespace characters, as defined in HTML, XML, and other standards.
\S	Any non-whitespace character	Every character bar whitespace: A%&g3:, etc.

Table continued on following page

Character Class	Characters it Matches	Example
.	Any character	"." matches any single character, except a newline character (unless the Multiline option has been set).
[...]	Any one of the characters between the brackets	[abc] will match a single character a, or b, or c, but nothing else. [a-z] will match any character in the range a to z.
[^...]	Any character, but not one of those inside the brackets	[^abc] will match any character except a or b or c, but A or B or C could be matched by this pattern. [^a-z] will match any character that is not in the range a to z, but all uppercase letters could be matched by this pattern.

Repetition Characters

Below, you can see the repetition characters.

Repetition Character	Meaning	Example
{n}	Match n of the previous item	x{2} matches xx, but not x or xxx
{n,}	Match n or more of the previous item	x{2,} matches two or more xs, that is xx, xxx, xxxx, xxxxx, ...
{n,m}	Match at least n and at most m of the preceding item; if n is 0, that makes the character optional	x{2,4} matches xx, xxx, and xxxx, but not x or xxxxx
?	Match the previous item zero or one times, essentially making it optional	x? matches x or zero x
+	Match the previous item one or more times	x+ matches x, or xx, or any number of x greater than zero
*	Match the previous item zero or more times	x* matches zero x, x, xx, or any number of x

Positional Characters

Below are the various positional characters. These apply to the character or group to the immediate left or right, depending on the character, and as described below.

Position Character	Description
^	The following pattern must be at the start of the string, or if it's a multiline string, at the beginning of a line. For multi-line text, (a string that contains carriage returns) we need to set the `Multiline` flag.
$	The preceding pattern must be at the end of the string, or if it is a multiline string then at the end of a line.
\A	The preceding pattern must be at the start of the string; the `Multiline` flag is ignored, if present.
\z	The preceding pattern must be at the end of the string; the multiline flag is ignored.
\Z	The preceding pattern must be at the end of the string or before a newline at the end of a string.
\b	This matches a word boundary, essentially the point between a word character and a non-word character. Remember a word character is any of `[a-zA-Z0-9_]`. The start of a word.
\B	This matches a position that is *not* a word boundary; not the start of a word.

Grouping Characters

In the next table you can find the various grouping characters that can be used to collect together specific matches and which allow you to retrieve these specific matches.

Grouping Character	Definition	Example

( )	This groups together the characters matched by the pattern inside the brackets. It's a capturing group; this means the characters matched by the pattern become part of the final match, unless the ExplicitCapture option is set – which would mean that by default, the characters are not part of the match.	With input string:
		
		`ABC1 DEF2 XY`
		
		The regular expression that matches three characters A to Z and then one digit:
		
		`([A-Z]{3})\d`
		
		will produce two matches:
		
		`Match 1 = ABC1`
		`Match 2 = DEF2`
		
		with each match having one group:
		
		`Match 1's first group = ABC`
		`Match 2's first group = DEF`
		
		With backreferencing we can access the group via its number within the regular expression and also via C# and the Group and GroupCollection classes. If the ExplicitCapture option is set then the contents captured by the groups will not be available.

(?:)	This groups together the characters matched by the pattern inside the brackets. It's a non-capturing group this means the characters matched by the pattern will not be captured as a group though it will form part of the final match results. It's basically exactly the same as the group type above but as if the ExplicitCapture option was set.	With input string:
		
		`1A BB SA 1 C`
		
		the regular expression that matches a digit or a letter from A - Z, followed by any word character is:
		
		`(?:\d|[A-Z])\w`
		
		and this will produce three matches:
		
		`First Match = 1A`
		`Second Match = BB`
		`Third  Match = SA`
		
		but there will be no groups captured.

Grouping Character	Definition	Example

(?<name>)	This groups together the characters matched by the pattern inside the brackets, and gives the group a name, as specified between the angle brackets. Within the regular expression we can use the name for back referencing, instead of having to use a number. It's a capturing group, even if the `ExplicitCapture` option is set; this means the characters matched within the group are available for back referencing or via access from the `Group` class, as we'll see shortly.	With the input string:
		
		```Characters in Seinfeld included Jerry Seinfeld, Elaine Benes, Cosmo Kramer and George Costanza```
		
		the regular expression to match their first and last names and capture the last name in a group called `lastName` is:
		
		`\b[A-Z][a-z]+ (?<lastName>[A-Z][a-z]+)\b`
		
		This produces four matches:
		
		```First Match = Jerry Seinfeld Second Match = Elaine Benes Third Match = Cosmo Kramer Fourth Match = George Costanza```
		
		There is one group in each match, the `lastName` group:
		
		```First Match: lastName group = Seinfeld Second Match: lastName group = Benes Third Match: lastName group = Kramer Fourth Match: lastName group = Costanza```
		
		The groups will be captured regardless of whether the `ExplictCapture` option is set.

(?=)	Positive look-ahead assertion. To the right of the assertion must be the specified pattern in brackets. This pattern will not form part of the final match.	`\S+(?=.NET)`
		
		used with the input string:
		
		```"The languages were Java, C#.NET, VB.NET, C, JScript.NET, Pascal"```
		
		would produce the following matches:
		
		```C# VB JScript```

Table continued on following page

255

Grouping Character	Definition	Example

(?!)	Negative look-ahead assertion. This specifies that the pattern must not be found immediately to the right of the assertion. The pattern will not form part of the final match.	`\d{3}(?![A-Z])`
		
		used with the input string:
		
		`"123A 456 789 111C"`
		
		would produce the matches:
		
		`456`
		`789`

(?<=)	Positive look-behind assertion. To the left of the assertion must be the specified pattern in brackets. This pattern will not form part of the final match.	`(?<=New )([A-Z][a-z]+)`
		
		used with the input string:
		
		`"The following states, New Mexico, West Virginia, Washington, New England"`
		
		would produce the matches:
		
		`Mexico`
		`England`

(?<!)	Negative look-behind assertion. To the left of the assertion must not be the specified pattern in brackets. The pattern will not form part of the final match.	`(?<!1)\d{2}[A-Z]`
		
		used with the input string:
		
		`"123A 456F 789C 111A"`
		
		will produce the following matches:
		
		`56F`
		`89C`

Grouping Character	Definition	Example

(?>)	Non-backtracking group. Prevents the regex engine from going back and trying to make a match.	Let's say we want to match all words ending in "ing". With the input string:
		
		`He was very trusting`
		
		the regular expression:
		
		`.*ing`
		
		will find a match – the word `trusting`. The "." matches any character but unfortunately that also includes the "ing" that the expression needs to be successful. So the regex engine back tracks a bit and stops at the second "t" and then matches the "ing" as the pattern specifies.
		
		However if we turn off backtracking:
		
		`(?>.*)ing`
		
		and use this we will find no match – the "." consumes all the characters including the "ing" – this means the "ing" at the end of our pattern can't be matched and so the match is unsuccessful.

Decision Making Characters

In the next table are those characters that force the processor to make an `if...else` decision:

Character	Description	Example
(? (*regex*) *yes_regex*| *no_regex*)	If *regex* is matched, then matching the *yes* regular expression will be attempted. Otherwise, the *no* regular expression is attempted. The *no* regular expression is optional. It is important to note that *regex*, the pattern that makes the decision, is zero width. This means the *yes* or *no* regexs will commence matching from the same place as the *regex* expression.	(? (\d) \dA| [A-Z]B) with input string "1A CB 3A 5C 3B" will match: 1A CB 3A
(? (group name or number) yes_regex| no_regex)	If the regular expression in the group is matched then the *yes* regular expression match is attempted. Otherwise, the *no* regular expression is attempted. The *no* regular expression is optional	(\d7)?- (? (1)\d\d[A-Z] | [A-Z][A-Z]) with input string: 77-77A 69-AA 57-B will produce the matches: 77-77A -AA

Substitution Characters

Below are the various characters that can be entered as part of a substitution string.

Character	Description
$*group*	Substitutes with the group number specified by *group*
${ *name*}	Substitutes the last substring matched by a (?<*name*>) group
$$	Substitutes a literal $
$&	Substitutes the entire match
$`	Substitutes all the text of the input string before the match
$'	Substitutes all the text of the input string after the match
$+	Substitutes the last group captured
$_	Substitutes the entire input string

Escape Sequences

Below are the escape characters that may be needed in your regular expression.

Escape Sequence	Description
\\	Matches actual "\"
\.	Matches "." character
*	Matches "*" character
\+	Matches "+" character
\?	Matches "?" character
|	Matches "|" character
\(	Matches "(" character
\)	Matches ")" character
\{	Matches "{" character
\}	Matches "}" character
\^	Matches "^" character
\$	Matches "$" character
\n	Matches newline
\r	Matches carriage return
\t	Matches tab
\v	Matches vertical tab
\f	Matches form feed
\nnn	Matches an ASCII character specified by octal number nnn; so \103 matches an uppercase C
\xnn	Matches an ASCII character specified by hexadecimal number nn; so \x43 matches C
\unnnn	Matches the Unicode character specified by the four hexadecimal digits represented by nnnn
\cV	Matches a control character; for example \cV matches *Ctrl-V*

Option Flags

The following are the regular expression options that can be set in the pattern itself:

Option Flag	Name
i	IgnoreCase
m	Multiline
n	ExplicitCapture
s	Singleline
x	IgnorePatternWhitespace

The RegexOptions themselves mean the following:

Flag	Description
IgnoreCase	Makes the pattern matching case insensitive. The default is that matches are case sensitive.
RightToLeft	Searches input string from right to left. The default is from left to right, which suits languages like English that read from left to right but not languages like Arabic or Hebrew that read from right to left.
None	Sets no flags. This is the default.
Multiline	Specifies that ^ and $ can match the beginning and the end of lines as well as the beginning and end of the string. This means that you can get different matches for each line, separated with a newline character. However, the "." character will still not match newline characters.
Singleline	Specifies that the "." special character matches any character, not any character except a newline. Default is that the "." special character does not match a newline. This is often used with the MultiLine option.
ECMAScript	ECMA (European Computer Manufacturer's Association) has defined how regular expressions *should* be implemented and so they have been implemented this way in the ECMAScript specification, which is a standards-based JavaScript. This option can only be used with the IgnoreCase and MultiLine flags set. Using the ECMAScript flag with any other flags results in an exception being thrown.

Flag	Description
IgnorePatternWhiteSpace	This removes all unescaped whitespace characters from the regular expression pattern used. This allows for the expression to span multiple lines, although you will have to ensure that you do escape all whitespace in the pattern. You can also comment your regular expression using "#" characters if this option is set.
Compiled	This compiles the regular expression into something more closely resembling machine code. This makes it faster, but also doesn't allow for any changes to be made to it.

C#

Text Manipulation

Handbook

Appendix D

Managing Culturally Correct Date and Time Formats in C#

Throughout this book we have discussed text manipulation using C# and the .NET Framework. In this bonus appendix, we give you one of the articles published on the C Sharp Today web site (http://www.csharp.today.com). The article was originally published in November 2001, and has been fully updated for .NET 1.0, and gives you a flavor of the content to be found on web site.

In this article we examine elements of the rich feature set of the .NET **DateTimeFormatInfo** class using C# as the vehicle. The goal is to help you write code that behaves correctly in any world region. Why write it twice when we can do it right the first time with little extra effort? We'll start with something simple that we can use right away. This will be done using two console programs. After that, we'll look at two examples that do a few things in ASP.NET with dates and calendars. Along the way, we will dissect the DateSquares example that was originally presented at the beginning of Chapter 13 of the Wrox publication *C# Programming With the Public Beta* (ISBN 1-86100-487-7) to show how simple changes lead to culturally correct output.

Console Examples Using DateTime

Console programs provide a quick way to learn how to deal with some new concepts or programming tasks. Initially, it is not very obvious how `DateTimeFormatInfo` works with the **DateTime** structure, the basic container for time and date in .NET. An instance of `DateTime` stores a particular instant in time. Using `DateTime`'s methods and properties, we can then change a particular time instance by adding or subtracting a time interval. It is also possible to parse, compare, convert, and format the contents. `DateTime` inherits from `IFormattable` among other interfaces, and that is where `DateTimeFormatInfo` comes into the picture. `DateTime` values are formatted using standard or custom patterns stored in the properties of a `DateTimeFormatInfo` instance.

As it happens, `DateTime` has a number of built-in formatting methods obtained from its inherited `DateTimeFormatInfo`. So, without invoking the latter class directly, we can manage international date formats practically without thinking. The format of the output is determined by the thread's implicit `CultureInfo`, which can be overridden if necessary. Every running thread on any modern operating system has an associated default locale, which can be overridden if necessary; in .NET, locale is managed by the `CultureInfo` class.

By the way, if you are not familiar with using the `CultureInfo` class, you may find it helpful to read the *Internationalization with the .NET CultureInfo Class & C#* (http://www.csharptoday.com/content.asp?id=1635) article. `CultureInfo` affects the behavior of most members of the `System.Globalization` namespace and a basic understanding of this class will aid understanding of this article.

First Console Example

In this first example we use the facilities of `DateTime` to provide internationalized formats. Basically, we see how to use the ones most commonly used, namely the short and long date or time formats. Code is also provided to show how to generate all the forms that `DateTime` knows about for the culture in which it runs, although we really need the help of `DateTimeFormatInfo` to determine the use of so much information. We also demonstrate how to change the default culture so we can see results from other world regions.

If you want to follow along, create a C# Console project called `ConsoleDateTime`. In the class file add the code as shown below:

```
using System;
using System.Globalization;
using System.Threading;

namespace ConsoleDateTime
{
```

```
class Class1
{
  static void Main(string[] args)
  {
    // get the current time
    DateTime dt = DateTime.Now;

    // display the name
    Console.WriteLine("Current Thread Culture : {0}",
        Thread.CurrentThread.CurrentCulture.Name);

    // show the output from ToString() (not internationalized)
    Console.WriteLine("DateTime.ToString: {0}", dt.ToString());

    // show culturally correct short and long dates and times
    Console.WriteLine("DateTime.ToshortDateString: {0}",
        dt.ToShortDateString());
    Console.WriteLine("DateTime.ToLongDateString: {0}",
        dt.ToLongDateString());
    Console.WriteLine("DateTime.ToShortTimeString: {0}",
        dt.ToShortTimeString());
    Console.WriteLine("DateTime.ToLongTimeString: {0}",
        dt.ToLongTimeString());

    // enumerate all possible formats
    // not all of these are culturally useful
    string [] dtfmts = dt.GetDateTimeFormats();
    for (int i = 0; i < dtfmts.GetUpperBound(0); i++)
        Console.WriteLine("{0}", dtfmts[i]);
    foreach(string s in dtfmts)
        Console.WriteLine("{0}", s);
  }
}
}
```

```
C:\WINNT\System32\cmd.exe                                          _□x
Microsoft Windows 2000 [Version 5.00.2195]
(C) Copyright 1985-2000 Microsoft Corp.

C:\>csc ConsoleDateTime.cs
Microsoft (R) Visual C# Compiler Version 7.00.9254 [CLR version v1.0.2914]
Copyright (C) Microsoft Corp 2000-2001. All rights reserved.

C:\>ConsoleDateTime
Current Thread Culture : en-US
DateTime.ToString: 11/13/2001 12:51:26 PM
DateTime.ToshortDateString: 11/13/2001
DateTime.ToLongDateString: Tuesday, November 13, 2001
DateTime.ToShortTimeString: 12:51 PM
DateTime.ToLongTimeString: 12:51:26 PM
11/13/2001
11/13/01
11/13/01
11/13/2001
01/11/13
2001-11-13
13-Nov-01
Tuesday, November 13, 2001
November 13, 2001
Tuesday, 13 November, 2001
```

The output from this program can be quite extensive. The exact results depend on the startup thread culture, which is printed out as an RFC 1766 identifier on the first line of output. Read more about RFC 1766 style identifiers at http://www.ietf.org/rfc/rfc1766.txt?number=1766. After this program is run for the first time, change your default culture by selecting a new locale from Control Panel | Regional Options.

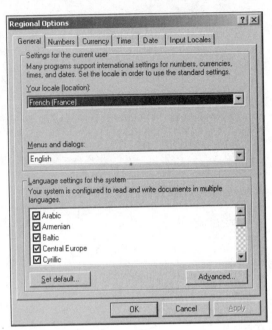

Choose a locale reasonably close to our default locale (as we are using the console, we may see only question marks instead of text if the locale we choose is radically different). For example, on my system, I usually develop with the English (United States) locale setting. If I change to French (France), which has a similar console code page, I can get useful output without adding any additional language support.

```
C:\WINNT\System32\cmd.exe                                    _ □ x
C:\>ConsoleDateTime
Current Thread Culture : fr-FR
DateTime.ToString: 13/11/2001 13:13:19
DateTime.ToshortDateString: 13/11/2001
DateTime.ToLongDateString: mardi 13 novembre 2001
DateTime.ToShortTimeString: 13:13
DateTime.ToLongTimeString: 13:13:19
13/11/2001
13/11/01
13.11.01
13-11-01
2001-11-13
mardi 13 novembre 2001
13 nov. 01
13 novembre 2001
mardi 13 novembre 2001 13:13
mardi 13 novembre 2001 13:13
mardi 13 novembre 2001 13.13
mardi 13 novembre 2001 13 h 13
13 nov. 01 13:13
13 nov. 01 13:13
13 nov. 01 13.13
13 nov. 01 13 h 13
13 novembre 2001 13:13
13 novembre 2001 13:13
```

As you may have guessed, the locale setting made here determines the startup thread's
CultureInfo instance. That is why we get different output.

Many, but not all, of the forms we will see, are acceptable for normal use. Some have
special uses that require an in-depth discussion of DateTimeFormatInfo. Also, in
some applications we may have to change the calendar type we use to get to specific
forms. DateTimeFormatInfo helps us sort it all out, but in most instances, the default
short and long date string methods of DateTime suffice to return useful default
behavior in the current thread. We will have a more in-depth look at
DateTimeFormatInfo in a future article.

Let's now look at an example that runs through the calendars available in our current
locale and displays a long date in a message box. (Many world regions use different
calendars to mark important national events or for religious purposes, and we mention
some of them further on.) With a message box providing the output, we have a better
chance of seeing the results correctly, especially when viewing 'exotic' locales.
However, we might have to install additional language support (details are given
below). Again, here is the code. We are using a console program but the output is
shown in a message box. Note the explicit use of DateTimeFormatInfo to get the
appropriate long date pattern and to act as the formatter for DateTime. Observe also
that we have added the line 'using System.Windows.Forms;' along with a
corresponding reference to the said .dll in the project:

```
using System;
using System.Globalization;
using System.Windows.Forms;

namespace ConsoleDateTimeCalendars
{
  class Class1
  {
    static void Main(string[] args)
```

```
{
    // Get the current date
    DateTime dt = DateTime.Now;

    // Create a writable cultureinfo according to the thread locale
    CultureInfo ci = CultureInfo.CreateSpecificCulture(
        CultureInfo.CurrentCulture.Name);

    // show the name
    Console.WriteLine("Current Culture: {0}", ci.DisplayName);

    // get the associated DateTimeFormatInfo instance
    DateTimeFormatInfo dtf = ci.DateTimeFormat;

    // enumerate the calendars
    Calendar [] cal = ci.OptionalCalendars;
    for (int i = 0; i < cal.GetLength(0); i++) {

        // select in each calendar
        dtf.Calendar = cal[i];

        // show the result
        MessageBox.Show(dt.ToString(dtf.LongDatePattern, dtf),
            cal[i].ToString());
    }

    foreach(Calendar c in cal) {
        // select in each calendar
        dtf.Calendar = c;
        // show the result
        MessageBox.Show(dt.ToString(dtf.LongDatePattern, dtf),
            c.ToString());
    }
  }
 }
}
```

Running the code returns a series of message boxes with the name of the calendar in the title and a long date format as the message. For example, here is the output on my machine if I set my locale to Japanese (use the Regional Options dialog again), where there are three calendars. The first one that appears is the Japanese Era calendar: the output reads Heisei 13th year, 9th month, 22nd day. Only the year differs; the days and months are the same as the Gregorian calendar. If you are targeting Japan, you may have to support this calendar.

The next result is a Gregorian date using English.

Finally, the last one is a Gregorian calendar in Japanese. The output reads as the 2001st year, 9th month, and 22th day. (Congratulations! You have just learned three useful Kanji (Chinese) characters).

We can view even more calendars if we set Arabic locales. Most of these have a Hijri lunar calendar and several Gregorian calendars in English, French, and French and/or English transliterated into Arabic. Other locales with perhaps surprising results to those new to internationalization are Chinese (Taiwan), Thailand, Korea, Farsi, and Israel. The latter also has a 13th month. In the next article we'll see how to find such information.

If you don't see these results very well or cannot find these locales on your system, you may want to install additional language support on your system. It is fairly easy to do. Just use the Regional Options dialog; check the additional languages you want to use (see the picture of the Regional Options dialog above) and have your installation CD handy.

A Note About Managing String Formatting

In the code samples above, you may have noticed the implicit use of the **String** (not string) class to manage formatting such as this example:

```
Console.WriteLine("Current Culture: {0}", ci.Name);
```

One of the biggest mistakes made by programmers is in using string concatenation to build a message. Assembling a sentence by successively adding fragments leads to translation hell because the result is entirely dependent on the word order and grammar rules of the underlying natural language. Unfortunately, programming languages such as VB, C#, and Java make such bad practices easy, but the result can be very costly when a program or web site has to be translated to several languages; a lot of code has to be rewritten to make the program independent of the underlying user interface. Fortunately, C# (and Java, too) provides a nice mechanism to get around the problem.

Let's see a simple example. Suppose we write code like this to produce the output "My name is Bill":

```
string myname = "Bill";
string greeting = "My name is ";
Console.WriteLine(greeting + myname);
```

In a well-written program, neither of these strings would be in the code but in a message table or resource file. But, even if the strings are stored in resources our problems are not over. Let's translate the desired output into Japanese (we'll use Romanized Japanese to illustrate). One possible translation is "Watashi no imeno wa Bill desu", which is something like "As for my name it Bill is". But, if you attempt to build the message by concatenation you would have to rewrite the code to concatenate **three** parts together instead of two because the value of the variable myname has to come before the verb:

```
string myname = "Bill";
string greeting = "Watashi no imeno wa ";
string tobe = " desu"
Console.WriteLine(greeting + myname + tobe);
```

Such word ordering is typical of Japanese, German to some extent, and many other world languages, but not of English. In other words, we have to change the code to render the message, an unacceptable solution, especially when it is not necessary.

How do we get around the problem? It is actually easy. Change the greeting string to be:

```
string greeting = "Hello, my name is {0}";
```

Translated into to Japanese it becomes "Watashi no imeno wa {0} desu". Now the same code will work for the original and the translated string, namely
`Console.WriteLine(greeting, myname);`

This technique becomes even more useful when multiple replacements are used. You may be reminded of using the `printf` family of API's in C and C++, FormatMessage in Win32, `CString::FormatMessage` in MFC, and the `MessageFormat` class in Java.

Some Examples from ASP

Since you are interested in C#, you may have read the Wrox publication *C# Programming with the Public Beta*, referenced above.

Early in Chapter 13, we are lead through the steps to create a web project. After that the authors ask us to rename the provided default .aspx file to DateSquares.aspx and add some C# code to display the date and to create a list of squares of the digits 1 to 10. Here is the code that was added:

```
<h1>First ASP .NET Page</h1>
Today's date is
<% = DateTime.Now.ToString() %>

<p>
First 10 squares are
<%
int i;
for (i = 1; i <= 10; i++) {
   Response.Write("<br> ", + i.ToString() + " squared = " +
   (i*i).ToString());
}
%>
```

Although there are lots of interesting internationalization problems (including the string concatenation combining both HTML and program output, which guarantees that your web site will be essentially untranslatable to another language!), the first item that caught my eye was the code for displaying a date, highlighted above. When I ran the code, I got the expected result: not even the slightest hint of a culturally correct date display. However, it is usually about as easy to do correctly from the beginning, and it certainly saves money and development time over the life of the product, especially when amortized over releases into other world regions.

So, let's see what is wrong with the date code above and examine how we can fix it with just a little bit more programming. The problem is the output. Regardless of any system or user locale settings I make on my system, the output of the line of code above always looks like a US style date and time string, 9/10/2001 7:04:35 PM. The separators between fields are ':' and '/', the time is based on a 12-hour clock, and worse, the date is ambiguous – is it the 10th of September or the 9th of October? If you lived in the US you would conclude the first but most people in Continental Europe would see the second. It could be even more confusing if a two-digit year had been used. For example, 9/10/01 could even be read as the 9th year, 10th month, 1st day of the Heisei era. How quaint you must be saying to yourself, but you may have to handle this issue if you are targeting one of the most important economies in the world – Japan! Finally, too much information is being displayed. Usually a user just needs a date or a time but rarely both together. Let's do two examples to see what can be done.

Revising DateSquares

In the first example, we will rewrite `DateSquares.aspx`. We replace the date portion with a line that produces a slightly more locale-aware display. We also move the text "Today's date is " into a `String.Format` call to make it more maintainable and translatable, and we use a formatter in the `ToString` statement. Indirectly, `DateTimeFormatInfo` comes into play here since `CultureInfo` has one as a member. Finally, we replace the table of squares with a list of all locales found on the server and show the local name, native name, and the full date and time for each. By the way, when we are mixing so many languages, we will want to set our page encoding (the document property is 'charset') to utf-8 as shown below.

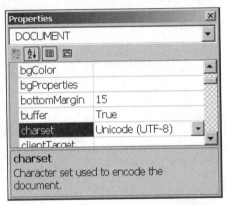

Here is the code. Note the `import` statement required to get access to the `Globalization` namespace and the `charset` declaration in the header. Also note how we have used the `String` class to eliminate the string concatenation problem of the original code and to isolate HTML statements. Here is the whole page:

```
<%@ Page language="c#" Codebehind="datesquares.aspx.cs"
    AutoEventWireup="false" Inherits="AspIntlDemo.datesquares" %>
<%@ Import Namespace="System.Globalization" %>
<!DOCTYPE HTML PUBLIC "-//W3C//DTD HTML 4.0 Transitional//EN" >
<HTML>

<HEAD>
  <meta http-equiv="Content-Type" content="text/html; charset=utf-8">
  <meta name="GENERATOR" Content="Microsoft Visual Studio 7.0">
  <meta name="CODE_LANGUAGE" Content="C#">
  <meta name=vs_defaultClientScript
        content="JavaScript (ECMAScript)">
  <meta name=vs_targetSchema
        content="http://schemas.microsoft.com/intellisense/ie5">
</HEAD>

<body>
```

```
<h1> First.ASP.Net Page </h1>
<% = String.Format("Today's date is {0}",
    DateTime.Now.ToString(CultureInfo.CurrentCulture)) %>

<p>
<%
  DateTime dt = DateTime.Now;
  CultureInfo [] ci =
      CultureInfo.GetCultures(CultureTypes.SpecificCultures);
  for (int i = 0; i < ci.GetLength(0); i++) {
    DateTimeFormatInfo dtf = ci[i].DateTimeFormat;
    Response.Write(String.Format("<br>{0} {1} {2}",
                      ci[i].EnglishName,
                      ci[i].NativeName,
                      dt.ToString(dtf.FullDateTimePattern, dtf)));
  }
%>
</body>
</HTML>
```

You may wonder why we have enumerated specific cultures instead of all cultures. A specific culture combines a language with a world region, whereas a parent culture has only a language. But, parent cultures have no associated DateTimeFormatInfo classes. One reason for this is that DateTimeFormatInfo contains the names of the weekdays and the months as well as numerous formats that have both language and regional dependencies. For example, en-US (United States) and en-UK (United Kingdom) have the same parent culture – en – but each has a different first day of the week (Sunday vs. Monday), and the default short date formats have different ordering (15/8/2001 vs. 08/15/2001).

The output from the program is pretty extensive. Included with the article is the actual page generated (datesquares_aspx.htm) and you can open it with your browser to see the output. Depending on the fonts and international support on your local system you may not see everything in its full glory.

Finally, observe that the steps to obtain a more culturally correct date display and to reduce the drawbacks of string concatenation do not really require much more code. The only problem with this example is that the output shows what the server can do but disregards client preferences. So, let's look at another example that reads the client language preferences and displays some date, time, and calendar information accordingly.

Another Date Example

In this example, we read the user's language preference in the browser and for each one found, a specific culture is created. For each such culture, all the calendars are enumerated, and for each calendar the full date and time string is displayed. We also show the names of the cultures in two formats (native and UI display) along with the calendar names.

You probably know how to set your language preferences in a browser. In Internet Explorer the steps are Tools | Internet Options | Languages | Language Preference. In the following screenshot, the ones I have set in my browser have associated RFC 1766 identifiers (en-US, ar-EG, ru, etc.) that can be read and used either as a constructor for a CultureInfo instance or passed to the static method CreateSpecificCulture. We should always do the latter as mentioned above. For example, if we simply use "ru" in the CultureInfo constructor we will end up with a parent culture, which, as noted above, cannot be used for date and time information. However, CreateSpecificCulture will actually create a writeable Russian language CultureInfo object with Russia as the default country. This is what we want.

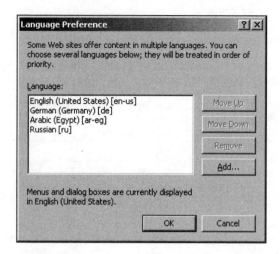

Below we see the source code that generates the output. Things to note are the isolation of HTML formatting using the `String` class and the parsing for the RFC 1766 identifiers. For brevity we leave out most of the boilerplate and the HTML header statements except the important **Import Namespace** directive:

```
<%@ Page language="c#" %>
<%@ Import Namespace="System.Globalization" %>
<body >
<%
  // get current date and time
  DateTime dt = DateTime.Now;

  // retrieve the server variables
  NameValueCollection coll = Request.ServerVariables;

  // get the accept_language string
  string s = coll.Get("HTTP_ACCEPT_LANGUAGE");

  // parse the strings and get the RFC 1766 ID's
  // which are comma separated.
  char [] sep = {','};

  // split the strings into an array and iterate over each element
  string [] langstr = s.Split(sep);
  for (int i = 0; i < langstr.GetLength(0); i++) {
    // the substrings may have additional data separated by ';'
    int pos = langstr[i].IndexOf(";");

    // use the 'name' variable obtained (RFC 1766 Id)
    // to create a CultureInfo instance
    string name = pos > 0 ? langstr[i].Substring(0, pos) : langstr[i];
    CultureInfo ci = CultureInfo.CreateSpecificCulture(name);
```

275

```
    // get the associated DateTimeFormatInfo object
    DateTimeFormatInfo dtf = ci.DateTimeFormat;

    // enumerate all the possible calendars in this culture
    System.Globalization.Calendar [] cal = ci.OptionalCalendars;

    // Show the user's languages in local and native formats
    Response.Write(String.Format("<h2>{0} : {1}</h2>",
        ci.DisplayName, ci.NativeName));

    // For each calendar, display some information
    for (int j = 0; j < cal.GetLength(0); j++) {
        // select the calendar into the DateTimeFormatInfo object
        dtf.Calendar = cal[j];

        // display the name of the calendar in bold type
        Response.Write(String.Format("<STRONG>{0}</STRONG>",
            cal[j].ToString()));

        // if the calendar is Gregorian append the type in parentheses
        if (cal[j].GetType().IsInstanceOfType(new GregorianCalendar()))
            Response.Write(String.Format("<STRONG> ({0})</STRONG><br>",
                ((GregorianCalendar)cal[j]).CalendarType.ToString()));

        else
            Response.Write("<br>");
            // Finally show the fully localized date for this calendar
            Response.Write(String.Format("{0}<br>",
                dt.ToString(dtf.FullDateTimePattern, dtf)));
    }
}
%>
</body>
```

Here is how the output looks for the Russian and Egyptian–Arabic cultures:

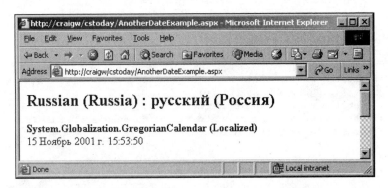

Summary

As you can see, it is about as easy to provide date and time formats that do the right thing automatically as it is to write code that has no cultural awareness. In most instances, the short and long date formatters from DateTime will suffice for rendering date and time displays in a culturally correct manner. If you need additional granularity, you must turn to explicit use of the DateTimeFormatInfo class. This class is also the repository of much incidental information such as weekday names, month names, abbreviated names, first day of the week, calendar, and an enormous number of specialized formats including those that can be parsed.

C#

Text Manipulation

Handbook

Appendix E

E

Support, Errata, and Code Download

We always value hearing from our readers, and we want to know what you think about this book and series: what you liked, what you didn't like, and what you think we can do better next time. You can send us your comments either by returning the reply card in the back of the book, or by e-mailing us at feedback@wrox.com. Please be sure to mention the book title in your message.

This is the first C# Handbook we've done, and it is almost a direct translation of the Visual Basic .NET Text Manipulation Handbook. Let us know how well you think we've done.

How to Download the Sample Code for the Book

When you log on to the Wrox site, http://www.wrox.com/, simply locate the title through our Search facility or by using one of the title lists. Click on Download Code on the book's detail page.

The files that are available for download from our site have been archived using WinZip. When you have saved the attachments to a folder on your hard-drive, you will need to extract the files using WinZip, or a compatible tool. Inside the Zip file will be a folder structure and an HTML file that explains the structure and gives you further information, including links to e-mail support, and suggested further reading.

Errata

We've made every effort to ensure that there are no errors in the text or in the code. However, no one is perfect and mistakes can occur. If you find an error in this book, like a spelling mistake or a faulty piece of code, we would be very grateful for feedback. By sending in errata, you may save another reader hours of frustration, and of course, you will be helping us to provide even higher quality information. Simply e-mail the information to support@wrox.com; your information will be checked and if correct, posted to the Errata page for that title.

To find errata, locate this book on the Wrox web site (http://www.wrox.com/ACON1.asp?ISBN=1861008236), and click on the Book Errata link on the book's detail page.

E-Mail Support

If you wish to query a problem in the book with an expert who knows the book in detail then e-mail support@wrox.com, with the title of the book, and the last four numbers of the ISBN in the subject field of the e-mail. A typical e-mail should include the following:

❑ The name, last four digits of the ISBN (8236), and page number of the problem, in the Subject field

❑ Your name, contact information, and the problem, in the body of the message

We won't send you junk mail. We need the details to save your time and ours. When you send an e-mail message, it will go through the following chain of support:

❑ **Customer Support**

Your message is delivered to our customer support staff. They have files on most frequently asked questions and will answer anything general about the book or the web site immediately.

❑ **Editorial**

More in-depth queries are forwarded to the technical editor responsible for that book. They have experience with the programming language or particular product, and are able to answer detailed technical questions on the subject. Once an issue has been resolved, the editor can post the errata to the web site.

❑ **The Authors**

Finally, in the unlikely event that the editor cannot answer your problem, they will forward the request to the author. We do try to protect the author from any distractions to their writing (or programming); but we are quite happy to forward specific requests to them. All Wrox authors help with the support on their books. They will e-mail the customer and the editor with their response, and again all readers should benefit

The Wrox support process can only offer support for issues that are directly pertinent to the content of our published title. Support for questions that fall outside the scope of normal book support, is provided via our P2P community lists – http://p2p.wrox.com/forum.

p2p.wrox.com

For author and peer discussion, join the P2P mailing lists. Our unique system provides Programmer to Programmer™ contact on mailing lists, forums, and newsgroups, all in addition to our one-to-one e-mail support system. Be confident that the many Wrox authors and other industry experts who are present on our mailing lists are examining any queries posted. At http://p2p.wrox.com/, you will find a number of different lists that will help you, not only while you read this book, but also as you develop your own applications.

To subscribe to a mailing list follow these steps:

- ❑ Go to http://p2p.wrox.com/
- ❑ Choose the appropriate category from the left menu bar
- ❑ Click on the mailing list you wish to join
- ❑ Follow the instructions to subscribe and fill in your e-mail address and password
- ❑ Reply to the confirmation e-mail you receive
- ❑ Use the subscription manager to join more lists and set your mail preferences

C#

Text Manipulation

Handbook

Index

Index

A Guide to the Index

The index is arranged hierarchically, in alphabetical order, with symbols preceding the letter A. Most second-level entries and many third-level entries also occur as first-level entries. This is to ensure that users will find the information they require however they choose to search for it.